'This book is important, timely and a very good read. The prominence given to the voices of trainees, trainers and practitioners, ensures the book is firmly grounded in experience and highly relevant to all interested in music therapy training.'

Claire Flower, PhD, *Chelsea and Westminster Hospital NHS Foundation Trust, London*

'The importance of learning to learn – and of training the trainers – is thoroughly unfolded in this excellent book: *Contemporary Issues in Music Therapy Training: A Resource for Trainees, Trainers and Practitioners*. With a focus on practice in the UK, international professionals will also benefit from its valuable and reflective insights.'

Professor Dr Hanne Mette Ridder, *Aalborg University, Denmark*

'The experienced authors of *Contemporary Issues in Music Therapy Training* are deeply practical and critically intelligent about engaging with the challenges of broadening the accessibility and diversity of music (and arts) therapy in training. Striking stories of learning and teaching and career paths of music therapists are woven elegantly throughout the book. An international resource for the future, and highly recommended for students, professionals and employers in arts therapies, health and education.'

Associate Professor Sarah Hoskyns, PhD, *Te Kōkī, New Zealand School of Music, Te Herenga Waka, Victoria University of Wellington, Aotearoa New Zealand*

'This book is a rare find. Very few books offer such thoughtful guidance for teachers and educators of music therapy clinicians. This book is a vital contribution to professional excellence in our field and to all those interested in improving their practice.'

Professor Hilary Moss, *University of Limerick, Ireland*

'Based on multiple perspectives, the information in this UK-based book includes learning and teaching music therapy, developing music skills, clinical placement and reflective practice throughout the career of a music therapist. Thoughtful reading for all entering or teaching in the music therapy profession.'

Professor Karen Goodman, PhD, *Montclair, New Jersey, USA*

Contemporary Issues in Music Therapy Training

Contemporary Issues in Music Therapy Training introduces approaches, practices and dilemmas in contemporary learning and teaching of music therapy with a focus on experiential learning, reflective practice and inclusion.

The book starts by setting out the pedagogical context for music therapy training, weaving together trainers' views with pedagogical theory and drawing in contemporary themes essential to music therapy education. This context leads to a detailed focus on the experience of music in training, work-based learning and the trainee experience. The final chapters consider the broader developing role of the music therapist beyond the work in the therapy room, presenting individual career case studies. Contemporary issues of pedagogy, diversity and sustainability are also thoroughly explored throughout. Drawing upon the voices of recent graduates, trainers and practice educators, this book is steeped in lived experience and practice.

The book will be of interest to current and future trainees, practitioners, placement educators and trainers of music therapy. It will also be relevant to readers across the fields of education, healthcare and social work.

Tessa Watson is a music therapy clinician, educator, cellist and vocalist currently working at the University of Roehampton as Associate Professor and Programme Leader for the MA Music Therapy Programme. Experienced in mental health and learning disability work her current clinical work is with the Alexander Devine Children's Hospice Service.

Catherine Warner is a music therapist, educator, cellist and music therapy researcher. She is Co-Programme leader for the MA Music Therapy Programme at the University of the West of England and Chair of the Training and Education Committee for the British Association of Music Therapy.

Contemporary Issues in Music Therapy Training

A Resource for Trainees, Trainers and Practitioners

Tessa Watson and Catherine Warner

LONDON AND NEW YORK

Designed cover image: Rawpixel

First published 2025
by Routledge
4 Park Square, Milton Park, Abingdon, Oxon OX14 4RN

and by Routledge
605 Third Avenue, New York, NY 10158

Routledge is an imprint of the Taylor & Francis Group, an informa business

© 2025 Tessa Watson & Catherine Warner

The right of Tessa Watson & Catherine Warner to be identified as author[/s] of this work has been asserted in accordance with sections 77 and 78 of the Copyright, Designs and Patents Act 1988.

All rights reserved. No part of this book may be reprinted or reproduced or utilised in any form or by any electronic, mechanical, or other means, now known or hereafter invented, including photocopying and recording, or in any information storage or retrieval system, without permission in writing from the publishers.

Trademark notice: Product or corporate names may be trademarks or registered trademarks, and are used only for identification and explanation without intent to infringe.

British Library Cataloguing-in-Publication Data
A catalogue record for this book is available from the British Library

Library of Congress Cataloging-in-Publication Data
Names: Watson, Tessa, 1967– author. | Warner, Catherine, author.
Title: Contemporary issues in music therapy training : a resource for trainees, trainers and practitioners / Tessa Watson & Catherine Warner.
Description: [1.] | New York, NY : Routledge, 2024. |
Includes bibliographical references and index. |
Identifiers: LCCN 2024030604 (print) | LCCN 2024030605 (ebook) |
ISBN 9781032853949 (hardback) | ISBN 9781032853963 (paperback) |
ISBN 9781003517962 (ebook)
Subjects: LCSH: Music therapists–Training of. | Music therapy.
Classification: LCC ML3920 .W315 2024 (print) | LCC ML3920 (ebook) |
DDC 615.8/5154071–dc23/eng/20240710
LC record available at https://lccn.loc.gov/2024030604
LC ebook record available at https://lccn.loc.gov/2024030605

ISBN: 9781032853949 (hbk)
ISBN: 9781032853963 (pbk)
ISBN: 9781003517962 (ebk)

DOI: 10.4324/9781003517962

Typeset in Times New Roman
by Newgen Publishing UK

This is dedicated to all our past trainees and those of the future.

Contents

List of contributors	*x*
Foreword	*xi*
Acknowledgements	*xviii*
Introduction	1
1 Learning and teaching in music therapy training	3
2 Theories and approaches for music therapy education	16
3 A historical context for music therapy training	33
4 Music in training	52
5 Work-based learning	78
6 The trainee experience	99
7 The reflective practitioner	123
8 The career of a music therapist	139
9 The broader role of the music therapist	159
10 Coda: The future	174
Index	*178*

Contributors

Kimberley Andrews
Tom Aplin
Alphonso Archer
Chris Atkinson
Emma Britton
Rebecca Burns
Tom Crook
Tilly Chester
Elizabeth Coombes
Philippa Derrington
Mary-Clare Fearn
Rebekah Gueye
Charlotte Hawkins
Alison Hornblower
Laura Howlett
Ming Hung Hsu
Karen Jones
Adrian Keefe
Claire Kelly
Jenny Kirkwood
Adam Kishtainy
Hesil Ko

Helen Loth
Sam Lowit
Risenga Makondo
Jill Moass
Deanna More
Gillian O'Dempsey
Helen Odell-Miller
Kate Pestell
Alliss Pollock
Alexia Quin
Reuben Quinn
Maria Radoje
Fiona Ritchie
Alex Roberts
Stephen Sandford
Ann Sloboda
Sophie Riga de Spinoza
Cerrita Smith
Eleanor Tingle
Garrick Wareham
Donald Wetherick
Bethan Wilson

Foreword

In keeping with the dialogic and collaborative spirit of this book, this Foreword includes the perspectives of recent graduates (Alex, Allya and Chloe) in conversation with music therapist and trainer (Claire).

Prelude

Alex: I kind of wish I'd read this book before I started if I'm honest, because it really gave such a great overview.

Chloe: I think a lot of the time when you're looking at recommended reading before you start the course, a lot of it can feel quite overwhelming or a bit academic. This book feels accessible and would've been a valuable resource both before and during the training.

Allya: In Chapter six, the authors write about the interview process and what is expected and what your interviewers are looking for. And that was so useful because it was set out in a way that you understood why the interviewers were asking the questions that they were asking and what they might be expecting from you.

Claire: It does present a very contemporary picture of the training process, but also one that is grounded in the history and the foundations of where it's come from. It highlights the reflexive processes sometimes that are being demanded of us in the training process.

Allya: And the book highlights the idea that the trainers are alongside you when you're training instead of it being a text where it's just the voices of the trainer and how things should be done.

When we were invited to write the Foreword, we spent time discussing and reflecting on the book, our experiences of training and practice and what stood out to us. Through our discussions, several themes emerged that we related to from our different perspectives. We wrote and reflected on these both individually and collectively. The four themes of wonder, diversity, the journey and the unknown emerged through our dialogue:

Allya: The idea of curiosity and staying curious – perhaps music therapy is so multi-faceted that it is important we continue to ask this question and be critical rather than feel the need to know the answer.
Chloe: Curiosity feels very important to not lose sight of, regardless of what stage of career you are at.
Alex: In practice, it's important to have a sense of wonder for the person or people you're working with. If that disappears, the capacity for change can also go.
Allya: The curiosity of being a trainee. The curiosity that remains for the trainer as well.
Alex: Having wonder for yourself and the whole of the world. Thinking about things from a systems perspective. How can this change and how do we fit into it?
Chloe: Part of the journey is to reflect and question.
Claire: And to embrace change which makes me think about change, diversity and looking forward in the profession which is also discussed in the book.
Allya: Something about sitting with the not-knowing.
Alex: The career of music therapy is such a broad church. It encompasses a wide range of backgrounds and aspirations. It's impossible to prepare for everything as there are so many different theoretical frameworks.
Chloe: Because music therapy can be so unknown. It feels helpful to have something concrete to hold onto, especially in the early stages of the career. There can however only ever be a 'guideline' of what to expect as each person's journey is different, meaning there will always be an element of mystery and wondering what is to come.
Allya: In terms of the role of music in the wider context, people might be able to use elements of this book to have a greater understanding of music therapy practice. It's often the case that when other professionals see music therapy they see the relationship the client has developed. That's when they see the lightbulb moment of seeing what it is.

These four themes are now explored by the individual contributors.

Wonder (Alex)

From the sparks of curiosity drawing trainees to the profession, to the reflective nature of practice, a sense of wonder will accompany the music therapist throughout their career. They will be open and receptive to what emerges within the relationships they form, having the courage to wonder and accept ambiguity.

As suggested in Chapter Six of this book, trainers may be drawn to prospective students that embody a sense of curiosity about themselves, those around them and the wider world. Staying with this curiosity can be a challenging prospect for the trainee as it may lead to feelings of uncertainty. This book is an invaluable resource, helping the reader to imagine the undiscovered and develop the necessary resilience to welcome it.

Whether exploring and critiquing theoretical frameworks with curiosity, finding ways to interpret the rich dynamics of experiential groups, or holding empathic regard for clients whilst on placement, nurturing the capacity to wonder is an integral part of the trainee experience. This extends beyond the training and into practice. The complex and varied career possibilities highlighted in Chapter Eight point to the importance of remaining professionally curious by engaging in continued professional development, guarding against complacency and raising awareness of potential power imbalances and biases.

The theme of wonder echoes through this book, placing the voices of trainers, graduates and placement educators at the forefront of the narrative to provide a wide-reaching illustration of music therapy training. This will be of interest to those across the profession and beyond, inspiring the reader to gaze across the landscape of music therapy with awe and wonder.

Diversity (Claire)

The case studies in Chapter Nine reveal the diverse possibilities to which a music therapy training and career may lead. If the reader started with this chapter, we might ask ourselves: Where do the diverse skills come from that can lead us into positions that influence and create change? Where do we find a sense of belonging within this profession that is so multi-faceted? We may find some answers in the stories presented here. We will definitely find answers in a training journey that aspires to a "willingness to learn from those in diverse and marginalised groups, including trainees and clients" (Chapter Ten), where training and practice can be co-produced.

The imperative that "understanding diversity, equity and inclusion" needs to be present at all stages of the training journey (Chapter Six) is clear. This book encourages a range of actions with which the reader can engage in relation to culture including being open, sensitive and humble. As skilled listeners, music therapists are well-placed to consider culture from many different perspectives and to create culturally safe spaces (Curtis et al., 2019; Lokugamage et al., 2023) with a view to addressing the inequities present in society.

Threaded through with a firm hand is attention to the vital role of reflexivity. In the production of professional selves (Crocket, 2007), we must consider the impact of the dominant discourses in which we and our practice sit. Standards, norms and governance shape our institutions and practice thus shaping ourselves. Learning to move fluidly between experiences of situated practice and wider critical perspectives, drawing our attention to the power relations and the different positions available (or not) to us and those with whom we work, is foregrounded in the writing and contributions of diverse voices and contemporary literature in this volume.

The journey (Allya)

Journeys are the constant of our life's stories, with beginnings and endings as their punctuation. As music therapists, we are seated parallel to the therapeutic journey of our clients, and much is written about this process. This book uniquely highlights a different side of that experience, that of the therapist themselves; be it from the amplified voices of the trainee, the trainer or those of the placement educator.

Through the discourse in Chapter Six, we are reminded of the preparation, effort and resources needed to train as a music therapist, even before a training may have begun. It is humbling to consider what is given of oneself upon entering the course and what is nurtured and expanded along the way. Additionally, real consideration is given to the barriers faced by trainees and pioneering ideas are suggested to broaden the accessibility of training for those in the future.

As a fledgling trainee, you turn to your training team for containment throughout the pilgrimage to qualification. Much like the client to therapist, you seek to see and understand the behaviours and boundaries modelled for you. The path can feel uncertain and daunting but, as suggested, a focus on self-care, personal therapy and a safe training environment lay the fertile groundwork from which to thrive. Chapter Nine illuminates the inspiring ways a career in music therapy can progress and what may be possible for the trainee as they move into the next phase of their career.

The unknown (Chloe)

Music therapy can feel like an enigma at times, and I have felt this at varying points throughout my own journey – from initially considering this career path, to training, to qualifying and embarking in my own practice. Many questions have come to mind, and frequently return to me. What exactly is music therapy? Am I doing the right thing? Where will we go from here? The artwork below is my reflection on these questions, considering the concept of the unknown in relation to my own journey. The silhouette of the person in the centre of the image has moved through the tunnel, into a lighter space, yet the darkness of the unknown still surrounds. Throughout the journey of becoming and practising as a music therapist, the darker and more unknown elements do not disappear, but we perhaps get better at sitting with and accepting them. There is light and hope in the future because of this.

The theme of the unknown also encapsulates questions regarding the future of music therapy. What will the field look like in 10 years, or even 50 years? This is a daunting yet exciting thought, and the answer is one that we can all contribute to shaping. Assessing the current training for music therapists is an essential place to start. How can we shape the future of music therapy without first looking at where it all begins – with the training itself?

This book is an essential tool for unmasking some of the mystery of music therapy training, providing potential trainees with a clearer idea of what to expect when considering this career path. The snapshot provided of the current training scene is also helpful for music therapists of all stages in their careers to reflect on how to move forward into the future of music therapy. The final chapter in particular pinpoints contemporary issues that are essential for all to contemplate, leading us in the direction of the change which needs to occur to make the music therapy field more diverse, sustainable and consequently impactful.

Figure F.1

Postlude

To conclude, we hope the reader will embrace this book with wonder and curiosity. At whatever stage one reads this book, it will act as a helpful navigator, seated beside you, revealing new pathways and steering you gently along the journey. We leave you with the words of the poet Rilke: 'Flow into the knowledge that what you are seeking finishes often at the start, and, with ending, begins' (Burrows and Macy, 2016).

Chloe Buttery graduated with an MA in Music Therapy from the University of the West of England in 2023. Prior to this she graduated with a BMus (hons) from the Royal Welsh College of Music and Drama in 2019. She currently works as a Music Therapist and Local Service Coordinator with Soundwell Music Therapy Trust, working with adults with a range of mental health needs, as well as a freelance Music Therapist with the charity Mindsong, working with adults living with dementia and family carers, and within mainstream primary education as part of Cardiff & Vale Music Education.

Allya Khammari graduated with an MA in Music Therapy from the University of Roehampton in 2023 previously gaining a BMus (hons) in 2015 from the University of Chichester. Following this, Allya worked as a musician and performer alongside her role as a Support Co-ordinator in a charitable organisation for young carers. Allya is currently working as a Music Therapist for Noah's Ark Children's Hospice (London) and as a Training and Development Co-ordinator for a Psychodynamic Counselling Centre (Kent).

Claire Molyneux is Course Leader for the MA Music Therapy and MA Dramatherapy courses at Anglia Ruskin University (ARU). She has over 25 years' clinical experience with people with diverse needs across the lifespan in both the United Kingdom and Aotearoa New Zealand. Claire completed doctoral research in 2023 exploring the impact of group music therapy for people living with dementia and their companions.

Alex Scott graduated from the University of the West of England in 2022, prior to which he worked extensively in the arts as an actor, musician, composer and creative facilitator. Since training, he worked within the prison service for Changing Tunes (Bristol, United Kingdom) and is currently employed by Raukatauri Music Therapy Trust (Auckland, Aotearoa New Zealand) working across a broad range of client groups and contexts.

References

Burrows, A. and Macy, J. (2016) *In Praise of Mortality: Selections from Rainer Maria Rilke's Duino Elegies and Sonnets to Orpheus*. Translated and edited by A. Burrows and J. Macy. Vermont: Echo Point Books & Media, p. 119.

Crocket, K. (2007) 'Counselling supervision and the production of professional selves', *Counselling and Psychotherapy Research* 7 (1), pp. 19–25.

Curtis, E., Jones, R., Tipene-Leach, D. et al. (2019) 'Why cultural safety rather than cultural competency is required to achieve health equity: a literature review and recommended definition', *International Journal for Equity in Health 18*, 174. https://doi.org/10.1186/s12939-019-1082-3.

Lokugamage, A.U., Rix, E., Fleming, T., Khetan, T., Meredith, A. and Hastie, C.R. (2023) 'Translating cultural safety to the UK', *Journal of Medical Ethics 49* (4), pp. 244–251.

Acknowledgements

Many music therapists have contributed to this book and we are grateful for their generosity and time in sharing their thoughts and ideas.
　We would like to acknowledge the Editorial Team at Routledge and John Lewis in Reading.

Introduction

This is the first book to comprehensively cover music therapy education in the UK and to include the voices of all those involved: trainers, graduates and placement educators. It is intended as a resource for all music therapists, and particularly to be of use to music therapy applicants and trainees, placement educators and arts therapies trainers. We know it will also have wider appeal as the central themes speak to all arts therapies education and indeed will provide resources for creative ways to learn and teach across postgraduate education. Practising music therapists and other health professionals will find much to consider as they move through their careers. Although the focus is on a particular arts therapy modality, music and concentrated on practice in the UK, it is written with an interprofessional and international audience in mind.

The book begins with an introduction to theories and approaches in learning and teaching in music therapy, and gives a historical context for music therapy training. Throughout these first three chapters, which draw upon historical and contemporary literature as well as the voices of trainers, graduates and placement educators, central principles for contemporary music therapy education are explored. Chapter 4 to 6 present experiences of training, specifically relating to music, work-based learning and student experience from diverse perspectives. Contributor voices are used to creatively convey key aspects of experience in music therapy education. When we conceived the book, the Covid 19 pandemic had not yet struck. As training experiences changed significantly during the pandemic it has been crucial to consider how they affected a generation of trainees and trainers. Chapter 7 considers a reflective stance, including the centrality of self-care. An understanding of career sustainability is essential during training, as this chapter explores. Chapter 8 and 9 explore careers in music therapy, with case studies included from music therapists who have developed their work in varied career pathways. The book covers the following central themes: approaches to learning and teaching, the importance of music in training, equality and cultural openness, E-learning and technology, interprofessional learning, reflective practice and self-care, research and evaluation, music therapy careers and continuing professional development. The book concludes in Chapter 10 with a look to the future, and imagines the ways in which this vibrant and improvisational profession might evolve.

We are grateful to all the many contributors to this book: recent graduates, trainers, placement educators and practitioners. Within the chapters we have kept contributions anonymous. This is partly to discourage comparisons across training courses; competition is not our intention. Both graduates and trainers are represented from every training course in the UK, and it is striking how much common ground there is between experiences and approaches. However, each voice is distinct and has a different story to tell. Our contributors' voices represent many different perspectives and experiences, some inspiring and some describing challenges, which adds to the authenticity of the text. We are also grateful to the many trainees and trainers from overseas with whom we have collaborated over our years as trainers, who have contributed richly to the perspectives explored.

The voices of the new generation of music therapists are strongly present throughout this book, alongside the perspectives of trainers, placement educators and experienced practitioners. Whilst comprehensively covering current issues in training, it is acknowledged that the book is of its time and will contribute to future discourse and debate. The book ends with a forward thinking vision; looking ahead to the ways in which this creative, improvisational and necessary profession might evolve. There is so much work to be done.

Catherine Warner and Tessa Watson
January 2024

Chapter 1

Learning and teaching in music therapy training

Tessa Watson

Introduction and some central principles

'Becoming a music therapy practitioner involves a process of learning that requires understanding the functions of music and the processes of therapy alongside the practice doing of music therapy through experiential learning student placements where observing and leading on-site music therapy occurs with individuals and groups'.

(Edwards 2016: 848)

The music therapy work that music therapists undertake with service users in diverse settings remains at the centre of the professional role, and gaining these skills sits at the heart of a training programme. In order to develop skills to work with the person in therapy, trainees also study topics in related areas, for example an appreciation of the idea of difference, diversity and power, knowledge of human development and growth, of theories of creativity, the healthcare landscape and context including systemic and institutional dynamics, interdisciplinary working and research. Trainees also engage in their own personal therapeutic work to develop a deep capacity for self-reflection. This chapter will present and discuss some central themes in music therapy education in preparation for the chapters that follow.

The importance of learning to learn

Argyris and Schon wrote that 'The foundation for future professional competence seems to be the capacity to learn how to learn' (1974: 157). A central principle of this book is the fact that a music therapy training is not an end point. A training prepares the graduate to embark on a career that will contain many more opportunities to learn and develop in varied roles, and that values the idea of lifelong learning. Tarrant suggests that: 'Having trained and qualified to do your chosen profession, it is important to realize that this is not the end of the journey. Becoming a professional is not the end, merely a step en route' (2013: 5). The ideas of engaging in a learning environment, of learning to learn and of life-long learning are all central to this chapter and the book as a whole. Macleod et al. consider the tension of supporting postgraduate students 'to become independent with them feeling ignored and overlooked' (2019: 495). Postgraduate students expect bespoke and specific support, and finding varied and creative ways to support trainees towards 'Mastersness' (Macleod 2019: 495) is a central issue for this book.

In his seminal text Freedom to Learn for the 1980s, Rogers wrote that:

> 'the primary task of the teacher is to *permit* the student to learn, to feed his or her own curiosity. Merely to absorb facts is of only slight value in the present, and usually of even less value in the future. Learning *how* to learn is the element that is always of value, now and in the future. Thus, the teacher's task is delicate, demanding, and a truly exalted calling. In true teaching there is no place for the authoritarian, nor the person who is on an "ego trip"'.
>
> (1983: 18)

Here Rogers' writing can be read as relating both to the role of music therapy trainer and music therapy clinician; the provision of a rich spontaneous learning or therapeutic environment, facilitating exploration and learning and putting the person in therapy/in training at the centre of the experience. This demands considerable skill as Macfarlane suggests; 'helping students to learn independently is a highly demanding activity for the teacher, requiring considerable investment in understanding the student's personal and academic objectives and in–depth knowledge of their academic field' (2017: 105). The provision of this bespoke type of learning is reflected in one graduate's account of their transformative experience of teaching:

> 'The practical musical training sessions were, to me, a fulfilment of the promise of a kind of education that I had not known during my schooling or undergraduate studies but had always wanted. There was a freedom to the discussions that reinforced the importance of materiality and experience in the moment, while also respecting the particular expertise and refined thinking of the tutors. It felt like apprenticeship in the best way – learning by doing, reflecting, trying again. More than good music therapy training, it was the best and most effective kind of musical education I've taken part in.'

The framework for learning – the past influences the future

There is a relationship between prior experiences of learning and future achievement (Prosser and Trigwell 1999). Writing about music therapy training Baker suggests trainees' 'personal backdrop profoundly influences their present responses', and that difficulties may 'be re-expressed in unconsciously generated local crises, via a well-worn, circular, compounding response-style' (2006: 173). Baker advises an understanding of the way in which the background and foreground are linked for trainees; another central principle for this book.

Expectations and motivation

All students are likely to have an expectation of what the learning environment will offer them, which may or may not be accurate. This may particularly be the case for those on a music therapy training where students may find that methods of learning, teaching and assessment and the requirement for personal engagement are different from previous educative experiences. When trainers spend time finding out about trainees' prior experiences of learning they help students to re-position their expectations of what learning can and will be.

Motivation is also central to success at university; Biggs and Tang write about the need for trainers to provide positive and hopeful learning, teaching and assessment support to support sustained motivation and to assist trainees in feeling they can own their learning (Biggs and Tang 2011). This idea is further explained by a music therapy trainer who said; 'we do a lot of preparation for learning; what we bring with us ... at the beginning of term, about learning styles and different layers, to get students to really think, right at the beginning, about how they learn and how they are taking in and doing everything, to set them up better I think for the training'. Another trainer noted that; 'as tutors we need to be aware of all the different ways in which people might be learning and try and adapt, put it into our seminar teaching and our teaching more generally. ... Over recent years ... there's much more of an openness around things such as dyslexia, dyspraxia: are the resources accessible for people'. Listening to and valuing trainees' past experiences of learning allows trainers to use this understanding as a springboard to move forward and develop bespoke and productive ways of engaging and learning.

Edwards writes that music therapy work can be 'wearying' (2016: 851) and it is clear that within the development of this new identity, self-care must be considered, to ensure that the trainee understands and develops their resources to work in a resilient way and to know how and when to seek support, including engaging in lifelong learning. This is explored further in Chapter 7.

Learning and identity

A trainer interviewed for this book suggested that 'we need to know music to be able to converse and be flexible. We need to be good at our techniques but it's not where I think the emphasis of teaching should be. It's a lot more about therapeutic attitude, how do we become therapists, personal development.'

From the first day of their training, trainees engage in a learning journey which will inevitably include developing a therapeutic identity and navigating personal obstacles to learning. They are active partners in the learning process, constructing their own knowledge and understanding of music therapy practice and deepening their understanding of the human condition through their own personal process work in therapy. Their progress through training includes exploration of their fundamental beliefs; about the world, about their own identity and the identity of others. Trainees may have well-established professional and personal identities (for example performer, teacher, carer, parent), and will go on to develop a new identity as a music therapist. This change will inevitably require the owning and exploring of vulnerabilities as part of the training journey and may be relished or resisted as detailed usefully in Bager-Charleson's writing (2010, 2020) and by Woodcock, who wrote that 'confronting the other's pain, and thus necessarily one's own, means the training itself becomes akin to a psychotherapeutic process. Change is inherently painful, as well as joyful, even the change in one's concepts of what music itself is' (Woodcock 1996: 24).

As Woodcock notes, the journey that trainees take includes new understanding of their own relationship with music and musical identity, and their perspectives about what music may be. Trainees must learn to attend and listen with detail and intensity in order to 'open their ears to really hear the messages in the music of their clients' (Wigram et al 2001: 274). Trainees may need to grapple with a musical ego and with their own possible judgement about different types of music in order to hold the service user at the heart of the work, as one trainer suggested; 'It is about your musicianship, and musical skills are absolutely crucial to what we're helping students to develop. It's not about their music being more important than the person they're working with. It's about not letting the therapist's music dominate.'

Musical identity

Reflection upon the trainee's own relationship with music is an important part of the training process, and may be undertaken as a private, or public endeavour, with some elements being assessed through written or creative assignments. Two graduates describe their experiences:

> 'before the training, my answer to "why I like music" was "I just like it". The training enabled me to thoroughly reflect on the whys. I became aware of how much music has given me an emotional support, particularly during the difficult times in my life. Singing, for example, was something I always enjoyed. Before the training, I was not aware that singing was something which gives me a time to breathe when it is hard to breathe, a sense of connection when I feel alone, a sense of being understood when I feel nobody understands me, and a tool to express myself when I do not have other means. In this way, I also reflected on the instruments I play, the songs I like, and any other musical experiences I had. This reflection allowed me to be aware of why I wanted to be a music therapist and how powerful it can be as a therapeutic tool.'

> 'The process of articulating my musical autobiography illuminated the central role of music in shaping my identity and coping mechanisms. It highlighted how I had used music to construct different versions of myself as a survival mechanism in white spaces where I did not want to stand out. This introspection was

juxtaposed with feelings of inadequacy, particularly when I compared my background to that of my predominantly white, conservatoire-educated peers. Their seemingly idyllic musical upbringings, captured in family photographs, starkly contrasted with my experiences. However, a profound shift in self-perception occurred during the course. I realised that my innate ability for improvisation, a skill honed in a chaotic family environment to drown out the noise and the ability to play by ear in the spontaneous musical environment of my church, was a valuable asset in music therapy. This understanding gradually dismantled my feelings of inadequacy, reshaping how I viewed my musical abilities. Rather than comparing myself to conservatoire-trained musicians, I began to embrace and value the unique perspective I could bring to music therapy.'

Diversity and power

In recent years, music therapy trainers in the UK and internationally have been informed by the social model of disability, the narrative of decolonisation and the BLM movement, and broader ideas of equality, diversity and inclusion. Training courses have changed teaching style and content in order to reflect learning and understanding of ableism, equality, diversity, inclusion. Literature from Cameron (2014 and 2015), Collier (2022), BAMT (2020), Myerscough and Wong (2022), Pickard (2022), Davies (2022), Lindo (2023), Roman (2022), Shaw et al (2022) and Vencatasamy (2023) has supported these changes. Pickard considers critical disability studies in relation to music therapy pedagogy in order to explore anti-oppressive pedagogy and to critique the use of a normalising discourse to pathologise those who use music therapy. This chapter includes useful recommendations for music therapy education (Pickard 2022: 12). As Myersough and Wong note (2022), lack of diverse representation in teaching institutions impacts upon narratives and culture which may lead to some trainees feeling othered; these authors make the case for more reflexive practice within training institutions to support positive experiences for minoritised groups.

Barriers to training, ideas about privilege

The scholarship noted above has supported training programmes in considering the ways in which all aspects of training may have replicated disadvantage or exclusion, and through educational exclusion may not have taken into account applicants' experience and emotional intelligence. Lindo's article notes how diversity issues within the profession can be traced to barriers presented by training programmes and institutions (Lindo 2023: 5). The social justice framework, explored usefully by Burke et al (2017) encourages educators to see that:

> 'inequity is perpetuated in teaching pedagogies that fail to recognise forms of privilege, normalisation, and compulsory heterosexuality, gender conformity, and whiteness; whilst these forms of inequity can be addressed when teaching

strategies specifically aim to develop social justice and disruptive encounters with students.'

(2017: 27)

Specifically referring to the upcoming Generation Z trainee cohorts, Camfield and Bayers (2023) encourage thinking about challenges such as the backdrop of the Covid 19 pandemic, the climate emergency, Black Lives Matter, economic uncertainty and the pressure and impact of social media which may lead to imposter syndrome and perfectionism. Literature and consideration of the climate emergency is now emerging in relation to the profession (Coombes 2023, Seabrook 2020, BAMT 2024).

Related to all music courses in higher education is a monetary privilege associated with progression through the grading systems that are frequently used to assess standards of playing and therefore allow access to further education (Lindo 2023, Wetherick 2016). This has led to lack of diversity throughout all areas of classical music, and many other areas of music work. Similarly, Bird and Pitman write about who and what requires better representation in the curriculum and resources across higher education that support student learning, and about the importance of these resources representing the perspectives and experiences of trainees. They note the challenge in providing accurately identified, relevant and up to date resources (Bird and Pitman 2020).

Sitting in the discomfort

The concept of power is a consideration for all therapeutic work and therefore also central within learning and teaching. Hadley's article introducing the special issue of *Voices on Music Therapy and Disability Studies* (2014) assists music therapy trainers to interrogate their positioning. Hadley questioned her understanding of therapy and her role as trainer, writing that 'I began to worry that I was actually training my students, even if inadvertently, to be oppressors who thought they were liberators' (2014: no page). Likewise, York's powerful chapter (2015) queries assumptions and lack of attention specifically related to LGBTQ+ issues. The profession is sometimes situated in a context that might inadvertently oppress; within HEIs, PSRBs, placement settings and employers such as the NHS, education and charitable foundations. As Hadley writes, 'we do not want to consider ourselves as part of an oppressive structure or as contributing to that oppressive structure. It is difficult to sit in the discomfort. It takes courage, strength and humility' (2014). Historical discourse about the relationship between music therapy and partner institutions gives a useful point of reflection, with disability studies scholars assisting music therapists in considering their power and positioning; 'from a disability studies perspective, the keenness of music therapists for acceptance, recognition and respect from the medical profession and its spin offs is intensely problematic' (Cameron 2014, 5). See also Barrington 2008, Procter 2002, 2008 and Hooper and Watson 2023. Cameron further states that the historical alignment of music therapy research with a medical model (for example gold standard traditional research and evaluation) is underpinned by a normalising ideology, thus further perpetuating ableist positioning (Cameron 2014). In the UK, Magee's keynote speech in 2021 (Cousins-Booth et al 2021) titled 'The work we have to do', for the British Association for Music Therapy's national conference sparked a process of work and reflection, added to by articles in the *British Journal of Music Therapy* (Pickard 2020 and *British Journal of Music Therapy* volumes 36, issue 1 and 37, issue 1). The valuing of this work, and of the central role of service user in co-producing training, is another central principle for this book.

Curiosity about past, current and future practice; curriculum design

The design of a music therapy curriculum is primarily informed by current practice, regulatory and evidence based/research context and is influenced by political and prevailing attitudes related to service users and the services they are offered, and to higher education and education per se. Wetherick reminds us that 'practice in the field is always ahead of training programmes'; ideally the two are linked (Wetherick 2009: 44). The training institution may also have a particular pedagogic music therapy approach. With these factors in mind, curriculum design should include consideration of what must be learnt and why this is so, how and when teaching and learning will be delivered and how trainee learning will be demonstrated or assessed (see Pokorny and Warren 2016: 17). Understanding how diverse trainees might demonstrate mastery of music therapy and an ability for critical thinking in different ways is important within the context of widening participation in the profession (2019 Macleod et al).

In the UK, music therapy is regulated by the professional, statutory and regulatory body (PSRB) HCPC. The Training and Education Committee of the British Association for Music Therapy (the professional body) updates the basic curriculum, informing the music therapy discipline specific HCPC Standards of Proficiency (HCPC 2023) and HCPC also provides Standards of Education (HCPC 2017). UK higher education institutions have governance processes to ensure quality and relevance to contemporary practice, usually involving engagement with stakeholders including service users, professional associations, placement educators and employers and trainees past and present. Thus multiple sources of governance and guidance come from the higher education institution, PSRB, professional association and profession. Some of these have been critiqued as working from colonialist and ableist perspectives (Pickard 2020).

Keeping things current

Educators have a responsibility to keep the curriculum current; Argyris and Schon wrote nearly 50 years ago that

> 'the professional skills of yesterday and today will not be adequate in the future, yet professional schools are preoccupied with the old to the exclusion of

emerging competences ... professions need innovators to improve practice and to clarify the professional's role in society'.

(1974: 143)

To support links with current practice, many trainers continue in a clinical role thus engaging in the double loop learning that Argyris and Schon consider is so important in assisting in the prediction of new professional role demands (1974: 153). This continual development of the trainer's own conceptualisation of the profession within a practice environment helps to ensure that the curriculum and teaching is relevant to current practice. Developments in the profession can provide a challenge for trainers who must choose what to include in the curriculum, as Biggs and Tang write: 'take your pick. Breadth: wide coverage and surface learning giving disjointed multi-structural outcomes. Depth: fewer topics and deep learning giving relational and extended abstract outcomes' (2011: 90). Wetherick more vividly conveys the experience of the trainer when he writes 'Here I see the poor music therapy programme leader throwing up their hands and crying "not more things to cram into the timetable!"' (Wetherick 2009: 44). Tensions may exist between existing curriculum and innovation that are experienced within the trainer, the team or the institution. Williams writes about the importance of disciplinary communities being open to change and development, because 'presented as dogma they can blindly enforce orthodoxies', and notes the narrow range of the academy (Williams 2016: 115). Trainers aim to remain alert and responsive to changes in practice, drawing changes into training as relevant.

The trainer's aim is not only to prepare trainees for readiness as independent practitioners, but to engender sustainability; a deep curiosity for future work and for lifelong learning. Readiness for independent practice involves the development of music therapy clinical skills, including critical thinking and clinical decision making, as well as the ability to take a role in working groups and teams, and to act as a leader and innovator when required (perhaps delivering training, supervising staff or developing initiatives and resources). Encouraging curiosity in the development of learning and mastery is a key skill for the trainer; therefore evidence of the trainer's own curiosity and commitment to the profession is a good model for trainees.

Underpinning ideas in learning and teaching in music therapy

Power and anxiety

In any learning experience there is a relationship to the idea of power, due to the transfer of knowledge (however much this is co-created) and the nature of assessment. This is likely to be more active within a training where trainees work with service users. Trainees are likely to find that they engage with perspectives around power as part of their process, including ideas about how much personal information to share with trainers and a sensitivity to judgement or assessment. Likewise, music therapy trainers may also feel there is a risk in being themselves in their work. It may be challenging to be creative around boundary issues (for example disclosure) whilst keeping the learning space safe. The importance of being reflective and honest is described by one trainer:

> 'the unconscious exists, transference and countertransference happen in everyday life, these are not just theoretical concepts, they are things that imbue everybody's interactions with each other, very strong feelings around all the time, and not just held by patients and clients, also held by us, so projective identification as an idea is very important.'

In interviews trainers recognised the need to reflect upon power in their own experience and relationships with students, and to use peer support to develop their ways of talking with and teaching students.

Power in higher education institutions

Trainers are also assessed and may feel they have little power within the context of the HEI. For example, trainers are required to obtain high levels of feedback from trainees in institutional evaluations that are published and scrutinised by HEIs and in some cases may be carried into appraisal or promotion systems. These evaluations are implemented to ensure that teaching is of high quality and to assist in improving standards and completion, however they can provide challenges for staff who are working to deliver high quality teaching across a wide curriculum with limited resources. The Teaching Excellence Framework is an additional evaluation in the UK. This assesses the quality of teaching in universities across some countries of England (McCabe and Bhardwa 2019 and Department for Business Innovation and Skills 2015). Some authors consider that the use of evaluation in this way has become reductive and unhelpful to lecturers who are striving towards student centredness and good teaching practice for their particular specific discipline (Barkas et al 2019, Wood and Su 2017). The complexity of the role, including pressures from management and the need to explain and defend practice and resource needs can be considerable when running a therapeutic training course. Edwards writes about the considerable responsibility that the course leader holds, including the 'expectation that the individual course leader will take responsibility to hold and resolve any tensions that arise' (2015: 50).

Trainers frequently work within a limited or rigid system within which to deliver learning and teaching. The staffing and resourcing implications within a pervasive business model are described by Bunt (2015), and more recently Berman considers concepts such as intersectionality and lack of openness to collaboration, noting how these might lead to defensiveness and poor mental health for staff in higher education (Berman 2022). Likewise, Edwards and Gilbertson suggest that a consumer based environment where high numbers are 'safe and successful' and with a high level of monitoring and low level of trust leads to a contagious sense of fear for academics who wonder whether their training programmes will be next for closure (Edwards and Gilbertson 2015). Academics must, within this picture, link the students to the institution (Macleod et al 2019). All these aspects lead to an experience of loss of power for trainers.

Over the past few decades, the higher education landscape in the UK has been challenging, particularly from a financial context. Challenges include a requirement for higher staff/student ratios (with larger cohorts), the adoption of a workload model for staff that allocates a specific amount of time for each task, and the neoliberal model (Brazzill 2020). In the UK funding structure has changed considerably (The Guardian, 2023) and all this pressure means that, as Risq expresses, 'an institution whose pre-eminent role is to think is forced to introduce practices and policies that make thinking impossible' (2007: 288). Within this context, it is interesting to note that Bunce et al found that higher consumer orientation was linked with a lower academic performance (Bunce et al 2017).

Learning and teaching as an iterative process

> 'Every single cohort of students teaches me something about the way that I teach' (trainer)

The role of trainer is a great privilege as well as a heavy task, and there is a cyclical process of learning for all involved; of 'teacher-student with student-teachers' (Friere 1970: 67). Mastering the role of a music therapist is complex and training is an iterative process, involving a variety of different approaches to learning. Theories and approaches to learning and teaching are explored in more detail in the next chapter.

References

Argyris, C. and Schon, D. (1974) *Theory in Practice. Increasing Professional Effectiveness.* San Francisco: John Wiley and Sons.
Bager-Charleson, S. (2010) *Reflective Practice in Counselling and Psychotherapy.* Exeter: Learning Matters Ltd.
Bager-Charleson, S. (2020) *Reflective Practice and Personal Development in Counselling and Psychotherapy.* London: Sage.
Baker, A. (2006) 'What else do students need? A psychodynamic reflection on students' need for support from staff at university', *Active Learning in Higher Education,* 7 (2), pp.171–183.
BAMT (2020) *Diversity Report.* London: British Association for Music Therapy.
BAMT (2024) *Conference Book of Abstracts, The Curve Theatre, Leicester 17th-19th May 2024,* London; BAMT.
Barkas, L.A., Scott, J.M., Poppitt, N.J. and Smith, P.J. (2019) 'Tinker, tailor, policy-maker: can the UK government's teaching excellence framework deliver its objectives', *Journal of Further and Higher Education,* 43 (6), pp.801–813.

Barrington, A. (2008) 'Challenging the profession', *British Journal of Music Therapy*, 22 (2), pp.65–72.

Berman, H. (2022) 'Traversing the unknown: group analytic approaches to intersectionality within tertiary education' in Collier, J. (ed.) *Intersectionality in the Arts Psychotherapies*. London: Jessica Kingsley Publishers, pp.137–144.

Biggs, J., & Tang, C. (2011). Teaching for Quality Learning at University. Maidenhead, UK: Open University Press

Bird, K.S. and Pitman, L. (2020) 'How diverse is your reading list? Exploring issues of representation and decolonisation in the UK', *Higher Education*, 79, pp.903–920.

Brazzill, M. (2020) 'The development of higher education in Japan and the United Kingdom: the impact of neoliberalism', *Higher Education Quarterly*, 75 (3), pp.381–397.

Bunce, L., Baird, A. and Jones, S.E. (2017) 'The student-as-consumer approach in higher education and its effects on academic performance', *Studies in Higher Education*, 42 (11), pp.1958–1978.

Bunt, L. (2015) 'The integration of art and science in music therapy training: some challenges in the UK' in Goodman, K. (ed.) *International Perspectives in Music Therapy Education and Training. Adapting to a Changing World*. Illinois: Charles C Thomas Publisher Ltd, pp.219–240.

Burke, P.J., Crozier, G. and Misiaszek, L.I. (2017) *Changing Pedagogical Spaces in Higher Education*. SRHE London: Routledge.

Cameron, C. (2014) 'Does disability studies have anything to say to music therapy? And would music therapy listen if it did?', *Voices: A World Forum for Music Therapy*, 14 (3). doi: https://doi.org/10.15845/voices.v14i3.794

Cameron, C. (2015) 'Why we are disabled people, not people with disabilities', *Disability Arts Online*, July 2, 2015. Available at: https://disabilityarts.online/magazine/opinion/disabled-people-not-people-disabilities/ (Accessed 1/8/22).

Camfield, E.K. and Bayers, L. (2023) 'From antagonist to protagonist: shifting the stories to support gen Z students', *Journal of the Scholarship of Teaching and Learning*, 23 (2), pp.1–14.

Collier, J. (2022) *Intersectionality in the Arts Psychotherapies*. London: Jessica Kingsley Publishers.

Coombes, L. (2023) 'Climate change and music therapy: a short report exploring considerations for the profession and clinical practice through the lens of a pilot research project', *Revista Portugesa de Musicoterapia*, 3, pp.29–40.

Cousins-Booth, J., Partridge, L. and Watson, T. (2021) *Open Ground: Music Therapy in Collaboration and Exchange*. London: British Association for Music Therapy. Available at: www.bamt.org/conference/past-bamt-conferences/bamt-conference-2021/conference-programme (Accessed 28 November 2022).

Davies, H. (2022) 'Autism is a way of being': an 'insider perspective' on neurodiversity, music therapy and social justice', *British Journal of Music Therapy*, 36 (1), pp.16–26.

Department for Business Innovation and Skills (2015) *Fulfilling our Potential: Teaching Excellence, Social Mobility, and Student Choice*. London: Department for Business Innovation and Skills. Available at: https://assets.publishing.service.gov.uk/government/uploads/system/uploads/attachment_data/file/474227/BIS-15-623-fulfilling-our-potential-teaching-excellence-social-mobility-and-student-choice.pdf (Accessed 20 December 2023).

Edwards, J. (2015) 'Paths of professional development in music therapy: training, professional identity and practice', *Music Therapy in Europe: Paths of Professional Development,* Approaches special edition 7 (1), pp.44–53.

Edwards, J. (2016) 'Training, education and professional issues in music therapy' in Edwards, J. (ed.) *The Oxford Handbook of Music Therapy.* Oxford: Oxford University Press, pp.847–852.

Edwards, J. and Gilbertson, S. (2015) 'Exploring resistance and change in music therapy learning for students and educators' in Goodman, K. (ed.) *International Perspectives in Music Therapy Education and Training. Adapting to a Changing World.* Illinois: Charles C Thomas Publisher Ltd, pp.219–240.

Friere, P. (1970) *Pedagogy of the Oppressed.* New York: Seabury Press.

Hadley, S. (2014) 'Shifting frames: are we really embracing human diversities?', *Voices: A World Forum for Music Therapy*, 14 (3). doi: https://doi.org/10.15845/voices.v14i3.801

HCPC (2017) *Standards of Education and Training Guidance.* Available at: www.hcpc-uk.org/resources/guidance/standards-of-education-and-training-guidance/ (Accessed 14 December 2023).

HCPC (2023) Standards of Proficiency Arts Therapists, The Health and Care Professions Council.

Hooper, J. and Watson, T. (2023) 'What are carers carrying?', *Unpublished Conference Workshop on 12/9/23: Co-Producing Professional Healthcare Education; How Do We All Work Together?*

Lindo, D. (2023) 'Examining the accessibility of MA Music Therapy training in the United Kingdom for ethnic minority communities', *British Journal of Music Therapy*, 37 (1), pp.5–16. doi https://doi.org/10.1177/13594575231154491

Macfarlane, B. (2017) *Freedom to Learn. The Threat to Student Academic Freedom and Why It Needs to be Reclaimed.* London: Routledge.

Macleod, G., Barnes, T. and Huttly, R.A. (2019) 'Teaching at Master's level: between a rock and a hard place', *Teaching in Higher Education*, 24 (4), pp.493–509.

McCabe, G. and Bhardwa, S. (2019) 'What is the TEF', *Times Higher Education blogs.* Available at: www.timeshighereducation.com/student/news/tef-2023-results (Accessed 20 December 2023).

Myerscough, F. and Wong, D. (2022) '(Un)learning from experience: an exposition of minoritized voices on music therapy training', *Music Therapy Perspectives*, 40 (2), pp.132–142.

Pickard, B. (2020) 'A critical reflection on the health and care professions council standards of proficiency for music therapists: a critical disability studies perspective', *British Journal of Music Therapy*, 34 (2), pp.83–94.

Pickard, B. (2022) 'Anti-oppressive pedagogy as an opportunity for consciousness raising in the music therapy profession: a critical disability studies perspective', *British Journal of Music Therapy*, 36 (1), pp.3–64.

Pokorny, H. and Warren, D. (2016) *Enhancing Teaching Practice in Higher Education.* London: Sage Publications Ltd.

Procter, S. (2002) 'Reparative musicing: thinking on the usefulness of social capital theory within music therapy', *Nordic Journal of Music Therapy*, 20 (3), pp.242–262.

Procter, S. (2008) 'Premising the challenge. A response to Alison Barrington's article challenging the profession', *British Journal of Music Therapy*, 22 (2), pp.77–82.

Prosser, M. and Trigwell, K. (1999) *Understanding Learning and Teaching: The Experience in Higher Education.* Bucks: SRHE/Oxford University Press.

Risq, R. (2007) 'On the margins: a psychoanalytic perspective on the location of counselling, psychotherapy and counselling psychology training programmes within universities', *British Journal of Guidance and Counselling*, 35 (3) pp.283–297.

Rogers, C. (1983) *Freedom to Learn for the 80s*. Ohio: Bell and Howell Company.

Roman, T. (2022) 'Developing a research approach to explore therapeutic relationships with children and young people with complex needs: a critical reflection', *British Journal of Music Therapy*, 36 (1), pp.27–36.

Seabrook, D. (2020) 'Music therapy in the era of climate crisis: evolving to meet current needs', *Arts in Psychotherapy*, 68. doi: https://doi.org/10.1016/j.aip.2020.101646

Shaw, C., Churchill, V., Curtain, S., Davies, A., Davis, D., Kalenderidis, Z., Langlois Hunt, E., McKenzie, B., Murray, M. and Thompson, G.A. (2022) 'Lived experience perspectives on ableism within and beyond music therapists' professional identities, *Music Therapy Perspectives*, 40 (2), pp.143–151. doi https://doi.org/10.1093/mtp/miac001

Tarrant, P. (2013) *Reflective Practice and Professional Development*. London: Sage Publications Ltd.

The Guardian (2023) 'Funding model for UK higher education is 'broken', say university VCs', *The Guardian*, 31/5/23 www.theguardian.com/education/2023/may/31/funding-model-for-uk-higher-education-is-broken-say-university-vcs (Accessed on 31 August 2023).

Vencatasamy, D. (2023) 'The importance of being diverse: exploring the journey from Brexit to belonging', *British Journal of Music Therapy*. doi: https://journals.sagepub.com/doi/10.1177/13594575231153558

Wetherick, D. (2009) 'A response to Nigel Hartley's article "The arts in health and social care – is music therapy fit for purpose"', *British Journal of Music Therapy*, 23 (1), pp.44–45.

Wetherick, D. (2016) 'Audition requirements of UK music therapy trainings', Poster presentation at *Revisioning our Voice: Resourcing Music Therapy for Contemporary Needs*. London: BAMT.

Wigram, T., Nygaard Pedersen, I. and Bonde, L.O. (2001) *A Comprehensive Guide to Music Therapy. Theory, Clinical Practice, Research and Training*. London: Jessica Kingsley Publishers Ltd.

Williams, J. (2016) *Academic Freedom in an Age of Conformity*. London: Palgrave MacMillan.

Wood, M. and Su, F. (2017) 'What makes an excellent lecturer? Academics' perspectives on the discourse of "teaching excellence" in higher education', *Teaching in Higher Education*, 22 (4), pp.451–466.

Woodcock, J. (1996) 'Stretto: Meet them where they are', *British Journal of Music Therapy*, 6, (2), pp.24–25.

York, E. (2015) 'Inclusion of lesbian, gay, bisexual, transgender, questioning content into the music therapy curriculum: resources for the educator', in Goodman, K. (ed.) *International Perspectives in Music Therapy Education and Training. Adapting to a Changing World*. Illinois: Charles C Thomas Publisher Ltd, pp.241–266.

Chapter 2

Theories and approaches for music therapy education

Tessa Watson

Introduction

This chapter includes discussion of theories of learning and teaching and assessment employed in music therapy education, as well as a consideration of the parallels between learning and teaching and therapeutic facilitation.

Constructive alignment

A central idea in curriculum design is the use of a constructive alignment; a focus on ensuring that the outcomes trainees must achieve are driving the planning of the curriculum, teaching, assessment and the teaching environment (Biggs 1999, Biggs and Tang 2011, Goodman 2011). Trainees benefit from knowing at the beginning of each stage of their learning how they are required to evidence their learning and to understand what is required to gain each competency. This alignment throughout teaching and assessment helps trainees to engage deeply with their learning in the present moment, and to understand the competencies that will be required for professional practice.

Learning in different ways

Describing the concept of deep and surface learners, Prosser and Trigwell write of the deep learner that:

> 'They have an intrinsic interest in the task and an expectation of enjoyment in carrying it out. They adopt strategies that help satisfy their curiosity, such as making the task coherent with their own experience; relating and distinguishing evidence and argument; looking for patterns and underlying principles; integrating the task with existing awareness; seeing the parts of a task as making up the whole; theorizing about it; forming hypotheses; and relating what they understand from other parts of the same subject, and from different subjects.'
>
> (1999: 3)

Concepts of learning and teaching such as this can contribute to trainers' understanding of their role in encouraging learning. As trainers we may recognise the trainee described above as one who has a 'need to know' (Biggs 1999: 16, and see Goodman 2011), who is looking past the factual information given, to understand the meaning and concepts beneath. This trainee works to make links between the different elements that they are learning, comparing it with their prior knowledge. They use their knowledge to populate the bigger picture of their music therapy learning and can apply their learning to practice. Theories of learning and teaching can assist trainers in understanding how to assist trainees in achieving this deep learning.

Exploring the varying levels of a topic being taught can encourage deep learning. A specific, detailed topic or technique may be taught and then contextualised within the discipline. Moving between the general and specific, or utilising the helicopter technique of moving further out to see the bigger picture and then back again to confirm details and strengthen understanding (Misseyanni et al 2018) can allow trainees to build a more complete picture of their role as practitioners. In time trainees develop their own skills in holding awareness of the background as they study or consider something in the foreground, a skill relevant both for training and lifelong learning.

Whilst there has been critique of the idea of learning styles (Newton 2015) it is evident that trainees learn in different ways. Some jump into a topic and immerse themselves; others hold back, listening and reflecting; some want to be involved in experiential learning. Trainees may be visual, auditory or kinetic learners. However they engage, trainees who learn skills at a deep level theorise, relate and apply their new learning to practice in a broad context (Biggs 1999). They use their newly learnt skills to problem solve and to generate new ideas for themselves. Prosser and Trigwell note that the deep learner will do better than the trainee who adopts a surface approach to learning, who is seeking only to meet the demands of the specific task with the least effort and without reference to other areas of their learning (Prosser and Trigwell 1999). In addition, learning is a social experience and interaction with figures in the environment (including self-reflection) assists in the development of deep learning (Tarrant, 2013). Honey and Mumford's model (1982), which draws upon Kolb's model of experiential learning delineates four learning styles: activist, reflector, pragmatist and theorist. It can be useful for both the trainee and trainer respectively to have an awareness of their own personal learning styles in order to develop their own learning, and to reflect upon and vary the teaching and learning experiences offered to trainees. Assisting trainees to understand their own learning patterns, their expectations of what learning will be and how trainers will teach is an important part of the introduction to a training. Workshops and reflection on this topic can usefully be embedded in the introductory weeks of a training course.

Trends in teaching

Trends in teaching evolve as in any profession and Fischer and Hanze (2019) note the move to and from educator as 'guide on the side' to 'sage on the stage' and back again, with their student reported study noting success with both methods. Other pedagogical ideas in learning and teaching are summarised in Ryan and Tilbury's writing (2013). These include learner empowerment (and co-creation), the importance of de-colonising higher education, transformative learning (linked with lifelong learning), crossing disciplinary boundaries and the need to consider future-facing education. Flipped classroom techniques, where trainees are introduced to teaching and learning material prior to the learning and teaching taking place, are useful in assisting trainees in independent study and in preparing for teaching. These may involve reading, viewing lecture videos or using other technology to explore ideas prior to and alongside formal teaching. Lastly Bovill (2019) writes about whole class co-creation in learning and teaching, a method that might provide good opportunities for inclusive teaching and building positive relationships.

Modelling a music therapy approach through teaching

A central idea in work with trainees is that the teaching that is delivered models principles of music therapy practice. Relationships between trainers and trainees on a therapeutic training course are quantitatively and qualitatively different from many other courses in higher education. The tutorial system is central within this as it allows trainee and tutor to take both a micro and macro view of the trainee's learning to consider what might need further development. Trainees meet with tutors and talk in depth about their experience and progression on the training, including exploring issues that emerge in their personal process. In order to manage this learning and development, trainees must be provided with an emotionally safe learning environment, with appropriate relational security through tutorial support and relationships that allow them to be open about their process through the training. Edwards and Gilbertson suggest that music therapy education has the potential to model 'not a perfect therapist, nor a perfect student, but the paths of human learning and change within a relational existence, one of the key aspects of music therapy itself' (2015: 232).

This was a topic of particular interest to the trainers interviewed for this book, as one explained:

> Modelling a kind of thinking in depth, thinking of a range of possibilities, being open to a range of possibilities, a kind of listening and enquiring and wanting to know and find out attitude, I think that's what I would want us all to be modelling, and a creative way of thinking. And I suppose giving, trying to give students a range of tools and attitudes that they can take with them and develop, rather than creating a fully finished product at the end of 2 years, that goes

around with all these skills and competencies, I mean they will have those, but they have got the capacity to grow and use their judgement...

Another trainer spoke about the importance of modelling a professional but warm attitude, describing how their staff team would aim for a boundaried but friendly approach to trainees. They noted that 'I would certainly model things like turning up on time, and being a professional in the teaching setting as well as being warm and friendly, and enabling people to come [to discuss issues]. It's an interesting boundary and can be pushed a lot.'

Trainers, graduates and placement educators who contributed to this book communicated the importance of supporting trainees to think about 'what goes where'; identifying appropriate settings in which to explore different challenges or issues whilst managing appropriate boundaries. Likewise, in group teaching the topics covered may sometimes be difficult to introduce and consider, provoking personal responses in learners that may relate to their own circumstances. Whilst it is important to ensure that trainees do not re-experience trauma as part of their learning (Bentley 2017 and Rae 2016), a capacity for openness about gaps in knowledge and the challenges that might arise in training is necessary to develop a reflective stance. The careful construction of a relationally safe teaching environment for each new cohort is important in order to allow this work, as thoughtfully described by one trainer:

There are things that need to be delivered, and need to be delivered at different times, it's different thinking about safeguarding for example which is this mandatory thing that's very serious, to thinking about something like spirituality and intimacy in music. Very different types of seminars which have to be thought about in terms of the way in which they are set out and how much time you allow for people to put things together... One thing I've really learnt is that ... we're trying to encourage critique and grappling with some really difficult issues, but we're encouraging people to do that with each other and with us, of course acknowledging our positionality in it but also perhaps setting out at the beginning of a situation where you are going to be asking people to grapple with things, kind of setting that scene ... and ... within it are these really difficult issues around assumptions and biases, so as part of it we're going to be thinking about that too.

Relational work and facilitation

Edwards and Gilbertson (2015) explore issues relating to relational work in training, and provide their own experiences, suggesting that trainers should be aware of the impact of patterns of attachment on trainees' ability to engage with and learn from those who are in authority and on learner confidence. Whatever their stage in life, trainees may find themselves drawn into a particular relationship with the programme team and to the authority expressed through the training institution.

Past experiences may be drawn into the training experience. Trainees may find themselves taking an adolescent position, feeling judged or defensive, or needing to rework their identity and confidence. Likewise the trainer may feel pulled into a particular position in relation to specific trainees or groups of trainees and will need to work reflectively and with colleagues to interrogate and process their experiences.

In his seminal text, Freedom to Learn for the 1980s, Rogers wrote about his change from being a teacher and evaluator to being a facilitator of learning, as he did when laying out his principles for client-centred therapy (1983: 26 and 1995). Rogers encourages educators to focus on facilitating, and on learning 'how, why and when the student learns, and how learning seems and feels from the inside' (1983: 133). Many of the same qualities that Rogers felt were needed as a therapist are included in this text: realness, prizing, acceptance, trust, empathic understanding and the importance of 'puzzlement' for the teacher in trusting the potential of the learner (1983: 119–134). Rogers' book, written over 40 years ago, contrasts with the recent trend of higher education as having an input-output production function, with students and trainees as consumers. This consumer culture is referred to by Brooks et al (2021, see also Brooks 2017), who write about the dominant discourse that students 'place much more emphasis on their rights rather than their responsibilities, and on *having* a degree rather than *being* a learner' (1376). Brooks' research also showed that in line with Rogers' views in 1983, contemporary students described the function of higher education as being for personal growth and enrichment, and societal development and progress, alongside preparation for the employment market (Brooks et al 2021: 1382 and 1382).

Experiential learning

> 'Challenge, success, failure, conflict and harmony can all provide powerful opportunities for experiential learning'.
>
> (Hutchinson and Lawrence 2011: 4)

Working as a music therapist involves the use of specific music approaches and skills and it is important that trainees have many opportunities to develop existing skills and abilities and gain new skills through practical experiential teaching, taught in large and small groups. Trainers frequently use experiential learning to assist the trainee in thinking about their relationship to a topic, thus moving the learner to the centre of the meaning making process. One trainer interviewed for this book considered that experiential work allows theory and practice to be integrated and embodied and considered it fundamental; 'you teach theory and then you workshop it'. This chimes with Murphy's consideration that experiential learning 'weaves together cognitive insight and emotional understanding' (2007: 54). For example, trainees about to begin placement might explore the clinical context in teaching, and then engage in experiential learning where reflection upon identities and ways of engaging with service users is encouraged and trainees hear from service users as teachers and discuss their own experiences as service users. Or following a seminar about a specific music therapy technique or approach, trainers might support trainees to think about instrumentation and set up a music therapy room, and then engage in role play, experiencing the role of service user and music therapist. Kolb's ubiquitous idea of the cycle of experiential learning is of concrete experience, reflective observation, abstract conceptualisation and active experimentation (1984). This cycle allows for creative teaching in response to a variety of trainee experience. This process of creatively working to integrate theory and practice is described by one trainer who spoke about trainees bringing their experience from placement to their learning: "there's a lot of discovery learning too. We won't have a clinical seminar and I'll say 'right, this is what you've got to do', it's more 'what have you been doing, come and tell us about it, let's see how that could be understood and developed."

Even within this spontaneous style of teaching, when planning experiential learning trainers should be alert to the teaching and learning issues they are addressing. Likewise, to ensure alignment of learning and teaching experience and assessment, trainers can usefully communicate what a successful outcome or assignment will be in relation to experiential learning. Trainees are helped to engage in experiential learning by an explanation of how to use experiential learning, their peers, any equipment and the setting to develop their learning. This clarity is usefully established through introductory sessions where trainers demonstrate and take part in experiential exercises to show the type and level of engagement required. Additionally, in designing this kind of learning the individual qualities of the group should be considered; for example, how established and experienced are the trainees, is this learning suitable for everyone, does it suit the working relationships in the cohort, might it present barriers to some? Trainers should also consider risk; what might go wrong, and how can this be prevented, managed and supported.

Problem based learning

Another method of learning and teaching used in music therapy is problem based learning or case based learning (Ridder 2015, Baker 2007). Ridder describes how 'the learner's "puzzlement" and problem formulation is the stimulus and motivation for learning in this situation' (Ridder 2015: 87). For example, trainees might work in small groups to consider an authentic case example, working through and reporting on different aspects in order to build a potential practice pathway for music therapy work, which is then discussed. This is used extensively in music therapy training, and one trainer explained their use of this approach:

The idea is that you have a small group of students, 8 maximum, and you present a case study to them, and they discuss it. They pull apart what they need to find out. What are the key words? Therefore the wording of that case paragraph is critical. What are the key things we need to find out? Then they go away, and during that week each person takes responsibility for finding out certain things, which they agree as a group. Then they come back and discuss what they've found out, how that might inform what they do and they come to some conclusions, depending on what you've asked them.

This type of self-directed problem-based learning develops knowledge for use in professional practice and is nearly always conducted in groups. Bunt perhaps refers to this when he writes about historical teaching styles in UK music therapy, and of the vigorous and deep discussion from different perspectives that was involved in early training programmes (Bunt 2015: 291). Savin-Baden presents a detailed exposition of problem-based learning, suggesting different constellations of this approach, all of which begin with a problem to solve (Savin-Baden 2014).

Quiet learning

Music therapy learning and teaching is frequently active and collaborative, and indeed increasingly in higher education students are required to be seen to be learning actively. But learning can be a private, as well as a public endeavour. Macfarlane (2014) notes the hidden curriculum and the requirement for trainees to learn in a particular way, helpfully cautioning against reductive assumptions that active learning and participation is necessarily a marker of achievement, and noting the difficulty for trainees who find it hard to participate in class discussion, assessment or to be filmed for assessment or future study.

Trainers as improvisers

The idea of improvisation, central to music therapy, is also frequently present in the teaching experience. Trainers might fluidly adjust their teaching to address a topic, technique or learning point that has been raised or evidently needs further exploration in order to progress. They improvise; spontaneously drawing upon examples from their practice, or bringing in an experiential exercise. This allows bespoke moments of teaching that might address a complex learning point, move perspective, slow down a process, refer back to something learnt earlier, or consider a new idea.

Schon, a philosopher and educator, was also a musician interested in improvisation and performance in different settings. His writing explored the idea of the reflective practitioner, with the following quotations speaking to music therapists' experiences in training and practice: 'phrases like "thinking on your feet," "keeping your wits about you," and "learning by doing" suggest not only that we can think about doing but that we can think about doing something while doing it. Some of the most interesting examples of this process occur in the middle of a performance' (1991: 54), and 'practitioners like architects, musicians and therapists construct virtual worlds in which the pace of action can be slowed down and iterations and variations of actions can be tried' (1991: 279). Improvised moments in learning allow trainers to explore ideas, questions and challenges as sources of discovery and learning. This allows trainees to build a repertoire to add to their memory schema when undertaking clinical work.

Creative conflict and anxiety

> 'Music Therapists are masters at discovering and devising creative solutions to problems'.
>
> (Hanser 2016: 857)

Improvisational and experiential learning can also engender conflict where there are different perspectives and strong feelings. Conflict can be experienced as creative and as leading to developmental learning and thinking, but it may also confront trainees with challenges, as new and different ways of thinking about a concept or experience are explored. Trainers therefore need the skills to hold and contain the anxiety and emotions provoked by this kind of creative and experiential learning. Trainees can begin to feel particularly anxious once they have enough knowledge to understand what they do not know (this idea is referred to as conscious incompetence by Williams and Rutter 2021). This anxiety may be particularly active during the beginning of placement, where trainees become aware of the knowledge and experience of their placement managers and others around them, and feel anxious about achieving this themselves. This can lead to challenges for the trainee in feeling that the training is good enough, and for the trainer in managing communications and projections about the failure to provide adequate teaching and learning. As trainees gain more experience they move towards greater confidence and begin to perform the role of music therapist with more reflection and understanding (Goodman 2011).

Experiential group and personal therapy

An experiential group is frequently a central learning and teaching experience on a music therapy training, although the length and style of the group varies. Rogers described the experiential or encounter group as fostering 'a climate for significant learning' (1983: 158) and his writing is useful to quote at length here:

> 'It is difficult to describe briefly the nature of such a group experience because it varies greatly from group to group and from leader to leader. However, the group usually begins with little imposed structure; the situation and the purposes are up to the group members to decide. The leader's function is to facilitate expression and to clarify or point up the dynamic pattern of the group's struggle. In such a group, after an initial "milling around," personal expressiveness tends to increase. As increasingly free, direct, and spontaneous communication occurs between members of the group facades become less necessary. Defences are lowered, and basic "encounters" occur as individuals reveal hitherto

hidden feelings and aspects of themselves and receive spontaneous feedback – both negative and positive – from group members. Some or many individuals become much more facilitative in relationship to others, making possible greater freedom of expression.'

(1983: 158)

An experiential group is not a therapy group but a reliable and regular place of attentive support for the process of training and growth, which trainees may use differently as they progress through their training (Edwards 2016). It is recommended that the facilitator is external to the core staff team. Streeter writes about the different experiences that we have of groups over our lives and considers that 'usually it is not until one decides to become a therapist that these kinds of continuous, relatively unconscious experiences of group membership are thrown into relief' (Streeter, 2002: 263). Issues relating to the purpose of the group, to not knowing, boundaries, power, achievement and competitiveness and personal past experiences may all be explored. Davies, an experienced facilitator, suggests that the experiential group provides a space for trainees to reflect upon their capacity to relate and communicate – specifically within the pressure of their developing learning and development in a new profession, and upon all the uncertainty that this brings (2002: 275). Davies also notes that the work and learning that the cohort is engaged in outside the group leads to the whole training experience being central to the themes explored in the group (2014).

A graduate remembered that:

> the process group was incredibly helpful both professionally and personally. Without it, all the other learning would not have been as meaningful. It was helpful not only to have the experiential group and personal therapy, but also to write about it as an assignment. Once I wrote my learning experience down, what seemed chaotic was more manageable to understand. It was such a unique and personal learning experience and I feel lucky to be able to explore myself in a professional and supportive environment. Exploring myself was most challenging. Exploring all the pains, sufferings, and scars I have was part of the process to be a music therapist, which was exhausting. The training required me to grow as a person, musician, and consequently, as a music therapist.

The experiential group (and personal therapy) allow the trainee to have their own experience of a therapist and containing therapeutic space in both an individual and group setting, and give support for the trainee to work through issues that might present obstacles to their development as trainee music therapist. Individual personal therapy gives therapeutic support external to the training that allows exploration of past and present experiences and anxieties. Making links between the trainee's own experience and the experience of service users in beginning, using and ending a process of therapeutic work, and exploring their relationship to a therapist is a uniquely valuable part of learning. However, the cost of individual personal therapy presents a considerable barrier to training for some, potentially limiting the diversity of trainees. Brand et al (2023) write about this, including a list of recommendations relating to personal therapy on music therapy training programmes. These include trainers providing guidance for finding a personal therapist, exploring funding support, providing ideas about the benefits and challenges of personal therapy, giving background reading and encouraging students to reflect upon their experiences (Brand et al 2023: 236).

Online learning

International learning

The global music therapy landscape is one of the perspectives that trainers offer to trainees. Moving between a micro (small scale interactions between individuals), meso (groups, communities, institutions) and macro level (large scale disciplinary practice) of information is rich but can be daunting for trainees, engaged as they are in the detail of learning about particular theories or practices. With greater ease in using technology to connect and dialogue, international music therapy trainers, practitioners and researchers have developed significant links over the past 10 years, and trainees can research music therapy worldwide to find out about varying practice and topics of interest.

Covid 19 and online learning

In 2020, the Covid 19 pandemic crisis drew international trainers more closely together. McFerran and MacCaffrey initiated a series of meetings for international trainers in order to share knowledge and skills. McFerran (in Australia, with a long experience of running online learning), and MacCaffrey (in Southern Ireland), brought together more than 70 music therapy trainers to share and learn from each other in managing the urgent task of moving teaching, learning and assessment online, following the Covid 19 lockdown (McCaffrey et al 2020). Benner et al (2022: 37) refer to the 'extraordinary pivot' that UK universities made to swiftly move teaching online at this time. During the Covid 19 pandemic there was an urgent requirement to innovate in order to assist trainees in maintaining and developing their music therapy skills whilst the majority of teaching was online and the majority of placements were paused. Staff and trainees were pushed fast into using unintegrated digital tools within a digital learning space without having time to consider how this might be best pedagogically constructed and how roles might emerge in this new teaching practice (Bygstad et al 2022). Simulated clinical skills (always a central part of training) were developed for online use to allow trainees to continue to learn and perform their skills whilst isolated from the face to face learning situation (see Gaba 2004, who notes 11 dimensions within this technique).

Blended learning

There is currently little evidence to show efficacy of online learning for health professions training although more studies are emerging that consider relevance and impact (Regmi and Jones 2021). Benefits include greater accessibility for trainees and opportunities to use online resources in the trainee's own time and space and at their own pace. The Covid 19 pandemic pushed trainers into more serious consideration of online learning, and with time for reflection and planning, some music therapy programmes now employ a blended approach, utilising both online and on campus learning. This can allow wider participation in training programmes particularly in more geographically isolated areas.

Assessment of learning

Assessment tasks aim to develop independent and autonomous practitioners who can manage their own professional practice once qualified. A wide range of assessment methods are used in music therapy training, including essays, reflective narratives, live in-class assessments and performances, presentations and viva examinations. Accountability from PSRBs and HEIs requires that assessments are attempted and passed, with HCPC Standards of Proficiency (HCPC 2023) being central to ensuring safe and effective practice in the UK.

Formative assessment, which offers students feedback on ungraded work, is essential to give trainers and trainees opportunities to see how learning is progressing before summative work is graded. It assists trainees in their learning, and assists trainers to adjust and reposition their teaching. Trainees can also adopt a formative process for themselves, monitoring their progress as they learn; a useful habit that is a good model for future professional practice.

Summative assessment is usually carried out after learning and teaching has ended, providing an assessment grade. Trainers use learning outcomes and marking criteria to provide feedback and feedforward, and to moderate across the cohort. Assessments allow trainers to see how well trainees have understood, synthesised and performed their learning of the concepts and practices taught. Feedback helps trainees to see where they have areas for development. Torres writes about feedback being an open ended conversation. It can promote meaningful learning, prompting independent learning, including the trainee's own response to the feedback given (Torres 2022). Another useful tool in assessment is peer feedback, which can be used both as collaborative learning and formative feedback. Ion et al state that peer feedback can support trainees in becoming 'more active and involved in their learning' (2018: 134).

Reflective writing as assessment

The development of reflective practice is central within a therapeutic training, and reflective accounts may be used in assessment, or to consider incidents or critical experiences in relation to learning (Biggs 1999). Some authors have criticised the emergence of reflective writing across higher education per se. Macfarlane cautions against the requirement for trainees to show how their thinking has been transformed by sharing their experience, noting that this may threaten a trainee's privacy, cause anxiety about what should be shared or lead a trainee to shape their assignment accordingly. Macfarlane writes that 'the grading of self-reflective assignments may be perceived by a student as a judgement about them as a person as opposed to a grade for an academic piece of work' (Macfarlane 2017: 101). Here the idea of power should be considered with clear and relevant marking criteria given.

Placements, supervision and reflective practice

Work-based learning

Work-based or industry learning is a central part of the education of health professionals (Williams and Rutter 2021, Roth et al 2021) and is considered in depth in Chapter 5 of this book. Placement based learning supports trainees to develop skills and knowledge in the practice setting to a professional level. It also allows an experience of the role and work of the music therapist in a contrasting range of settings, assisting trainees in considering their preferred destination for employment.

Placement organisation and engagement is complex and unpredictable, and trainees can have varying experiences, including receiving conflicting advice and guidance. Parity of experience cannot be predicted or controlled across training placements as these occur across a diverse range of practice settings with varied approaches, support and opportunities. Regular contact with placement educators, including discussion of trainees' progress is an important element of the trainer's work, requiring considerable time resource. To ensure equality for trainees and alignment with learning outcomes, detailed information about the curriculum, placement requirements, learning outcomes and assignments should be provided for placement educators along with the provision of timely meetings, including training about changes and innovations in the programme. These resources allow the building of a shared understanding of the competencies and progress required.

Trainee's experiences of placement

Little has been written about music therapy trainees' placement experience. Bae's 2012 article studying trainee experience on placement in South Korea found that trainees move towards a more proactive and reflective stance as subsequent placements progress, and need correspondingly detailed teaching and feedback. Roth et al (2021), focusing upon USA training programmes, write that trainees on placement had central concerns about their musical ability and an understanding of their role in the specific placement setting. Goodman writes about the stages that can be experienced by trainees on placement, noting the end of month 4 as being a characteristic low point before confidence and competence grows (Goodman, 2011: 23–24).

Trainees may experience a disjunction in having to learn (in the classroom) and perform (on placement) at the same time; this uncomfortable experience frequently resolves as experience is gained. One graduate summarised their experience thus:

> Placement was where all the learning came to life and made sense. I cannot imagine the training without placement. I felt honoured to have worked in two different areas; children and adults, verbal clients and non-verbal clients, and education and hospital settings. The whole process was thoroughly supported. Not only the on-site experience, but also the on-campus experience was useful; to write case study essays and to give a presentation.

Triangulation of trainee support between trainees, trainers and placement educators

Finch (2017) outlines some of the issues that arise for trainees who struggle on placement, pointing to the strong emotions that may be experienced by trainee, trainer and placement educator and the tensions relating to assessment. The responsibility to support high standards for service users is evident and essential; any concerns about competence must be explored in order to ensure good practice on placement and safe and effective professional practice following graduation. Therefore communication should be open and active between trainee, trainer and placement educator to enable exploration of any issues raised. At times, difficulties experienced in relation to placement may be managed by any of those involved through splitting, with particular qualities being identified in another. Close and open communication is needed at these times to untangle communications and find a productive way forward, with trainers working sensitively and authentically to offer enough support without disempowering the trainee.

It can be challenging and stressful for placement educators and trainers to fail a trainee on placement and support appropriately; indeed in some professions the challenge in failing trainees has become known as failure to fail (Finch 2017). Williams and Rutter (2021) note the emotional experience that a failure may involve for the trainee and the trainer, resulting perhaps in a lack of confidence, sense of incompetence or of internalised failure. With reflection, the failure of an assignment or module related to placement may later be experienced by the trainee as having been useful in their development.

Supervision and reflective practice

Along with placement work, supervision or reflective practice sits centrally in training programmes, and is considered in more detail in Chapter 5. Whilst clinical responsibility may be held within the placement setting, all programmes have a seminar setting where trainees bring, present and discuss their work. This allows trainees to continue to learn, develop their music therapy skills and explore both the specific and broad context of their work (Odell-Miller and Richards 2009). Different placement settings will have specific objectives for the work which can be considered and compared with other trainee experiences within the supervision group. Ala-Ruona (2015) notes the value of observers within group supervision, specifically in relation to the idea of parallel process (a replication of the dynamics in the work within the supervision group). The supervision group provides an opportunity for trainees to consider multiple perspectives.

Placement educators may feel involved or observed by their trainee's reflection on and reporting of the work and setting. When these different roles, responsibilities and sensitivities are present for all involved, it is essential that reflective practice takes place both within the seminar and the staff team in order to manage the dynamics and complexities of the work. One graduate remembered how they had 'found supervision to be quite difficult sometimes, as I was led to confront aspects of my character that had previously been insulated from criticism at work/in education. Insights into musical tendencies that resonated strongly with long-term personal challenges both validated the idea that a musical analysis could provide an extra-musical understanding and made me feel uncomfortably exposed. I did however value this a lot, even more so now that I'm working.'

Conclusion

This chapter has considered theories and approaches to learning and teaching within music therapy education. In the UK as in other countries (see Goodman 2015) there is a historical tradition of different training and practice styles and lenses through which trainers view music therapy. This has impact through the generations of trainees who may feel the need for a home, and an allegiance. It is not possible, particularly with the growth of the professional role, to cover all aspects or models of music therapy within a training programme, but programmes cover enough of a variety of perspectives, allowing trainees to explore more in their chosen direction. This UK and international history and context will be explored further in the following chapter.

References

Ala-Ruona, E. (2015) 'Multilevel learning in intensive clinical training: music therapy training model of the University of Jyvaskyla' in Goodman, K. (ed.) *International Perspectives in Music Therapy Education and Training. Adapting to a Changing World.* Illinois: Charles C Thomas Publisher Ltd, pp.40–74.

Bae, M.-J. (2012) 'Student music therapists' differences in their clinical reflections across practicum levels', *Music Therapy Perspectives*, 30 (1), pp.89–93.

Baker, F. (2007) 'Enhancing the clinical reasoning skills of music therapy students through problem-based learning: an action research project', *Nordic Journal of Music Therapy*, 16 (1), pp.27–41.

Benner, M., Grant, J. and O'Kane, M. (2022) 'Higher education in the UK' in Benner, M., Grant, J. and O'Kane, M. (eds.) *Crisis Response in Higher Education*. London: Palgrave Macmillan, pp.25–40.

Bentley, M. (2017) 'Trigger warnings and the student experience', *Learning and Teaching in Politics and International Studies*, 37 (4), pp.470–485.

Biggs, J. (1999) *Teaching for Quality Learning at University*. Open University Press: Buckingham.

Biggs, J. and Tang, C. (2011) *Teaching for Quality Learning at University*. Maidenhead, UK: Open University Press.

Bovill, C. (2019) 'Co-creation in learning and teaching: the case for a whole-class approach in higher education', *Higher Education*, 79, pp.1023–1037.

Brand, M., Clarke, V. and Warner, C. (2023) '"Surprisingly helpful": an exploration of trainee and registered music therapists' perspectives on the current role of personal therapy in music therapy training in the United Kingdom', *Approaches: An Interdisciplinary Journal of Music Therapy*, 15 (2), pp.219–240.

Brooks, R. (2017) 'The construction of high education students in English policy documents', *British Journal of Sociology of Education*, 39 (6), pp.745–761.

Brooks, R., Gupta, A., Jayadeva, S. and Abrahams, J. (2021) 'Students' views about the purpose of higher education: a comparative analysis of six European countries', *Higher Education Research and Development*, 40 (7), pp.1375–1388.

Bunt, L. (2015) 'The integration of art and science in music therapy training: some challenges in the UK' in Goodman, K. (ed.) *International Perspectives in Music Therapy Education and Training. Adapting to a Changing World*. Illinois: Charles C Thomas Publisher Ltd, pp.219–240.

Bygstad, B., Ovrelid, E., Ludvigsen, S. and Daehlen, S. (2022) 'From dual digitalization to digital learning space: exploring the digital transformation of higher education', *Computers and Education*, 182 (104463), pp.1–11.

Davies, A. (2002) 'A group analytic look at experiential training groups: how can music earn its keep?' in Davies, A. and Richards, E. (eds.) *Music Therapy and Group Work Sound Company*. London: Jessica Kingsley Publishers, pp.274–287.

Davies, A. (2014) 'Experiential groups on music therapy trainings' in Davies, A., Richards, E., and Barwick, N. (eds) *Group Music Therapy: A Group Analytic Approach*. London: Taylor and Francis Group, pp.149–162.

Edwards, J. (2016) 'Training, education and professional issues in music therapy' in Edwards, J. (ed.) *The Oxford Handbook of Music Therapy*. Oxford: Oxford University Press, pp.847–852.

Edwards, J. and Gilbertson, S. (2015) 'Exploring resistance and change in music therapy learning for students and educators', in Goodman, K. (ed.) *International Perspectives in Music Therapy Education and Training. Adapting to a Changing World*. Illinois: Charles C Thomas Publisher Ltd, pp.219–240.

Finch, J. (2017) *Supporting Struggling Students on Placement: A Practical Guide*. Bristol: Policy Press.

Fischer, E. and Hanze, M. (2019) 'Back from "guide on the side" to "sage on the stage"? Effects of teacher-guided and student-activating teaching methods on student learning in higher education', *International Journal of Educational Research*, 95, pp.26–35.

Gaba, D. (2004) 'The future vision of simulation in health care', *Quality and Safety in Health Care*, 13, i1–i10.

Goodman, K. (2011) *Music Therapy Education and Training: From Theory to Practice*. Springfield Illinois: Charles C Thomas Publisher Ltd.

Goodman, K. (2015) *International Perspectives in Music Therapy Education and Training. Adapting to a Changing World.* Springfield Illinois: Charles C Thomas Publisher Ltd.

Hanser, S. (2016) 'Music therapy training requirements' in Edwards, J. (ed.) *The Oxford Handbook of Music Therapy.* Oxford: Oxford University Press, pp.853–874.

HCPC (2023) *Standards of Proficiency Arts Therapists.* Available at: www.hcpc-uk.org/globalassets/standards/standards-of-proficiency/reviewing/arts-therapists---new-standards.pdf (Accessed 20 February 2023).

Honey, P. and Mumford, A. (1982) *Manual of Learning Styles.* Maidenhead: Peter Honey.

Hutchinson, S. and Lawrence, H. (2011) *Playing with Purpose. How Experiential Learning can be More than a Game.* Surrey: Gower Publishing Ltd.

Ion, G., Marti, A.S. and Morell, I.A. (2018) 'Giving or receiving feedback: which is more beneficial to students' learning?', *Assessment and Evaluation in Higher Education,* 44 (1), pp.124–138.

Kolb, D.A. (1984) *Experiential Learning: Experience as the Source of Learning and Development.* Englewood Cliffs, NJ: Prentice-Hall.

Macfarlane, B. (2014) 'Speaking up for the introverts', *Times Higher Education,* 25th September 2014, pp.43–45.

Macfarlane, B. (2017) *Freedom to Learn. The Threat to Student Academic Freedom and Why it Needs to be Reclaimed.* London: Routledge.

McCaffrey, T., McFerran, K., Gattino, G. and Sundar, S. (2020) 'The global music therapy educators network', *British Journal of Music Therapy,* 34 (2), pp.80–81.

Misseyanni, A., Lytras, M.D., Papadopoulou, P. and Marouli, C. (2018) *Active Learning Strategies in Higher Education.* Bingley: Emerald Publishing Limited.

Murphy, K. (2007) 'Experiential learning in music therapy: faculty and student perspectives' in Meadows, A. (ed.) *Qualitative Inquiries in Music Therapy, A Monograph Series,* Gilsum NH: Barcelona Publishers, Volume 3, pp.31–61.

Newton, P.M. (2015) 'The learning styles myth is thriving in higher education', *Frontiers Psychology, 6.* doi: https://doi.org/10.3389/fpsyg.2015.01908

Odell-Miller, H. and Richards, E. (2009) *Supervision of Music Therapy: Theoretical and Practical Handbook.* East Sussex: Routledge.

Prosser, M. and Trigwell, K. (1999) *Understanding Learning and Teaching: The Experience in Higher Education.* Bucks: SRHE/OUP.

Rae, L. (2016) 'Re-focusing the debate on trigger warnings: privilege, trauma and disability in the classroom', *First Amendment Studies,* 50 (2), pp.95–102.

Regmi, K. and Jones, L. (2021) 'Effect of e-learning on health sciences education: a protocol for systematic review and meta-analysis', *Higher Education Pedagogies,* 6 (1), pp.22–36.

Ridder, H.M. (2015) 'Doctoral education: a model of problem based learning' in Goodman, K. (ed.) *International Perspectives in Music Therapy Education and Training. Adapting to a Changing World.* Illinois: Charles C Thomas Publisher Ltd.

Rogers, C. (1983) *Freedom to Learn for the 80s.* Bell and Howell Company: Ohio.

Rogers, C. (1995) *On Becoming a Person: A Therapist's View of Psychotherapy.* New York: Mariner Books.

Roth, E.A., Hua, X., Lu, W., Novak, J.B., Wang, F., Mehnert, T.N., Morano, R.K., Fiore, J. and Sterenberg Mahon, A.J. (2021) 'Clinical training in music therapy: perceptions of preparedness and satisfaction', *Voices: A World Forum for Music Therapy,* 21 (3), pp.1–21.

Ryan, A. and Tilbury, D. (2013) *Flexible Pedagogies: New Pedagogical Ideas.* York: The Higher Education Academy.

Savin-Baden, M. (2014) 'Using problem-based learning: new constellations for the 21st century', *Journal on Excellence in College Teaching,* 25 (3/4), pp.197–219.

Schon, D. (ed.) (1991) *The Reflective Turn: Case Studies in and on Educational Practice.* New York: Teachers College Press.

Streeter, E. (2002) 'Some observations in music therapy training groups' in Davies, A. and Richards, E. (eds.) *Music Therapy and Group Work Sound Company.* London: Jessica Kingsley Publishers, pp.262–273.

Tarrant, P. (2013) *Reflective Practice and Professional Development.* London: Sage Publications Ltd.

Torres, J.T. (2022) 'Feedback as open ended conversation: inviting students to co-regulate and metacognitively reflect during assessment', *Journal of the Scholarship of Teaching and Learning,* 22 (1), pp.81–94.

Williams, S. and Rutter, L. (2021) *The Practice Educator's Handbook.* London: Learning Matters SAGE.

Chapter 3

A historical context for music therapy training

Tessa Watson

Introduction

This chapter will provide a context for the UK training experience, including a historical pathway through the development of training and regulation in the UK. Consideration of the current climate in higher education in the UK, and the opportunities and pressures that this brings for staff and trainees will be explored. The context for music therapy training in Europe and internationally will be considered. The chapter will conclude with some central principles for contemporary practice such as cultural openness, e-learning and technology, interprofessional learning and service evaluation and research.

The history of music therapy training in the UK

From short introductory courses arranged by the society for Music Therapy and Remedial Music (later the British Society for Music Therapy, BSMT), came the first music therapy training programme in London in 1968 at the Guildhall School of Music and Drama, run by Juliette Alvin (a professional cellist). In 1974 a Nordoff and Robbins training began at Goldie Leigh hospital, led by American composer Paul Nordoff and British teacher Clive Robbins. This moved to Southlands College, Roehampton Institute of Higher Education in 1978 where two cohorts trained before moving to north London (Fraser 2007: 2009). Nordoff and Robbins now has three cohorts in London, Manchester and Newcastle. At Roehampton (now University of Roehampton) a programme continued, developing its own identity following the short collaboration with Nordoff and Robbins. In 1976 the Association of Professional Music Therapists (APMT) was formed, and in 1987 the professional journal, titled *Journal of British Music Therapy* was begun. This is now titled the *British Journal of Music Therapy*. In 1991 a part time training began at Bristol University (now University of West of England) and in 1994 a further training began at Anglia Polytechnic University Cambridge (now Anglia Ruskin University). Other new programmes followed in 2002 at University of Edinburgh (until 2015 identified with Nordoff and Robbins, and now at Queen Margaret University, Edinburgh), in 1997-2008 at the Royal Welsh College of Music and

Drama and from 2010 at University of South Wales, in 1998 at University of Limerick and in 2018 at University of Derby. In 2011 BSMT and APMT merged to form the British Association for Music Therapy (BAMT), now with five paid positions (one full time and four part time) representing 1200 members, of which 860 were working music therapists and 160 trainees in 2023.

There are currently eight qualifying training programmes in music therapy in the UK, all approved by HCPC, and one in Limerick in Southern Ireland. All have common curriculum guidance (TEC 2023). At the time of writing, new apprenticeship trainings, considered important for widening participation in training, are being developed in the UK at University of Roehampton and at Teeside University (Gov UK no date).

These historical developments are documented by authors such as Tyler (2000), Darnley-Smith and Patey (2003), Bunt and Hoskyns (2002), Bunt (2015) and are vividly conveyed in the historical perspectives interviews in the *British Journal of Music Therapy* (Wigram and Loth 2000, Bunt and Durham 2000, Odell-Miller and Darnley-Smith 2001, Warwick and Simmons 2001). Reviews of the profession tracking the development of areas of work, roles and job satisfaction have been conducted by Stewart (2000) and Carr et al (2017). The approaches and history of some specific training programmes have been documented (Sobey and Woodcock 1999, Simpson 2007) with a European perspective being provided in Stegemann's book (2016).

A narrative of difference

For those who trained in the UK in the early years, there was a strong narrative of difference between the training programmes. A small amount of literature relating to one's own tradition of training was studied in great depth, without the access that trainees now have to online publications in the UK and internationally. Wigram said in 2000 that 'there was very little literature compared with now when we've got a lot of books and texts on music therapy, and the journals. In those days there was very little, and it was putting it all together and believing what the tutors told you' (Wigram and Loth 2000: 5). Warwick describes how 'there seemed to be so much emphasis on how much each [programme] was different from the other, including some misinformation, rather than looking at the similarities' (Warwick and Simmons 2001: 49). Other interesting accounts of training in the early years can be read in Bunt and Hoskyns (2002, Chapter 3).

Odell-Miller remembers a series of APMT residential weekends in the mid-1980s that included music therapy groups, presentations and debates (Odell-Miller and Darnley-Smith 2001), and describes that during the weekend:

> 'there were some difficult arguments and debates between different schools of thought on music therapy. We were at this 'child-like' stage where we were all being very competitive and people would say things like, 'well, I've just been listening to you present and what you've been saying isn't music therapy

in my view.' Some people's research was denigrated to 'just playing a numbers game' and not being 'proper' music therapy, and there was a lot of upset, and disagreement. There were also some very interesting, less controversial discussions'.

(Odell-Miller and Darnley-Smith 2001: 12)

Finding the middle ground

As Waller notes (1991) part of becoming a profession is the political and passionate dialogue that takes place from strongly held positions, enabling a secure middle ground to be found. Under Ansdell's Editorial guidance, the *British Journal of Music Therapy* published a fascinating series of historical perspectives interviews which provide a rich repository of fact and experience relating to the profession's development. In an interview in 1999 Eisler spoke about 'a measure of antagonism between the different types of music therapy, each trying to assert and validate themselves theoretically at a time of considerable financial insecurity in the early days of the profession as a whole' (1999: 45). In 1999 editions 1 and 2 of volume 13 of the *British Journal of Music Therapy* set out some of the positions to which Eisler refers (1999). These editions – noted wittily by Ansdell as being both most read, and most stolen, from the Nordoff and Robbins Library (Ansdell 2015a) – included an article by Streeter titled 'Finding a Balance between Psychological Thinking and Musical Awareness in Music Therapy Theory — A Psychoanalytic Perspective' in volume 1 (1999) and four lively responses in the following Edition from Pavlicevic, Brown, Ansdell and Aigen (all 1999). Brown wrote of the 'danger of a situation whereby the "rules" regarding appropriate therapeutic behaviour are generated from within a theoretical model itself, whether psychological or musical. Inevitably these will be affected by the situation and needs of the client' (Brown 1999: 65). Similarly Darnley-Smith and Patey wrote about their reluctance to nail their colours to any particular mast, noting how the 'pioneers of music therapy were enriched by their wide-ranging musical, philosophical and psychological experiences' (2003: 2).

In 1999, in a chapter that outlined the Roehampton approach, Sobey and Woodcock suggested that 'an agreed core syllabus for training is precise enough to ensure adequately high standards but sufficiently flexible to embrace some strongly defined different philosophies of work' (1999: 132). They suggested that these shared aspects were an emphasis on the interactive use of music and the centrality of the relationship between the service user and music therapist, whilst noting differences in emphasis and theory. In 2000 Bunt hoped for a 'place where we can cherish and respect differences' (Bunt and Durham 2000: 61), and Odell-Miller noted that 'we have got better at doing this – more professional and more aware of boundaries …. I hope that we will never lose some tension because difference is how you learn, change and learn new things' (2001: 12). However, perhaps it was at times, easier to reject or ignore rather than assimilate; Wetherick writes about the idea of silencing as a contrast to the challenging task of integration (2019: 72).

All this writing and thinking developed music therapy discourse and enabled frameworks to be held alongside each other and further explored. In contemporary training there is openness and exchange and trainees are interested in other approaches as one of our graduates explained:

> I'd be interested to know about the extent to which each approach to music therapy introduces its students to other approaches. We did have some good seminars on other approaches, but I would have been interested to know more to help me to put my approach into context – and to meet students from other approaches.

The journey to regulation

To develop a career structure in line with other paramedic professions Tony Wigram and Helen Odell-Miller led APMT work with the Department of Health (paramedic professions such as Occupational Therapy, Speech and Language Therapy and Physiotherapy are now usually referred to as allied health professions or AHPs). Wigram was appointed the Music Therapy Advisor for the Department of Health (Wigram and Sutton 2011). His work was not straightforward as music therapists were already working in a wide range of settings, not just within the National Health Service (NHS). In order to progress this project it was considered necessary to align music therapy as a paramedic partner contributing to treatment within medicine, psychiatry and psychology. This began a positioning which Wigram notes was contentious to some (Wigram and Loth 2000) and that contemporary authors continue to consider misrepresents music therapy (Procter 2001 and 2008, Ansdell 2015b). Wigram spoke of this alignment with paramedics as nearly leading to music therapy being subsumed within occupational therapy, and describes the campaign that needed to be undertaken to avoid this happening (Wigram and Loth 2000). Despite setbacks, in 1991 Tony Wigram and Rachel Darnley-Smith (the Chair of APMT at that time) began a process of applying for state registration that was concluded in 1996 when state registration of music therapy (alongside art psychotherapy and dramatherapy) was formally ratified in parliament (Barrington 2015). This process involved considerable work including the definition of qualifications, of basic or specialised work and agreement about good practice. This work led to continued collaboration between training courses in the form of the Courses Liaison Committee of APMT (now the Training and Education Committee of BAMT) and to the Basic Module of Training document (Wigram and Loth 2000), now revised and titled Curriculum Guidance (TEC 2023). Roberts writes about this thoughtful process of development that it 'involved great care to establish unity amidst diversity ... reducing cherished ideals to formulations in legal documents must have seemed at times an impossible task' (Robarts 1997: 35). Despite these developments, a formal career structure remains elusive leading to employment attrition. In 2000 Stewart noted low levels of recognition, poor employment prospects and poor morale, and noted the 'highly flexible, imaginative attitude to employment' that was needed (2000: 14). In 2017, Carr et al also noted the adaptability of music therapists and the challenges of provision across all areas of the UK (especially in rural areas).

10th World Congress as a benchmark

Perhaps the 10th World Congress of Music Therapy, held in Oxford in 2002 and titled 'Dialogue and Debate – Music Therapy in the 21st Century: a contemporary force for change' (Goodman 2011, Sutton 2002), stands as a benchmark for collaboration and development in the profession in the UK. Introducing the congress in the *British Journal of Music Therapy*, Sutton wrote that 'the Oxford congress offers us a setting within which we can "come together around music therapy without having to agree about it"' (Sutton 2002: 4). At the time of writing, all training courses in the UK are approved by HCPC and work with shared curriculum guidance and the HCPC Standards of Proficiency (which apply to Art Psychotherapy, Dramatherapy and Music Therapy; HCPC 2023a and 2023b). The most recent version of the HCPC SOPs took effect in September 2023 (HCPC 2022), and the most recent Curriculum Guidance is also dated 2023 (TEC 2023).

Following state registration being achieved in 1996, discourse within the profession has continued to interrogate the relationship of music therapy to professions, healthcare models and more recently to power. Barrington's article in 2008 set out some of these issues noting that eternal pressures (government, employers and bodies such as education, the NHS and social care) could 'cause music therapy to be defined in a manner which is incompatible with the clinical ethos of the work involved' and that 'seeking and gaining approval from others is a pragmatic means of survival' (2008: 67 and 70). This article prompted responses from other authors which discussed ideas such as the resistance of professions to change, concepts of expertise, status and power and indeed the complexity of the whole picture (Ansdell and Pavlicevic 2008, Procter 2008). Changing ideas about power in healthcare, and service user and carer involvement have been usefully explored in recent years (Johnstone and Boyle 2020) with a considerable shift both in perspective, content and delivery of teaching in music therapy training programmes. The first conference on service user and carer co-production in healthcare education recently took place (Cadogan et al 2023). Involving service users in co-production of teaching and in delivery of teaching is now seen as a central principle for music therapy training. The importance of authenticity within this process is noted in the ladder rung process, moving from coercion through to engagement and with co-production as the final goal (We Coproduce no date).

European and international context

Wigram's work as Chair of both the EMTC and World Federation of Music Therapy contributed much to understanding and collaboration across countries. Authors have drawn together overviews of European and international training in literature and presentations. For example in presentations at the World Congress of Music Therapy in Hamburg in 1996 and at the European Music Therapy Confederation in 2005, in Ridder and Tsiris (2015), Stegemann et al (2016, including maps of music therapy training courses in Europe), Hanser (2016) and with the Aalborg programme being described in detail in Wigram et al 2002. De Backer noted that 'the courses differ in many ways and a training in one country might not be at all comparable with that in another area of Europe' (Sutton et al 2003: 61). Differences and changes within political and health care systems across Europe are noted as a barrier to drawing parallels between countries. There is variation between undergraduate and postgraduate levels of training within Europe and internationally; for example in the UK the training is only provided as a Masters qualification and in Austria there are both BA and MA levels of training (Nocker-Ribaupierre 2016). The International Interview Series in the *British Journal of Music Therapy* (2003–2005) provides a vivid account of work in Europe and internationally, with reflection upon themes of training and practice. Within these interviews Sutton et al raise issues such as broadening music therapy training, advanced music therapy training, post training supervision framework and standards of training and practice across Europe (Sutton et al 2003). The European Consortium for Arts Therapies Education was founded in 1991 and represents and encourages the development of the Arts Therapies at a European level (ECArTE 2023). Internationally, Goodman's comprehensive texts set out the training picture across a range of countries (2011 and 2015), and Hanser includes a timeline of development in the USA, and the voices of international trainers.

European Music Therapy Confederation initiatives

Various initiatives from the European Music Therapy Confederation (EMTC) have aimed to support parity of qualification or standards, the most recent being a research project which suggests standards for safe and effective music therapy practice, drawing upon 116 data responses from 78 training courses across Europe (Dowling et al 2022: 53). This project, undertaken by an international group of music therapist colleagues, aimed to support both the development of music therapy in countries where it was emerging and the diversity of cultural and geographical practice within music therapy across Europe (and indeed worldwide). Projects such as this have allowed knowledge and expertise to be shared, and questions such as those posed by Stegemann, to be answered:

> 'Working in the field of education – designing, revising or streamlining a curriculum – some questions come up repeatedly: How do they do it in other institutes or in other countries? How do others deal with a certain issue? Who is experienced with a distinct problem? Does one really have to reinvent the wheel?'
>
> (Stegemann 2016: 13)

The current climate in higher education in the UK

It is useful to shift focus slightly here to consider in more detail the UK current higher education climate and its impact upon music therapy training. The management of higher education in the UK is led by four bodies, one in each of the countries making up the UK, with different structures and arrangements across each country. These were previously governed by QAA (Quality Assurance Agency), now the Office for Students (QAA and Office for Students 2023). There are currently approximately 285 higher education providers in the UK, funded through student tuition fees and grants, and additional grants and income. There has been a considerable reduction since 2012 in any governmental funding, leading to increased tuition fees (including an emphasis on the recruitment of international students, challenging in the context of Brexit and visa restrictions), a push to increase knowledge exchange funding, and challenges to sustainability for many institutions. Additionally, support for strategically important subjects and an aversion to high cost non-strategic subjects has led to the increased demise of subjects in the arts and humanities.

In their policy paper setting out data and strategy Atherton et al (2023) state that there are over 2 million higher education students in the UK, an increase in numbers (most consistently in Wales), with most studying in England and approximately 20% of these students being postgraduate. These authors estimate there are around 230,000 staff working in the UK sector.

Pressures within higher education in the UK

The standard of teaching in HEIs is assessed every four years using the gold, silver, bronze or requires improvement ratings of the REF (Research Excellence Framework) and TEF (Teaching Excellence Framework). It seems that all parties involved are unsatisfied (Crown Copyright 2021). Student satisfaction is falling, with students questioning the value of their education and the impact of stress on their mental health (particularly relating to cost of living and value for money of fees and teaching). University management points to the funding gap leading to deficits in budgets and challenges in maintaining resources and finding new income streams. Lecturers complain about managerialism with no focus upon scholarship, accuse management of bullying and of requiring impossible productivity, and in 2022–2023 resorted to Union action to gain security of employment, reasonable workload and pay (Mahony and Weiner 2019, UCU 2023). In December 2022 a national conversation was launched to find bold and innovative solutions for the future (Universities UK 2023), however this conversation and the issues have been ongoing for years (DES 2003) with no easy solution. Along with the aim to provide more equitable access to particular groups of students (specifically disabled students, those with particular experiences such as those from minority ethnic groups and care leavers), to raise graduate outcomes and to fund scientific research, the agenda is ambitious. One important development has been the increasing introduction of apprenticeships. These are emerging in the arts therapies with the first training courses planned to begin in 2024 and 2025, anticipated to bring the benefits of widening participation and accessibility. The context described here provides both limitations and innovative opportunities for trainers.

Plurality as the future?

Ansdell wrote in 1999 of the need for 'a creative and vibrant plurality of both practice and theory' (1999: 75) and the idea of plurality continues to be relevant for the development of the profession. Using this ancient idea, Dryden and Cooper (2015) write about pluralism in psychotherapy as having a premise that each person will need something different from their therapy, with plurality celebrating diversity for clients and practitioners, and encouraging the integration of different approaches into practice. Dryden and Cooper also consider that plurality is a 'direct challenge to the "schoolism" that has been endemic in the field of counselling and psychotherapy' (2016: 3); likewise in music therapy. It was to this schoolism that Pavlicevic referred to in speaking about moving past historic debates in music therapy (in Butterton 2008). In 2014 Maratos challenged the BAMT conference audience, asking:

> 'What if we said to ourselves that it's time to move on. Yes, we had squabbling parents. They shaped our lives. But that was a long time ago… What if we literally put the two bits together? We would not stop competing or developing new approaches, but the competition would not be from old sensitivities but from what works best for the patient'.
>
> (2014: 7)

In this presentation Maratos also referred to the interesting Schesi graduate group made up of graduates from across the training programmes that ended the 2002 BAMT conference (Maratos 2014).

Authors such as Pavlicevic (2008), Maratos (2014) and Lawes (2021) suggest that rather than being linked to traditions, schoolism or how the practitioner wishes to work, a pluralistic approach could respond to what the service user needs, using what Aigen terms a 'situationally determined approach' (2005: xx). The centralising of the needs of the service user is at the centre of music therapy practice and is now one of the HCPC standards of proficiency (HCPC 2023a). It is of course not new; many music therapists (including the authors of this book) have drawn upon diverse approaches and techniques throughout their practice. This response to need has also seen the role of the music therapist expanding to include not only direct work with service users but also diverse roles such as collaborative work across disciplines, work with families and carers, with staff teams, in leadership and strategic roles and in delivering training. Chapter 9 in this book includes stories from music therapists who have taken different pathways in their careers, including in leadership roles.

Mary Priestley wrote in 1988 that 'Music therapy as a profession is feeling secure enough to take a long look at itself and be open – where necessary – to change and development': some of this change has taken rather a long time (Priestley 1998: 3). In 2002 Bunt and Hoskyns suggested future developments in relation to greater diversity of musicianship, diversity of those who make up the profession, and the development of advanced clinical trainings, all issues that continue to need attention today (2002: 317). In 2016 Sandford suggested future directions for the profession might be to support equality and diversity (including music therapists supporting marginalised service users and staff), cultural commissioning, social psychiatry and the centralising of the service user's voice (2016: 63). Some of these issues are now considered briefly.

Central principles for future music therapy education

This chapter has traced the journey of music therapy from its beginnings in the UK to the current state of regulation and contemporary training. The development of context, discourse and practice, and access to online and international resources which have grown exponentially have meant that the original training courses would now be unrecognisable to the current trainee. Trainers continually develop programmes in order to reflect change, and over the past few years there have been a number of influences that have necessitated development of many aspects of training programmes. Influences from the information age, from contemporary research across a broad range of disciplines, from disability studies, from service user and carer involvement and from contemporary cultural changes (such as ideas about equality, gender, the use of technology and changes in the economy) have considerably influenced practice and training, with programmes interrogating their positioning and making positive changes to all aspects of their provision. Four of these areas are now briefly explored.

Cultural openness and availability

A central principle of this book is the importance of cultural openness and humility across the profession; in training and practice. Sundar usefully defines culture as 'belief systems, philosophical orientations, tradition, religion, art, values and societal normal for behaviour' (2015: 204). For many years the interaction between the concept of culture and the profession seemed challenging. The idea of cultural sensitivity or availability was not explored in detail on early training programmes and the majority of conceptual models used were not sufficiently able to afford reflection upon oppressive practice. Stige's book in 2002 perhaps provided impetus for change (Stige 2002). Another piece of writing which prompted discussion and reflection was Pavlievic's chapter about work with the Thembalethu community, which opened dialogue about the relevance of transporting models into different cultural settings and about the importance of considering the different ways in which music is used in varied cultures (2004). Knowledge of and availability to multi-cultural music began to be considered more fully on training programmes (see Loth, 2006). Perhaps because of Loth's specific engagement with music from different cultures the programme at Anglia Ruskin was notably open to accepting trainees with a range of cultural traditions and instruments.

More recently referring to music therapists practicing in countries other than their own, Fitzsimons notes the different ways in which authors have reflected upon their own position and expectations, their roles and the effectiveness of therapy when working in different cultures (2016). Issues relating to boundaries, language, collaboration and the framing of theoretical approaches are raised by Fitzsimons as useful points for meeting cultural difference. These ideas are relevant for all music therapy practice. Development of understanding of the impact of cultural wealth in music therapy work has developed considerably since this time, with HCPC including the necessity to 'recognise the impact of culture, equality and diversity on practice and practise in a non-discriminatory and inclusive manner', noting the importance of intersectionality and stating that music making should be culturally informed (standards 5 and 7 and 12 respectively, HCPC 2023a).

Likewise, the personal identity of the music therapist, which in the early days of training was perhaps considered best kept out of the picture, is now considered essential to value and explore during training, with difference being welcome and celebrated. One trainer explained how this has been explored in their training programme:

> We get students to think about their own diversity, who are you? So thinking about race, culture, language, political opinion, religion, spirituality, gender, sexual orientation, etc. And then we think about that as therapists and we think about it as clients as well, and how those come together. Students have to read about experiencing race as a Music Therapist. We look at the psychology of diversity beyond prejudice and racism, learning and intercultural arts therapies and so on. So we really try and embed students thinking about what they bring and how they work with their clients. In the second year I get them to all go and look at music from other cultures, find recordings and think about what it means, and how it is used, and how that is experienced by the people of that culture and then how, if there's anything from that we can use that translates or that would be useful but also to reflect on how our clients might be experiencing the music and the assumptions we make about what music means.

Another programme runs a series of reading seminars that explores issues of cultural wealth such as race, gender, sexuality, disability and music, giving opportunities to explore central principles of equality that underpin the training. Literature further articulates the value of teaching about these issues, with writing about sexuality (York 2015, Baine et al 2016), gender identity (Voices edition 19, 3, 2019 and Myerscough 2023), racial identity (see CAMTI 2023, Lindo 2023, Vencatasamy 2023) disability (Davies 2022) and models of practice (Pickard 2020, 2022). The construction of a safe space where trainees feel able to bring and explore different aspects of their identity is now understood to be an important part of training, and this links with ongoing self-care for music therapists in professional practice. Gilboa proposes three layers of cultural exploration for trainees; the clinical, programme and personal (Gilboa 2015). Chances for the trainee to develop an appreciation and awareness of cultural wealth (including their own, and including music) and to become aware of their own identifications and perspectives is now part of the training process and is undertaken in varied and creative ways.

E-learning and technology

As technology advances there are both benefits and challenges in society. Music therapy training has largely been seen as important to teach face to face; however for many, large parts of life are now conducted online. Trainees will need to learn safe and effective practice in the online age, maintaining for example a safe online clinical practice (including safe storage of confidential data), along with managing their own social media and online identity as a health professional. Currently, the advantages and disadvantages of AI (artificial intelligence) are being debated, with some authors considering that the strategic use of AI can be appropriate in training and can support practitioners (Blyler and Seligman 2023) and individualised healthcare (Dave and Patel 2023).

Many trainers prefer to teach music skills on campus, to maximise the participatory, collaborative and embodied qualities of music. Within practice, despite some moves towards online work (Baker and Krout 2009) music therapists have generally been reluctant to embrace this development. But in 2020 the Covid 19 pandemic required trainers and clinicians to quickly adapt practice in order to support service users, manage multiple lockdowns and continue their work (Cousins-Booth and Rizkallah 2020). This period of change was extreme and stressful for many however valuable knowledge and experience was gained about working online. The importance of offering online contact for service users who, for a range of reasons may not be able to access face to face work is evident. Training programmes now include consideration of online working, and may also provide some training content online when relevant.

Interprofessional learning and practice

In order to trace the pathway of collaborative working in music therapy we might start with Priestley, who wrote in 1993 'The multidisciplinary team – I loved it and hated it, but we music therapists could not and cannot do without it, so the more young music therapists have time to get to know and work with its members, the better' (Priestley 1993: 27). Perhaps having to work so hard to develop the discipline of music therapy made early practitioners unsure about diluting their work by collaborating with others. However, the richest parts of professional work can be with colleagues, as one graduate explained:

Working with other disciplines has been the most important aspect of my work in any clinical settings. I feel grateful for having an opportunity to write an essay on this topic during the training. I considered the issues of communication, flexibility, group dynamics, projection, self-care in my essay, which has provided me a framework of working with others. Reflective practice has been the most important principle.

Other arts media and health and care approaches implicitly and explicitly emerge in our work (Cobbett 2007, Watson 2017). Collaborative work can greatly support service users, and many authors have now written about this creative and fruitful way of working (Twyford and Watson 2008, Strange et al 2017, Colbert and Bent 2018, Oldfield and Carr 2018). The HCPC require that music therapists 'work appropriately with others' (2023a: 12), referring to co-production with service users, the importance of valuing other disciplines and the need for leadership in collaboration. Training must therefore provide teaching and opportunities to explore this rich area of practice. Trainers are now frequently able to draw in colleagues from linked disciplines to provide teaching. The majority of music therapy training programmes across the UK are embedded in schools or departments that also teach some or all of Art, Dance Movement and Dramatherapy, Play Therapy, Psychotherapy and Counselling, or other AHPs such as Nursing, Physiotherapy and Occupational Therapy. This collaboration during training assists understanding of other disciplines and of how they might work together, as one graduate suggested:

> I felt fairly well prepared to work with other disciplines, as the interprofessional module gave us the opportunity to experience workshops in the other arts and play therapies. This provided me with new perspectives and a glimpse what it might be like for a client who is not an expert in that modality. The most important principles for this work are consistent communication, preparation in advance and balancing different approaches alongside each other.

Research, service evaluation and their role in professional practice

In 1985 Leslie Bunt was awarded the first music therapy PhD in the UK; this is now a well-trodden path, although PhD studies are still rarely funded despite the need for research. The current economic picture is challenging and this impacts upon funding for music therapy posts across the health and care landscape. In 2022 the Care Quality Commission wrote of the UK that 'the health and care system is gridlocked, unable to operate effectively' (2022: 4). They referred to workforce shortages in all sectors and barriers to accessible health and social care across the UK, with child and adult mental health and learning disability and autism services being areas of particular concern (CQC 2023). The Kings Fund explore how funding of health and social care in the UK has failed to keep up with inflation, and how the delay in social care reforms in particular has led to great pressure on the system (2023). These pressures mean that services face greater scrutiny for evidence of efficacy in order to be commissioned. Research and service evaluation are therefore key components of professional practice and employability for graduates.

Service evaluation

HCPC (2023a: 18 and 19) requires music therapists to engage in evidence based practice, and to be able to monitor and evaluate their own practice, including quality management and improvement. HCPC also refer to knowledge of research methodologies that may be relevant to the role (HCPC 2023a: 18). This does not mean that trainees have to be researchers or have completed research prior to qualifying, but that they should know how to draw upon appropriate resources in order to evaluate their practice. Abrams writes about the different music therapy evidence that is available (2010), and Aigen argues for the relevance of the evidence hierarchy for music therapy in working with each service user's unique needs (2015). Skills in searching, critiquing and using a range of resources, including literature and research, are embedded within academic work during training. These skills support the trainee's ability to work in co-production with service users to formulate, assess, carry out and evaluate music therapy clinical work. Research skills contribute to evidence based practice, including 'asking questions, acquiring, appraising and applying evidence to patient care decisions', and communicating information to service users in order to make shared decisions about the music therapy work to be undertaken (Lehane et al 2018: 2).

Patient reported/experience outcome measures (PROMs/PREMs) are increasingly viewed as important but have not yet been fully explored within music therapy (Andsell and Meehan 2010, Clifford et al 2021, Havsteen-Franklin et al 2021). These might include pre and post therapy questionnaires or other indicators which could be adapted for service users with complex communication needs. A range of patient reported outcome measures are used, often within NHS settings, however these are generally not specifically developed for music therapy. Music therapy measures have been developed for some specific areas of work (Compton Dickinson et al 2017, Kirkwood et al 2019 and Millstein et al 2020).

In challenging economic times practitioners will need to make a financial and strategic argument for their jobs, and Odell-Miller advises it is important that music therapists can engage with appropriate guidance and link their practice to these as they may 'point to roles for Music Therapy' (2018: 72). Wood et al write about their strategies for engaging with commissioners and funders, describing how they provided feedback and reports and developed their service in line with trends (2016: 44). This ability to engage with learning resources and to critique and apply evidence to practice is not only part of gaining music therapy resources, but also part of life-long learning, essential to the continued development of the music therapist (Linsley et al 2019).

Coda

'When you first train it's rather like learning to drive a car: at first you think you must 'do this; do that' then you get beyond that and it begins to flow, things happen more instinctively and you're off''

(Eisler and Verney 1999: 46)

Leading on from this exploration of the rich history of UK music therapy, and some central considerations for contemporary music therapy practice, the next chapters will consider in detail aspects of the training journey, beginning with music and improvisation.

References

Abrams, B. (2010) 'Evidence-based music therapy practice: an integral understanding', *Journal of Music Therapy*, XLVII (4), pp.351–379.

Aigen, K. (1999) 'The true nature of music-centred music therapy theory', *British Journal of Music Therapy*, 13 (2), pp.77–82.

Aigen, K. (2005) *Music-Centred Music Therapy*. Barcelona: Gilsum.

Aigen, K. (2015) 'A critique of evidence-based music therapy practice in music therapy', *Music Therapy Perspectives*, 33 (1), pp.12–24.

Ansdell, G. (1999) 'Challenging premises. A response to Elaine Streeter's "Finding a balance between psychological thinking and musical awareness in music therapy theory – a psychoanalytic perspective"', *British Journal of Music Therapy*, 13 (2), pp.72–76.

Ansdell, G. (2015a) 'A useful and lively period of controversy: reflections on editing the BJMT 1998-2001' within 'Looking back: reflection from previous editors of the British Journal of Music Therapy', *British Journal of Music Therapy*, 29 (2), pp.4–5.

Andsell, G. (2015b) *How Music Helps in Music Therapy and Everyday Life*. Surrey: Ashgate.

Andsell, G. and Meehan, J. (2010) '"Some light at the end of the tunnel": exploring users' evidence for the effectiveness of music therapy in adult mental health settings', *Music and Medicine*, 2 (1), pp.29–40.

Ansdell, G. and Pavlicevic, M. (2008) 'Responding to the challenge: between boundaries and borders', *British Journal of Music Therapy*, 22 (2), pp.73–76.

Atherton, G., Lewis, J. and Bolton, P. (2023) *Higher Education in the UK: Systems, Policy Approaches, and Challenges*. London: House of Commons Library. Available here: https://researchbriefings.files.parliament.uk/documents/CBP-9640/CBP-9640.pdf (Accessed 20 June 2023).

Baine, C.L., Grzanka, P.R. and Crowe, B.J. (2016) 'Toward a queer music therapy: the implications of queer theory for radically inclusive music therapy', *The Arts in Psychotherapy*, 50, pp.22–33.

Baker, F. and Krout, R. (2009) 'Songwriting via Skype: an on-line music therapy intervention to enhance social skills in an adolescent diagnosed with Aspergers', *British Journal of Music Therapy*, 23 (1), pp.3–14.

Barrington, A. (2008) 'Challenging the profession', *British Journal of Music Therapy*, 22 (2), pp.65–72.

Barrington, A. (2015) 'Perspectives on the development of the music therapy profession in the UK', *Music Therapy in Europe: Paths of Professional Development*, Approaches special edition 7 (1), pp.118–122.

Blyler, A.P. and Seligman, M.E.P. (2023) 'AI assistance for coaches and therapists', *Journal of Positive Psychology*, 14/9/23. Available here: www.tandfonline.com/doi/full/10.1080/17439760.2023.2257642 (Accessed 20 December 2023).

Brown, S. (1999) 'Some thoughts on music, therapy and music therapy', *British Journal of Music Therapy*, 13 (2), pp.63–71.

Bunt, L. (2015) 'The integration of art and science in music therapy training: some challenges in the UK' in Goodman, K. (ed.) *International Perspectives in Music Therapy Education and Training. Adapting to a Changing World.* Illinois: Charles C Thomas Publisher Ltd, pp.267–300.

Bunt, L. and Durham, C. (2000) 'Historical perspectives interview series Leslie Bunt interviewed by Cathy Durham', *British Journal of Music Therapy*, 14 (2), pp.56–61.

Bunt, L. and Hoskyns, S. (2002) *The Handbook of Music Therapy.* London: Routledge.

Butterton, M. (2008) *Listening to Music in Psychotherapy.* London: CRC Press.

Cadogan, H., Price, A. and Watson, T. (2023) Book of Abstracts: Co-producing Professional Healthcare Education; How Do We All Work Together? Conference held at University of Roehampton on 12/9/23.

Care Quality Commission (2023) *The State of Health Care and Adult Social Care in England 2021/2022.* London: Crown Copyright.

Carr, C., Tsiris, G. and Reigersberg, M.S. (2017) 'Understanding the present, re-visioning the future: an initial mapping of music therapists in the United Kingdom', *British Journal of Music Therapy*, 31 (2), pp.68–85.

Clifford, A.M., Shanahan, J., Moss, H., Cleary, T., Senter, M., O'Hagan, E.M., Glynn, L., O'Neill, D., Watts, M. and Ni Bhriain, O. (2021) 'Insights from an early-stage development mixed methods study on arts-based interventions for older adults following hospitalisation', *Complementary Therapies in Medicine*, 60, 102745, ISSN 0965-2299. Available here: https://doi.org/10.1016/j.ctim.2021.102745

Cobbett, S. (2007) 'Playing at the boundaries. Combining music therapy with other creative therapies in individual work with children with emotional and behavioural difficulties', *British Journal of Music Therapy*, 21 (1), pp.3–11.

Colbert, T. and Bent, C. (2018) *Working Across Modalities in the Arts Therapies, Creative Collaborations.* London: Routledge.

Colonialism and Music Therapy Interlocutors (CAMTI) Collective (2023) *Colonialism and Music Therapy.* Dallas, Texas: Barcelona Publishers.

Compton Dickinson, S. and Hakvoort, L. (2017) *The Clinician's Guide to Forensic Music Therapy: Treatment Manuals for Group Cognitive Analytic Music Therapy (G-CAMT) and Music Therapy Anger Management (MTAM).* London: Jessica Kingsley Publishers Ltd.

Cousins-Booth, J. and Rizkallah, M. (2020) 'Covid 19: notes from the United Kingdom', *British Journal of Music Therapy*, 34 (2), pp.77–79.

Crown Copyright (2021) *Independent Review of the Teaching Excellence and Student Outcomes Framework (TEF).* London: Crown Copyright.

Darnley-Smith, R. and Patey, H.M. (2003) *Music Therapy.* London: Sage Publications.

Dave, M. and Patel, N. (2023) 'Artificial intelligence in healthcare and education', *British Dental Journal*, 234 (10), pp.761–764.

Davies, H. (2022) '"Autism is a way of being": an "insider perspective" on neurodiversity, music therapy and social justice', *British Journal of Music Therapy,* 36 (1), pp.16–26.

Department for Education and Skills (2003) *The Future of Higher Education.* Norwich: HMSO.

Dowling, M., Hussey, C., Maclean, E. and Tsiris, G. (2022) 'Abstracts of the 12th European Music Therapy Conference', *British Journal of Music Therapy,* Online special edition 1-315. Available here: https://journals.sagepub.com/page/bjmb/abstractsofthe12theuropeanmusictherapyconference (Accessed 21 December 2023).

Dryden, W. and Cooper, M. (2015) *The Handbook of Pluralistic Counselling and Psychotherapy.* London: Sage Publications.

Eisler, J. and Verney, R. (1999) 'Historical perspectives interview series. Jean Eisler – Interviewed by Rachel Verney', *British Journal of Music Therapy,* 13 (2), pp.44–48.

European Consortium for Arts Therapies Education (2023) *European Consortium for Arts Therapies Education.* Available here: www.ecarte.info/ (Accessed 22 December 2023).

Fitzsimons, B (2016) 'Approaching music therapy in a different country: a literature review on cultural considerations when practising in a developing country', *British Journal of Music Therapy,* 30 (2), pp.83–88.

Fraser, S. (2007) *Every Note Counts, The Story of Nordoff-Robbins Music Therapy.* London: James and James Publishers Ltd.

Fraser, S. (2009) *The Nordoff-Robbins Adventure. Fifty Years of Creative Music Therapy.* London: James and James Publishers Ltd.

Gilboa, A. (2015) 'Ebony, ivory and other shades of music therapy training in Israel: some multicultural thoughts and considerations' in Goodman, K. (ed.) *International Perspectives in Music Therapy Education and Training. Adapting to a Changing World.* Illinois: Charles C Thomas Publisher Ltd, pp.130–158.

Goodman, K. (2015) *International Perspectives in Music Therapy Education and Training. Adapting to a Changing World.* Illinois: Charles C Thomas Publisher Ltd.

Goodman, K.D. (2011) *Music Therapy Education and Training from Theory to Practice.* Illinois USA: Charles C Thomas Publisher Ltd.

Gov.UK (no date) *Apprenticeship Training Course Arts Therapist (degree) (level 7).* Available here: https://findapprenticeshiptraining.apprenticeships.education.gov.uk/courses/432 (Accessed 5 May 2023).

Hanser, S. (2016) 'Music therapy training requirements' in Edwards, J. (Ed) *The Oxford Handbook of Music Therapy.* Oxford: Oxford University Press, pp.853–874.

Havsteen-Franklin, D., Oley, M., Sellors, S.J. and Eagles, D. (2021) 'Drawing on dialogues in arts-based dynamic interpersonal therapy (ADIT) for complex depression: a complex intervention development study using the Medical Research Council (UK) phased guidance', *Frontiers in Psychology,* doi: https://doi.org/10.3389/fpsyg.2021.588661

HCPC (2022) *Revisions to the Standards of Proficiency.* Available here: www.hcpc-uk.org/standards/standards-of-proficiency/reviewing-the-standards-of-proficiency/ (Accessed 2 May 2023).

HCPC (2023a) *Standards of Proficiency, Arts Therapists.* Available here: www.hcpc-uk.org/standards/standards-of-proficiency/arts-therapists/ (Accessed 21 December 2023).

HCPC (2023b) *Education. We Approve and Monitor Programmes within the UK for the Professions We Regulate.* Available here: www.hcpc-uk.org/education/ (Accessed 2 May 2023).

Johnstone, L. and Boyle, M. (2020) *The Power Threat Meaning Framework: Overview.* London: British Psychological Society.

Kings Fund (2023) *Health and Social Care in England: Tackling the Myths*. London: Kings Fund. Available here: www.kingsfund.org.uk/publications/health-and-social-care-england-myths (Accessed 8 September 2023).

Kirkwood, J., Graham-Wisener, L., McConnell, T., Porter, S., Reid, J., Craig, N., Dunlop, C., Gordon, C., Thomas, D., Godsal, J. and Vorster, A. (2019) 'The MusiQual treatment manual for music therapy in a palliative care inpatient setting', *British Journal of Music Therapy*, 33 (1), pp.5–15.

Lawes, M. (2021) 'Trends of differentiation and integration in UK music therapy and the spectrum of music-centredness', *British Journal of Music Therapy*, 35 (1), pp.4–15.

Lehane, E., Leahy-Warren, P., O'Riordan, C., Savage, E., Drennan, J., O'Tuathaigh, C., O'Connor, M., Corrigan, M., Burke, F., Hayes, M., Lynch, H., Sahm, L., Heffernan, E., O'Keeffe, E., Blake, C., Horgan, F. and Hegarty, J. (2018) 'Evidence-based practice education for healthcare professions: an expert view', *BMJ Evidence Based Medicine*, 24, pp.103–108.

Lindo, D. (2023) 'Examining the accessibility of MA music therapy training in the United Kingdom for ethnic minority communities, *British Journal of Music Therapy*, 37 (1), pp.5–16.

Linsley, P., Kane, R. and Barker, J. (2019) *Evidence-Based Practice for Nurses and Healthcare Professionals*. London: Sage Publications Ltd.

Loth, H. (2006) 'How gamelan music has influenced me as a music therapist – a personal account', *Voices: A World Forum for Music Therapy*. Available at: www.voices.no/mainissues/mi40006000201.html (Accessed 7 September 2023).

Mahony, P. and Weiner, G. (2019) 'Neo-liberalism and the state of higher education in the UK', *Journal of Further and Higher Education*, 43 (4), pp.560–572.

Maratos, A. (2014) 'MTUK: collaboration for the future: keynote speech, BAMT conference, February 2014', *British Journal of Music Therapy*, 28 (2), p.6–15.

Millstein, A., Myers-Coffman, K., Horowitz, S., Kesslick, A. and Bradt, J. (2020) 'Experiences of implementing treatment manuals: Clinician, supervisor, and researcher reflections', *Nordic Journal of Music Therapy*, 30 (2), pp.179–191.

Myerscough, F. (2023) 'Reflections on (in)visibility and (in)audibility in music therapy: Who? How? To whom?', *British Journal of Music Therapy*, 37 (1), pp.17–27.

Nocker-Ribaupierre, M. (2016) 'Recognition of music therapy in Europe' in Edwards, J. (ed.) *The Oxford Handbook of Music Therapy*. Oxford: Oxford University Press, pp.927–936.

Odell-Miller, H. (2018) 'Response to Justine Schneider's article "Music therapy and dementia care practice in the United Kingdom: a British Association for music therapy membership survey"', *British Journal of Music Therapy*, 32 (2), pp.70–73.

Odell-Miller, H. and Darnley-Smith, R. (2001) 'Historical perspectives interview series Helen Odell-Miller interviewed by Rachel Darnley-Smith', *British Journal of Music Therapy*, 15 (1), pp.8–13.

Office for Students (2023) *About us*. Available at: www.officeforstudents.org.uk/ (Accessed 27 June 2023).

Pavlicevic, M. (1999) 'Thoughts, words and deeds: harmonies and counterpoints in music therapy theory', *British Journal of Music Therapy*, 13 (2), pp.59–62.

Pavlicevic, M. (2004) 'Learning from Thembalethu: towards responsive and responsible practice in community music therapy', in Ansdell, G., and Pavlicevic, M. (eds.) *Community Music Therapy*, London: Jessica Kingsley Publishers, pp.35–47.

Pickard, B. (2020) 'A critical reflection on the Health and Care Professions Council Standards of Proficiency for Music Therapists: a critical disability studies perspective', *British Journal of Music Therapy*, 34 (2), pp. 83–94.

Pickard, B. (2022) 'Anti-oppressive pedagogy as an opportunity for consciousness raising in the music therapy profession: a critical disability studies perspective', *British Journal of Music Therapy*, 36 (1), pp.3–64.

Procter, S. (2001) 'Empowering and enabling. Improvisational music therapy in non-medical mental health provision', *Voices A World Forum for Music Therapy*, 1 (2). doi: https://doi.org/10.15845/voices.v1i2.58

Procter, S. (2008) 'Premising the challenge. A response to Alison Barrington's article challenging the profession', *British Journal of Music Therapy*, 22 (2), pp.77–81.

Priestley, M. (1998) 'Foreword', *British Journal of Music Therapy*, 2 (1), pp.3–4.

Priestley, M. (1993) 'Stretto. Music therapy in the context of the multidisciplinary team: music therapy in the multidisciplinary team', *British Journal of Music Therapy*, 7 (1), pp.26–27.

QAA (2023) *The UK's Expert Quality Body for Tertiary Education*. Available at: www.qaa.ac.uk/ (Accessed 27 June 2023).

Ridder, H.M. and Tsiris, G. (2015) *Music Therapy in Europe: Path of Professional Development*, Approaches special edition 7 (1). Available here: https://approaches.gr/special-issue-7-1-2015/ (Accessed 21 December 2023).

Robarts, J. (1997) 'Naming things… but can we astonish the gods?', *British Journal of Music Therapy*, 11 (2), pp.34–35.

Sandford, S. (2016) 'Music therapists marching, running and playing with the beat: BAMT Conference Plenary Session – April 2016', *British Journal of Music Therapy*, 3 (2), pp.57–64.

Simpson, F. (2007) *Every Note Counts. The Story of Nordoff-Robbins Music Therapy*. London: James and James Publishers Ltd.

Sobey, K. and Woodcock, J. (1999) 'Psychodynamic music therapy. Considerations in training', in *Process in the Arts Therapies*. Cattanach, A. (ed.) London: Jessica Kingsley Publishers, pp.132–154.

Stegemann, T. (2016) *Music Therapy Training Programmes in Europe*, Zeitpunkt Musik. Germany: Verlag Publications.

Stewart, D. (2000) 'The state of the UK music therapy profession. Personal qualities, working models, support networks and job satisfaction', *British Journal of Music Therapy*, 14 (1), pp.13–27.

Stige, B. (2002) *Culture Centred Music Therapy*. Illinois: Barcelona Publishers.

Strange, J., Odell-Miller, H. and Richards, E. (2017) *Collaboration and Assistance in Music Therapy Practice, Roles, Relationships, Challenges*. London: Jessica Kingsley Publishers.

Streeter, E. (1999) 'Finding a balance between psychological thinking and musical awareness in music therapy theory – a psychoanalytic perspective', *British Journal of Music Therapy*, 13 (1), pp.5–20.

Sundar, S. (2015) 'Music therapy education in India: developmental perspectives' in Goodman, K. (ed.) *International Perspectives in Music Therapy Education and Training. Adapting to a Changing World*. Illinois: Charles C Thomas Publisher Ltd, pp.203–216.

Sutton, J. (2002) 'Editorial. Dialogue and debate', *British Journal of Music Therapy*, 16 (1), pp.4–6.

Sutton, J., De Backer, J., Hartley, N. and Wigram, T. (2003) 'Introducing the new interview series: the UK and a European perspective', *British Journal of Music Therapy*, 17 (2), pp.60–66.

Training and Education Committee, British Association of Music Therapy (2023) Personal communication via email regarding BAMT Curriculum Guidelines.

Twyford, K. and Watson, T. (2008) *Integrated Team Working: Music Therapy as Part of Transdisciplinary and Collaborative Approaches.* London: Jessica Kingsley Publishers.

Tyler, H.M. (2000) 'The music therapy profession in modern Britain' in Horden, P (ed.) *Music as Medicine. The History of Music Therapy since Antiquity.* Aldershot, Brookfield, USA: Ashgate, pp.375–393.

UCU (2023) *UCU Rising.* Available at: www.ucu.org.uk/rising (Accessed 27 June 2023).

Universities UK (2023) *Opening the National Conversation on University Funding.* Available at: www.universitiesuk.ac.uk/what-we-do/policy-and-research/publications/opening-national-conversation-university (Accessed 27 June 2023).

Vencatasamy, D. (2023) 'The importance of being diverse: exploring the journey from Brexit to belonging', *British Journal of Music Therapy,* 37 (1), pp.28–35.

Voices (2019) *Special Issue on Queering Music Therapy,* 19, p.3. doi: https://voices.no/index.php/voices/issue/view/373

Waller, D. (1991) *Becoming a Profession: The History of Art Therapy in Britain, 1940–82.* London: Routledge.

Warwick, A., and Simmons, M. (2001) 'Historical perspectives interview series Auriel Warwick interviewed by Mary Simmons', *British Journal of Music Therapy,* 15 (2), pp.42–50.

Watson, T. (2017) 'Supporting the unplanned journey. Music therapy as a developmental resource with people with profound and multiple learning disabilities and their carers and staff' in Strange, J., Odell-Miller, H. and Richards, E. (eds.) *Collaboration and assistance in music therapy practice: roles, relationships, challenges.* London: Jessica Kingsley Publishers Ltd, pp.169–187.

We Coproduce (no date) *The Art of Coproduction A Guerrilla Guide,* We Coproduce/NHS England.

Wetherick, D. (2019) 'Are UK music therapists talking past each other? A critical discourse of three book reviews', *British Journal of Music Therapy,* 33 (2), pp.67–73.

Wigram, T. and Loth, H. (2000) 'Historical perspectives interview series Tony Wigram interviewed by Helen Loth', *British Journal of Music Therapy,* 14 (1), pp.5–12.

Wigram, T., Nygaard Pedersen, I. and Bonde, L.O. (2002) *A Comprehensive Guide to Music Therapy. Theory, Clinical Practice, Research and Training.* London: Jessica Kingsley Publishers.

Wigram, T. and Sutton, J. (2011) 'A dialogue with Professor Tony Wigram. Considering music therapy and music therapy research in a changing world. A review of publications and their related links with the development of the music therapy profession over 3 decades', *British Journal of Music Therapy,* 25 (1), pp.8–31.

Wood, J., Sandford, S. and Bailey, E. (2016) '"The whole is greater". Developing music therapy services in the National Health Service: a case study revisited', *British Journal of Music Therapy,* 30 (1), pp.36–46.

York, E. (2015) 'Inclusion of lesbian, gay, bisexual, transgender, questioning content into the music therapy curriculum: resources for the educator' in Goodman, K. (ed.) *International Perspectives in Music Therapy Education and Training. Adapting to a Changing World.* Illinois: Charles C Thomas Publisher Ltd, pp.241–266.

Chapter 4

Music in training

Catherine Warner

Selection for training

Qualities and skills required to train

This chapter draws upon ideas about music within music therapy and explores the central role of music in music therapy training from preparation for training to professional practice. The act of co-creating music together between client and therapist forms the central relationship-making process in music therapy as taught in UK based training (Bunt and Hoskyns 2002, Wigram 2004, Bunt 2015, Edwards 2016). Music therapy trainees are expected to have skills and capacities in active music making before training. These are defined in various ways on course websites for prospective applicants. Wetherick's research (2016) identifies three discourses on music therapy Masters course webpages in the UK and in other recruitment material. The first narrative emphasises that the applicant must have existing musical skills and experience; the second, that trainees develop their musical skills during their music therapy training 'in order that they can use their music to help their clients' (Watson 2005: 10), and the third discourse, which is more hidden, that at audition, 'actual or potential relevant musical skills are selected for' (Wetherick 2016). Not all candidates will show these skills or potential sufficiently to be accepted, while successful candidates will develop them further in training.

During selection, to showcase existing musical skills, candidates are asked to prepare and perform music of their choice.

> A rounded musician who could be good at one instrument and competent with voice and competent with keyboard if their main instrument is a melody one. That is the ideal. (Trainer)

> There's a creative task on the keyboard, which is not about being harmonic, it's about being expressive, although people often think it is about being harmonic, but that's not what we look for. And then interactive role play – clinically based. (Trainer)

This requirement links to one of the music therapy specific Standards of Proficiency of the UK accrediting body, the Health and Care Professions Council (HCPC). Music therapists are required, by the time they qualify: *to be able to play at least one musical instrument to a high level, and to use their singing voice and a keyboard / harmonic instrument to a competent level* (HCPC Standard 13.34). This is interesting in contrast with other arts therapies. There is perhaps not such a strong requirement in art therapy for a background as a professional artist although applicants for arts therapy training are typically expected to be actively involved in some kind of art-making.

> I speak to my colleagues who are teaching Dramatherapy, Dance Therapy or Art Psychotherapy and they say 'actually you can have someone who hasn't been taught art or hasn't been to drama college or… but they can come with the talent and they can produce a portfolio or a video and you can see the potential'. And I don't think you can do that with music. Because of the actual technical [aspects of] how you hold the bow, you know, where you find the note… (Trainer)

The co-creation of the moment-to-moment interaction in clinical improvisation, particularly central in the UK models of practice, may require a number of interpersonal qualities as well as skills. Trainers spoke about this, saying 'I'm looking for an ear and a sensitivity and <u>listening</u>; more than just skill' and 'When we talk to people who are applying we say … the main thing is that we want you to be *generous* in your music, and we want to help widen your musical skills or widen your musical repertoire, or thinking about music so you can be as available as possible to the people you are working with.'

The importance of musical communication

One trainer described valuing an applicant's communicative or interpersonal potential even when some technical knowledge was lacking: 'A singer-songwriter who doesn't necessarily read music, who definitely doesn't have too many piano skills and maybe not another instrument, yet you see such a fantastic quality of music in terms of their interpersonal skills… their musicianship is in their interpersonal way; I think it's all about them, so it's much more [important] for me than whether they can play three instruments. They need to be able to communicate their music and be really flexible with their musicianship.' Her words relate to another music therapy-specific Standard of Proficiency requiring music therapists to: *Understand the practice and principles of musical improvisation as an interactive, communicative and relational process, including the psychological significance and effect of shared music making* (HCPC Standard 13.32).

Arguably, the potential or capacity to understand musical improvisation in relational and communicative terms does need to be present in training applicants, even if they have no history of being involved in musical improvisation. Lockett's research shows that development of musical improvisation capacity may develop early in childhood, through play. An applicant who is sufficiently in touch with their playfulness is more likely to be able to engage in improvisation (Lockett 2023). This will then allow them to engage with learning about musical therapeutic processes, significance and effect during their training.

During the Covid 19 pandemic, trainers were faced with selecting applicants who had not engaged in interactive music-making with others for some time, and had little prospect of doing so. This raised questions about not only their readiness to practise, but also the lack of opportunity to develop interactive processes during lockdown periods in their training. The dilemma led to trainers developing innovative practices such as recording improvisations, sending them to students, and students recording 'response improvisations' (Annesley and Haire 2021). Although musical improvisational responses to another person could not happen online in a sufficiently synchronous way in real time due to time lags, it was possible for the improvisational and relational aspects to be preserved and newly created in sequence through the recordings.

The selection process

In a detailed ethnographic study of the selection process of one institution, Wetherick constructs a notion of 'music therapy musicianship' which includes interpersonal skills in music-making and body language, a capacity to use simple musical resources creatively (rather than just an instrument where the candidate has developed significant skill), and the potential to find ways of responding musically to unexpected situations. These situations might be role-played in the audition (Wetherick 2023). Wetherick argues for the need for course literature to develop a clearer narrative about music therapy musicianship to assist future applicants.

Overall, the selection process is wide-ranging. Different courses may emphasise contrasting aspects.

> Face-to-face in a group to begin with, a couple of improvisations, activities where we've had discussion after each one, and then after that they have their individual audition/interviews, all done in one day. We might have 5 or 6 [applicants] in a day, starting with the group. Play prepared pieces, have an improvisation task as well, and a fairly structured interview as well where everyone's asked the same sort of questions although we might add others as well (Trainer).

Group improvisation for all candidates together on a particular audition day is a common practice; it can help people settle their nerves, but crucially can allow the trainers to observe and experience how candidates respond to their fellow applicants and interviewers in musical meetings, and how they contribute to the music. For example, do they dominate or do they disappear into the background? How do they connect with others?

I honestly think that playing music in that group is one of my best thermometers of whether people are ready [to train] (Trainer).

This small group improvisation approach to interview selection bears some similarity to small group experiential musical teaching on the programmes themselves and gives the candidate a taste of what is to come.

Musical preparation and inclusion for training

UK based trainings have developed introductory courses to music therapy for people interested in a music therapy career, such as at the University of Roehampton, The Guildhall School of Music and Drama, the University of South Wales and the *Futurelearn* Nordoff and Robbins courses. Courses may be in person, hybrid or online, typically running between 6 and 18 weeks. They provide introductions to some of the musical improvisatory experiences and skills as well as sharing examples of case work. For those who can access these courses, their chances of selection are possibly enhanced.

Applicants from a background other than classical, jazz or rock music do not necessarily see themselves represented on course webpages unless there is specific mention of different traditions. As a response to promoting equity across different musical traditions, the grade requirement as a guide for the musicianship level has recently been dropped from some course documentation.

The idea of a 'high level' of musicianship identified in the standards of proficiency harks back to the classical roots of the music therapy pioneers, such as Juliet Alvin, who was a concert cellist, and Paul Nordoff, an established composer and pianist, as discussed in Chapter 3. The authors' own experiences of training in the 1990s involved encountering a notion that music therapy clients *deserve* therapists who have a high level of musicianship. This was taken to mean, among other attributes, an acute sensitivity to sound, a strong capacity to express the sound they can hear in their head, and technical proficiency on at least one instrument to bring that to fruition, as well as the capacity to play rhythmically and in tune. The thinking is that the client will be more likely to feel that there is musical space for them, that the therapist can attune skilfully to the nuance of their playing, and that the therapist's music can reach them in terms of shape, gesture and form of their music. Arguably this may be akin to the kind of attunement talking therapists also aspire to, and in particular the use of silence (Sutton 2002).

The timing of a musical entry and the capacity to imagine musical sound can be linked to ability in composition or free improvisation but essentially arises out of a universal bond of sharing that connects all humanity (Nachmanovitch 1991; 2019). Musical capacities and sound worlds developed through varied musical traditions may emphasise different skills such as improvisation and memorisation, or various ways of thinking of musical structure. It is interesting that trainers note a growing number of people who are singer-songwriters entering the music therapy profession. These include some who have focused mainly on composition through production using digital software and therefore do not represent the traditional idea of a music therapy trainee who has a classical background and strong competence on the piano. Music therapy training courses tend to specify that musicians also demonstrate strong competence on at least one acoustic instrument, but are less likely to preclude those from a production background as long as they pass the audition.

Equity of access

Equity of access to training is an issue that has been debated in earnest recently. In the UK, entry level to the profession is at Masters degree level. In June 2016 a postgraduate loan became available for UK citizens who do not already have a Masters degree, allowing some financial barriers to be overcome. Early evaluations identified that this increased the overall numbers of Masters degrees being taken up, and that over a third of applicants would not even have considered a Masters degree without the loan (Adams *et al* 2019). Since then the number of people training in music therapy from less wealthy backgrounds has increased. Part-time training courses, which may involve only a day a week on campus, make this experiential training more accessible for people with, for example, caring responsibilities or health conditions that affect fatigue levels, as is the case at the University of the West of England, the University of South Wales and the University of Roehampton (in this case alongside a full-time course option). In a recent publication, Lindo also examines accessibility to training for people from ethnic minority communities (Lindo 2023).

The barrier identified by trainers as the most problematic in preventing access to training, other than financial, is in relation to the musical background of the applicant. People with a background in punk, rock, hip hop or rap, popular music and folk music traditions have not traditionally fitted so clearly into the musical skills entry criteria identified by some courses until recently as 'grade 8 minimum level'. This is partly problematic owing to the traditional emphasis on a classical music background. Although in recent years, grade exams have been available to cover jazz (Associated Board of the Royal Schools of Music 1999) and rock music (RSL Awards 1991), these grade exams are traditionally associated with classical music; in contrast, the ABRSM was formed in 1889 and instigated the first grade exams a year later.

Applicants from a background other than classical, jazz or rock music still do not see themselves represented on course web pages unless there is specific mention of different traditions. The grade requirement as a guide for the musicianship 'level' has recently been dropped from some course documentation. There has been some debate about the idea that each person has a 'first study'.

> You can be 'first study anything'; we don't even say 'study' because that has connotations; maybe we should say 'preferred instrument' (Trainer).

The idea of a preferred instrument is not confined to particular instruments or voice, and there is little expectation that applicants need to read specified musical notation. This means that full-time training courses have traditionally offered several training places a year to international trainees who play instruments from different traditions. Unfortunately, visa requirements restrict this for part-time courses.

> We have a lot of students from Asia [sometimes] people whose first study is the erhu or the guzheng or the harp, and then come and say 'well actually I don't read Western notation'. We've always been really interested in what that brings. And then a lot of their Major Projects [dissertations] during training end up being about their instrument and how they have used it in the UK, so we've always been very interested in that (Trainer).

Performance anxiety

Performance anxiety is not necessarily discussed at audition, yet the authors, as trainers ourselves, have often heard trainees talk about how this has affected them in the past, and during training. There is some evidence that performance anxiety can have a negative impact on a musician's capacity to stay in a state of flow (Cohen and Bodner 2021). Flow is often important for the music therapist in order to maintain being in the present moment and attentive to the client and is part of a mechanism for therapeutic change (Silverman and Baker 2018). Therefore, there is a need for trainers to provide safe but reflexive spaces for this to be explored during music therapy training, both in small groups and in tutorials. Personal therapy, and in particular their own music therapy can also be crucial for the trainee to interrogate and explore the root of past performance trauma, and how it contributes to their identity as a musician and a music therapist.

Training as a music therapist may, for some trainees, address performance anxiety, as the meaning of the music-making can change so much as a therapist, with less emphasis on performance, technical brilliance and conveying an interpretation of an artist and more on listening and making use of one's musicianship for others. However, the competitiveness between trainees experienced in previous musical training, especially from those graduating from a conservatoire may continue to play out in a music therapy training, as this graduate describes.

> One of the most difficult parts of the training involved me feeling vulnerable and exposed in front of others and navigating the more performative aspects of the training. It also seems a lot of music therapists struggle with confidence in their musical abilities (despite spending their time building other people's musical confidence!) and I saw the seeds of this in the training, as we learnt to think more critically about the music we're offering and as we started to realise our limitations and have experiences that led us to question if our music was 'enough'. I think a learning environment in which there was rarely a clear right and wrong could be very freeing, but in some ways it may also have fed into these insecurities. It could be hard to know exactly how we were doing or what we were comparing ourselves to, especially when we had limited exposure to

music therapy, only getting to witness the highlights and moments of interest in recorded extracts (not the 'lost' or mundane moments in between) (Graduate).

Musical learning during training

The musical identity of the trainee

Once a cohort begins training, all UK training courses emphasise the importance of the trainee critically engaging with their own musical identity, and finding ways of explaining this to others.

For example, in Amelia Oldfield's 'letter to my instrument' Oldfield describes how she asked students at Anglia Ruskin University to write a letter to their instrument and share this with their peers by reading it out: 'For us as music therapists, it is essential for us to be aware of our feelings towards our instruments and our playing, and to be able to harness the healthy and positive aspects of these relationships so that we can connect effectively through our playing with our clients' (Oldfield 2015; 310). Musicians may have conflicted relationships with their instruments and need opportunities to explore this as budding therapists.

It is also common practice to introduce some kind of presentation of a musical autobiography which can generate formative or summative feedback from trainers and formative feedback from peers. For example, the 'autobiography' at the University of the West of England asks each trainee to prepare three choices of music that are particularly significant and present recordings or perform them to peers and trainers, supported by a reflexive narrative. This provides an opportunity to practise talking about personal emotional significance in music; by selecting autobiographical music and events in their lives which are important to them and may be highly sensitive. Therefore a safe and supportive environment for this presentation is crucial, as is the presence of the peer group.

> Hearing and seeing what everyone else in the group brings… is often a very rich experience (Trainer).

Timing of a biographical exploration within the training journey can vary: it appears later on at another course.

> They all do their own biographies to one another, and we've now moved that to second year, so they do look back, but it's also about how their music is changing, being influenced by the first year, so it's a different sort of emphasis. It's not just about necessarily about their background or their musical background, it's much more linked to the course and ongoing musical development (Trainer).

Focus on the personhood of the musician within the peer group is promoted as well as the growing individual awareness of how their musicianship might be constructed and therefore developed.

> What I see fundamentally the course being about is the person becomes the therapist they should be and not how anybody else thinks they should be (Trainer).

At one university, new trainees are asked to write two sides of A4 on 'my relationship to music'. An assessed reflective journal can chart the exploration of the trainee's musical identity, allowing them to connect with the main theoretical focus of the training.

> The training gave me a tool to see my musicianship and relationships to music from a psychodynamic point of view. Before the training, my answer to "Why I like music" was [not] anything more than "I just like it". The training enabled me to thoroughly reflect on the whys. I became aware of how much music has given me an emotional support, particularly during the difficult times in my life (Graduate).

One recent graduate reflects on a move away from an identity as performer and expansion of musicianship whilst training.

> The training also helped me to connect with my fuller musical identity, as I could rely more on my ear and incorporate non-classical styles. I enjoyed having the chance to be a 'scrappy musician', embracing my vulnerability and imperfection, drawing from all of my musical skills and influences as well as those of my client, and prioritising creative process over a final refined product. It also opened up possibilities for musical connection with a much more diverse group of people than I'd ever connected with before – in and outside of music – which has been a real joy of the work (Graduate).

In contrast, another experienced themselves reconnecting with themselves as 'musician' through the training.

> My relationship to music changed and deepened whilst training. It became much more a part of my everyday life in new ways, and I fell in love with making music again. I was much more open to spontaneous musical improvisations at home with my partner which was something that made me very nervous before training (Graduate).

Peer learning

Any musical meeting between two people could be seen as a meeting of two cultures, because of the individual musical history of each person. As students are strongly influenced by their own peers, a diverse musical intake is seen as crucial for a rich learning experience as a music therapist, even though we will always view culture through our own cultural lens (Stige 2016). This trainer aims to encourage this at a recruitment stage:

> So to also say 'from your own genre' or 'from your own tradition' on the website; hopefully that will expand [recruitment] a bit, because we are keen to have a wider diversity of students (Graduate).

Another trainer remembers her own experience of learning from a fellow trainee when she trained.

> He was a jazz musician, and I remember feeling as though... that when we improvised, it was like he was coming from a different country. He had no hang ups... We were in this room that had a sink and we did this improvisation, it was absolutely beautiful and at the end of it he went and turned the tap on, and it made this beautiful sound and somebody laughed and he said 'don't laugh, this is part of the music'. And I remember that; it changed my whole perspective about what music was.

For international students in particular, there is a possibility that assumptions can be made by trainers and trainees about their musical backgrounds, and this may be effectively or sensitively addressed through an exploration of musical biography with the community of learners.

> Those experiences led me to reflect on my musical background from an ethical point of view. As an international student, you automatically become a representative of your home country. People would assume you know everything about your home country, which is not true. Music education in my home country, for example, I did not necessarily see as something influenced by Western music; rather, something normal. In music classes, we would learn the history and songs of Western music. We would play Western instruments. My school was not Christian or international school, but in the choir club, we sang hymns and Western musical songs without question. There were some opportunities to learn the music of my home country, though it was rare. This realisation involved a sense of loss; what is my people's music? Why do I not know it? Where do I belong? Do I belong at all?
>
> I do not, however, recall this experience as an experience of racism or discrimination. I would like to emphasise this point because it was truly a joy to be asked and be interested in something from my home country (Graduate).

> Everybody comes from a different background. So they're all adjusting aren't they? They're all thinking about this new way of being with people (Trainer).

The change of identity to music therapist can be usefully thought about in terms of a professional role.

> If your role as a music teacher is to help someone build up a skill, then there are really important steps that you have to follow. If [as a trainee therapist]

you're trying to enable someone to communicate through music, then it's important to allow them more space to do that and facilitate differently [to a teacher]. You still need to provide but not necessarily in the same way. And I think that the same adjustments are necessary for performers when people are coming from a perspective of playing to people, giving their music to people, and wanting them to like it [laughs]; there's a lot of adjustment for roles there (Trainer).

Most programmes timetable opportunities for peer learning, acknowledging that trainees will hold different expertise which the course team cannot necessarily provide.

We highlight a very important part of that is the skills sharing between them. So we do have topics. And what we also say is that the studios we've got access to, we actively encourage them to use them outside those times, to come and practice (Trainer).

Lockett found that learning to improvise in communities broadened individual expression whether for music therapy trainees or other improvising musicians in higher education (2023). Similarly, sharing autobiographical experiences and explaining to others how we see our musical identity seems crucial for developing a cultural sensitivity when we train. This demonstrates the importance of trainee *commitment* to understanding, developing and improving their musicianship through the training and in practice afterwards.

Teaching and learning of improvisation

'Learning to improvise is nuanced and multi-faceted and can strongly influence the development of the self'.

(Lockett 2023)

Musical improvisation is a cornerstone in UK based music therapy training (Bunt and Hoskyns 2002, Wigram 2004, Nordoff and Robbins 2007). Improvisation in music therapy training may be conceived of and taught in varying ways depending on the philosophical and theoretical orientation, but there is considerable overlap between different UK trainings. This enables graduates from different training backgrounds to work together in a professional team on qualification, yet also provides an aspiring music therapy trainee with some choice of approach depending on where they decide to apply.

In this book we identify a common pedagogy when developing music therapy musicianship in European music therapy training; a facilitated, developmental approach. All trainers interviewed identified the importance of small musical experiential groups to workshop skills, interactive techniques, role play situations and experience flow states (Csikszentmihalyi 2014) essential to improvisation.

Improvisation is central to this, but also learning how to use structure within improvisation, including detailed awareness of different forms that can be used in song with clients who need extra structure and repetition for orientation. Musicianship training can include therapeutic songwriting, learning receptive approaches where client and therapist listen to recordings or pre-composed music, or where the client works towards performance. Facilitating group improvisation in itself requires practice and particular skills of containment and structuring, but also knowing when to facilitate space and freedom. All this can be taught within a music therapy training in developmental steps, or as and when the musical need arises on placement.

Approaches to improvisation

Darnley-Smith (2013) articulated two distinct approaches to clinical improvisation in the UK; music-centred and psychodynamic. The differences relate to where the therapeutic effect is situated; either in the music itself (music-centred) or in the therapeutic relationship (psychodynamic). The distinction is discussed in depth by Aigen (2013).

In terms of the teaching tradition, Nordoff made direct reference to classical works in his early music therapy teaching rather than his own compositions (Darnley-Smith 2013: 124). This tradition of learning from pre-composed music is still drawn upon today in Nordoff and Robbins teaching, and care is taken to integrate a culturally-informed stance.

> So at the outset, the first day, we do what we call like a learning from the music so we'll listen to some music, it could be anything, and then we'll think about how that makes us feel, and then we'll think about how we could use from that music in improvisation for example. And then that sort of runs throughout the whole programme really.
>
> And it's really important that we don't say we're going to teach you every kind of music, every kind of thing, and that actually when we draw on different genres and styles and things, we're just drawing on them for their affordances, we're not saying 'this is X Y Z', we're not treating things as nouns.
>
> We may focus upon specific devices, specific musical devices, like the affordances of drone, for example. Or it might be that we look to a particular genre, or a particular style and think about what that gives us, or what affordances that might bring. And then we workshop it. So we often listen to music, think about it, then we do a series of different scenarios, where we might think 'well where might this be interesting to use or what this affords in a situation' (Trainer).

Most UK based courses incorporate psychodynamic thinking into their training model, and for some this is central. Others involve a clear focus on the social model, or an integration of both.

This has implications for how music in the training is introduced and framed, and can take quite different forms.

> The key principle that we're asking for is to give yourself, allow yourself to be available to people musically, allow yourself to be influenced by their music, and actually it should be their music that you are beginning with, rather than 'I'm this particular musician and I can give this to you'.
>
> Training with a central social model foundation also promotes sensitivity to the power relationship between therapy trainee and client..I remember there was a brilliant musician, coming to supervision, sort of saying, I don't feel there's a connection here, and then listening to what was aesthetically beautiful music, because they've got such lush harmonies, and they're just, you know, beautiful. But the reason they're not connecting is because they're not listening (Trainer).

The British music therapist Mary Priestley has been strongly influential in Northern European training through the analytic training model (Priestley 2011, Eschen et al 2002, Alanne 2023), and ideas from this can be found in some UK training although none presently identify it as their dominant model. Some courses acknowledge a psycho-analytic influence, and others primarily a person-centred approach informed by psychodynamic thinking.

> What I think is important is that we need to know music to be able to converse and be flexible. We need to be really good at our techniques but for me that is almost like, that's the student's responsibility – it's also in our teaching, but it's not where I think the emphasis of teaching should be. I actually think it's a lot more about therapeutic attitude, how do we become therapists, such as your own personal development and understanding of your own experiences and how that's being played out – all the processes (Trainer).

An analytically or psychodynamically informed training will involve a number of different aspects of what free improvisational music can bring to the work. Key ideas include musical play enabling free association, and analytic listening where the music therapist listens both to the music and identifies the feelings, adapting their playing to the client's music. Alanne explains 'It is important for a music therapist to understand that if she is putting too much of her own personality into the therapy and its music, it may not be possible for the client to openly provide his or her own music and personality into the same space' (Alanne 2023).

> It's not about their music being more important than the person they're working with. It's about not letting the therapist's music dominate in a person-centred model (Trainer).

More analytic approaches include the following ideas: unconscious communication, symbolic understanding within the music, musical transference and countertransference and resistance and defences within the music (Alanne 2023). There is a particularly detailed focus on the influence of object relations;

in particular the idea of potential space and transitional objects (Winnicott 1971, Levinge 2015) and music and therapist as objects. And finally the growing understanding from neuroscience, including neuropsychiatry and neuropsychoanalysis allows trainees to develop their understanding of *affect attunement* (Stern 2004), which also links to the concept of *dynamic form* (Pavlicevic 1997), *communicative musicality* (Malloch and Trevarthen 2009) and *affect regulation* (Van der Kolk 2015).

Musical interaction techniques

These influences can be linked to many of the following musical interaction techniques, which can be taught and practised whilst training. These include attuning to, matching, reflecting and grounding the client's music through their own (Wigram 2004; Bruscia 2011). These techniques are based on studies of musical and gestural aspects of early infant and caregiver interaction based on the work of Pavlicevic, Trevarthen and Malloch and Daniel Stern.

> Central to this process is the concept of affect attunement as related to music therapy, reading the client's emotional state from their behaviour, playing or vocalisations, and responding musically in a way that seems to reflect these feelings, but without directly mirroring. This may help the client to perceive that the feeling content has been shared with the therapist, rather than that their actions have been directly mirrored. I find that music lends itself to this exchange of emotional information in a very direct way, with its properties of intensity, timing and shape, which can be shared across different instruments and other modes of expression. This theory is often in my mind when I find myself in a vocal dialogue with a non-verbal client, where their use of voice may be highly expressive, and is perhaps encouraged by my attuned responses (Graduate).

The importance of play and embodiment

If improvisation is a way a child can play in music, this allows mess and fun, and an opportunity to make sense of their previous lived experiences (Winnicott 1971; Levinge 2015; Edwards 2016; Annesley 2014; Annesley and Haire 2021; Haire and MacDonald 2021). Alternatively, when a trainee or therapist becomes aware of feelings they are sensing from the child but are unexpressed, the therapist can start to play music in response to this feeling; this is sometimes known as 'doubling' (Priestley 2011).

This allows embodied expression of the feeling: and another experience of embodiment can come from the trainee synchronising aspects of their music with the client, so that the client experiences being heard, as described by the graduate talking about affect attunement. This can be done cross-modally, such as when the therapist synchronises their music to match the speed and energy of the body movements of the child, as in stamping, running or waving. Cross-modal matching is a specific feature of early child-caregiver interaction (Stern 2004).

Containment

Other ways musical play can be understood and practically applied by trainees include the idea of *containment*; originally conceived by Wilfred Bion, containment in a musical sense is there to contain the anxieties of the client. In earlier music therapy practice and training, the piano was seen perhaps as an ideal instrument to provide harmony around the client's musical offering, however the idea of *single line containment* was developed by Oldfield and others which meant that single line instruments such as blowing or bowed instruments could be sufficient to hold or contain the client.

> We encourage trainees to pick up a recorder or something they haven't played for a while, as a single line instrument. This was ... developed from Amelia Oldfield's model, about how you improvise when you're holding a line, and how, when you might not have a piano, or you need to be able to move around the room, or get close to somebody to have this kind of melodic line (Trainer).

Similarly, the voice of a trainee could contain a client's feelings. Freedom to use the voice spontaneously as well as for song is an important aspect of music therapy technique in training.

> I also noticed as I trained that I listened to music differently, being more aware of the internal movement and relationship between melody, harmony and rhythm, and how this might impact on the flow of my feelings internally. I would often improvise vocally as I listened to music, following different harmony lines or creating my own (Graduate).

> The average expectation is that people will sing fluently and with warmth, or certainly be able to do that by the time they leave the training. It's something that we didn't really have in our training (Trainer).

Attunement and role play

Learning many ways of attuning and supporting the client musically takes time and experiences of playing and singing with different peers and clients. This then helps trainees meet the following Standard of Proficiency: *Understand the practice and principles of musical improvisation as an interactive, communicative and relational process, including the psychological significance and effect of shared music making* (HCPC Standard 13.32).

Exercises such as role play, pair work, voice-work, movement play, small group improvisation enacting written scenarios are all useful for experiential learning on a regular basis. Several trainers described role play.

> Clinical role play is very important in that, so can they think creatively about how they might use other instruments they are not trained in..... a few things that stand out in my mind when someone did something quite inspired and you think 'gosh, they've really got an imagination about how to accompany this particular thing', and that's about being able to think in the moment and just have an idea about 'what can I do with this person who's hiding under the piano?' (Trainer).

> Also thinking of clinical scenarios, so lots of role playing and then we do an improvisation assessment ...where they have these different scenarios, where we have a couple of actors who play the client and then they have to do this (Trainer).

Musical flexibility is particularly encouraged in training: 'A client's music can range from chaotic to structured, simple to complex, free improvisation to precomposed songs' (Wigram *et al* 2002).

Learning through the body

People learn to improvise musically through many experiences growing up, including responding musically to how people move (Lockett 2023). Recently LaCom and Reed (2014) considered unstable experiences of the body through, for example, autism, and Crohn's disease, arguing that a music therapist needs to address stability of their own body. Training courses can address this experientially through involvement of music therapist trainers who are open to sharing lived experiences and theoretically through engaging with the social model of disability. Explorations of a trainee's own physical and body responses to music are valued in training, and relate to particular techniques already mentioned such as attunement and cross-modal matching to movements. In relation to neurorehabilitation, the use of 'entrainment' may be introduced; a technique from neurologic music therapy (NMT) where the therapist plays a pulse at a particular speed that a client can use to help them coordinate movements, useful, for example in stroke recovery (Thaut 2015).

In addition, observing music therapists' work on placement or in videos, filming the trainee's own practice, noticing other trainee micro-interactions in their music or very specific improvisation exercises can all contribute to the development of these skills.

The importance of group work

Observation, acute listening, understanding of how the music is put together and a capacity to be free are all essential. Therefore trainers tend to structure improvisation classes so that trainees have the opportunity to work with many different people who are sharing the training.

Successful learning to improvise typically takes place in trusted communities (Lockett 2023). This is something that all trainers agreed upon. Here are four examples.

> We do a lot of group teaching and I think the group is really important in this. As well as you as a tutor, because reflecting on things as a group and becoming aware and vulnerable in the group is a big part.
>
> Not to say that there's one right way or a wrong way, but just to say that every decision we take in the music has impact, and it may not be obvious what the impact is, but our choices are so important. And part of the experiential learning, I think, goes towards forming our judgement in the moment.
>
> The learners identify at the start what they bring, what they have, what their resources are, and then we help them as well. They identify the resources they need to work on, so it's much more about the learners thinking for themselves.
>
> Reflecting on things as a group and becoming aware and vulnerable in the group is a big part. So a lot of it has got to be slightly stepping back and asking questions about what that was like, or can they think about this in another way, or 'ok that's really interesting but did you notice that there wasn't very much space for the person in that music so what do you think about that, how does that sit with you?
>
> (Trainers)

Structured improvisation

> *Be able to use a range of music and music-making techniques competently including improvisation, structured musical activities, listening approaches and creation and composition of material and music technology where appropriate and be able to help a service user to work with these* (HCPC Standard 14.20)

Often the people music therapists work with find it more accessible to engage if the music in the session is more structured. This can take many forms; singing songs together, songwriting together (Baker and Wigram 2005; Baker et al 2008), song-induced recall (Alanne 2023), song communication or simply providing musical parameters which restrict choice or provide a framework for an improvisation.

Examples of simple structure may include providing a tonal centre, a pulse or a mode in which all instruments are set. For example, use of the pentatonic scale of five notes is something that trainees can be encouraged to develop and question early on in training:

> What if your client's doing this [taps on desk] and setting up a pentatonic, and then what moods do pentatonics give and how can you set them up for your

client? So it's a mixture of developing [trainees'] musicality, to use it in much more flexible non-traditional ways, and simplifying often (Trainer).

The philosophy of teaching structured improvisation varies between training courses. In the Nordoff and Robbins tradition, improvising in styles has traditionally been important and resource books include study of classical pieces, many children's songs with specific therapeutic uses and form, and detailed material for practising the forms and styles of different idioms which a trainee needs to gain a strong grasp of (Lee and Houde 2011).

Conversely, in her analytic approach, Priestley didn't include stylistic elements to improvisations as this could divert clients away from exploring unconscious contents of the music (Alanne 2023; Aigen 2013), but acknowledged there may be times when the style can bring specific benefits to the particular client. Lee sees the skill of creating recognisable form in the music as providing essential emotional safety: 'as the music is created moment-by-moment, the therapist must be able to recapitulate themes and motives, thus providing security and containment for the therapeutic relationship and ongoing objectives' (Lee 2015). Psychodynamic training considers containment from a different variety of musical perspectives, including the use of single line, or therapeutic presence alone without music, and would emphasise the importance of thinking about symbolic meaning in the musical play and countertransference evoked in the trainee through musical encounter with the client.

In contrast Aigen questions the distinction made between clinical and non-clinical improvisation described by Brown and Pavlicevic, who characterised clinical improvisation as focused on the interpersonal contours of the music not musical ones (2013: 77). In relation to training, Aigen's view is that there may be no differences between improvisation in therapy and improvisation with other musicians in a non-therapeutic context. It is interesting that in Lockett's study she considers learning to improvise with both music students and music therapy trainees, and finds similarities between both (2023). However, the main distinction seems to be that the way the music is thought about, understood and co-created comes from a different place.

Performance

The opportunity to work towards performance may hold therapeutic meaning for some clients. Wetherick describes performance competence in a trainee's music therapy musicianship as 'a resource rather than an achievement and as requiring (inter)personal emotional capacity' (2023). Training courses do encourage the development of facilitation skills and leadership that involve performance.

We did a composition assessment that was a real eye opener and some of them [trainees] got really cross, obviously challenged because they were saying 'I don't notate'. And I said 'you don't have to notate, you can do a graphic score...' but it was very interesting because it really brought out who was happy with composing and leading and who... felt it was completely out of their comfort zone. Even though we said you can do it whatever way you like because you might be with a group of patients who need to...

And actually the leadership, being able to step into the sort of curation of a group piece is the useful thing.

(Trainers in conversation)

Songwriting

Songwriting intersects with creative writing, and is taught more widely in contemporary training courses than it used to be. The co-creation of a song with a client or group of clients allows the trainee therapist to develop a wide range of different skills and possibilities (Baker and Wigram 2005). The trainee, together with the client, can suggest ideas, use careful listening to fragments of client's music or speech to incorporate this into the song, to sense the underlying mood and help the client structure an end product that is felt by the client to be theirs.

Songwriting may encompass practice with a client who has no language, or a trainee may respond to poetry brought into a session by a client. Songs may be improvised or contain improvised elements. The process usually, but not always, ends up with a product, the song, which is an artefact; similar to the way an artefact can be created in art or drama therapy. This raises interesting therapeutic questions about who the client leaves the song with, who it is for and what the client wants to do with it. There is great potential for the song to hold significant symbolic meanings for the client, often unconsciously expressed, which can be explored in therapy (O'Callaghan 2009; Heath 2014). Conversely, the songwriting co-creation process itself may be more important, and the song can be very 'everyday' in the lyrics, as many songs are in culture. Songwriting can be taught in workshops and through the experience of writing songs directly with clients on placement.

Talking about, thinking about, evaluating and analysing music

Although improvisation may appear to be primarily intuitive, the music therapist needs to be able to think about and evaluate their decisions, so they can be communicated to others, and so that they are able to justify and develop their practice. Trainees are encouraged to find different ways of describing music and musical processes.

> Looking at ways of describing music, how do you write about it, how do you talk about it, purely technically, or emotively and descriptively, yeah in a colourful storytelling sort of way, or a more clinical way, such as you might write in a music therapy article, or a purely musically academically in terms of technical

musical terms? Looking at different ways that you might describe the same extract or piece of music (Trainer).

Bunt focuses on the musical elements in learning clinical practice as he argues this allows the music therapist to understand and articulate which aspects of the music are in particular being used to attune to the client at any particular point; for example rhythm, or loudness, or both (Bunt 2002, Bunt and Stige 2014).

As a development of this, microanalysis of a small clinical extract to explore microprocesses can be beneficial (Wosch 2007):

> We ask trainees to do a microanalysis, a short microanalysis that's part of a case study. It would be 'you must include some excerpts from your clinical work' and we offer the audio recording or video of it, we offer a little bit that we've done (Trainer).

Detailed analysis of even one minute of music from a therapy session can be surprisingly useful in helping a trainee develop confidence in their therapeutic work. As improvisation can involve 'special experiences' (Lockett 2023) it may be useful to analyse an extract that appears to be a turning point, or something puzzling in the therapy can be analysed in depth. Analysis may involve creating a notated, graphic or hybrid score (Bergstrom-Nielson 2010), and then looking for patterns, links and connections between the music and movement of the client and therapist, or reflections on the roles taken. There are a number of analytic approaches detailed by the contributors to Wosch's book (2007).

> I was working with a child who had experienced many losses and rejections during their time in care. I was amazed in my microanalysis assignment that from looking in detail at a few minutes of musical play, the child ended all our interactions abruptly, even at the level of a single note, and certainly in any phrase we played together. I couldn't believe how the difficulties he was having were shown at such a micro-level! (Graduate)

Analysis may also include a response improvisation to the extract for a reflexive exploration of the impact the process of analysis has had on a trainee, or a written reflection, which may be revealing in itself.

Lee (2015) writes about how music-centred therapy can involve two practices of systematic indexing for weekly evaluation of sessions. *Surface indexing* is completed as the recording of the session runs in real time, therefore corresponding to the flow of the session. *Inner indexing* requires the trainee to stop at a critical moment and analyse this point in the music in more depth. Lee also argues for the universal importance of continuing to use a music-centred approach as 'it is applicable to all models and approaches to music therapy' (Lee 2003, 2015: p8), making a plea for musical therapy evaluation of the music to take as important a place as psychodynamic or neuroscientific formulation.

In contrast, a music therapy trainer who is also a psychoanalyst identifies how her analytic training has influenced the way she thinks about analysing music, and passes it on to trainees.

> Something I have got from my psychoanalytic supervisors, a wish to want to go into real depth into clinical detail, musical detail, history, depth, really trying to think about all the influences that could have led to particular things happening and in sessions, what leads to what, in the way that one is taught to do in a psychoanalytic training. It's really laborious sometimes, but just to think 'oh, what might be the reasons behind someone playing like that and what are you actually doing to influence that? And what might be the impact of what you've done with your music on that person's music or indeed or what you've said to how they speak or play?' So to develop a heightened awareness I think of what's going on… And that should also apply to written and theoretical interactions as well (Trainer).

All trainers agreed that writing, evaluation and analysis of the work was essential for the trainee to develop an in-depth understanding of their music and crucially of the interaction between client and therapist. This also aided trainees in being able to explain processes to others, including carers, clients themselves or colleagues.

Embedding culturally informed practice

Cultural definitions and expectations about what music is, can be and crucially, how it can be used in music therapy practice, are undergoing a significant challenge (Trehub, Becker and Morley 2015). This is in part created by musicians who trained as music therapists recently who have applied different aesthetic and cultural expectations and parameters, and have shown a strong capacity to meet the therapeutic needs of the people with whom they work.

Music therapy has also lacked a cultural critique and has not always been reflexive enough to recognise quite how Euro-centric the expectations are (Hadley 2013). For example, even quite recent texts have often referred to 'world music' as if a myriad of different cultural practices and traditions can somehow be held together under an umbrella term. What seems important here is for trainers to promote cultural reflexivity within training, expecting trainees to engage with the training in a critical and culture-conscious way, and recognising that many training practices trainees inherit are steeped in the dominant paradigm of a Western classical tradition and are therefore limited. Here a trainer is talking about a person-centred model.

> This approach moves naturally away from saying 'Western music' or particular idioms or particular styles that take priority or should have more emphasis in the teaching (Trainer).

The example of how harmony is understood can illustrate the challenge of this. An ability to harmonise melodies was, and still is, an expectation of skills needed to train as a music therapist. Originally this was piano focused, broadened out to include a guitar as a substitute. Tony Wigram's book on improvisation methods (Wigram 2004) which is a core text in some UK trainings, provides resources which develop harmonic language, such as an exercise where a trainee on the piano finds as many different ways of harmonising a single unvarying note repeatedly played by another trainee, or client. This idea can be directly translated to a practice situation where a 'client' plays repeatedly on a single note, such as a bar on the xylophone, and the therapist is able, through harmony, to provide a different emotional and physical experience through introducing different harmonies.

As discussed above, harmony is often seen as the main approach to 'containment' of the client anxieties in psychodynamic practice but was challenged by Oldfield who developed training in the use of single line instruments which 'contain' in a different way. This idea has still to gain traction in some US music therapy training (Lee 2015). If the use of a single melodic line, or a drumbeat or a specific texture may also be conceived as containing, this opens up the potential for a frame for musicians who do not recognise harmony in a Euro-centric way.

If a trainee moves away from classical, jazz or rock traditions and critiques the concept of 'harmony' itself, there is an opportunity for the trainee to find many different understandings and opportunities for improvisation. There are music traditions where harmony is conceived differently such as Indonesian Gamelan, Indian Classical, Arabic and Persian, native American and Aboriginal Australian genres (Trehub et al 2013). Trainers and trainees who are both reflexive and communicative about the music traditions they have learned as musicians enrich and stimulate culturally reflexive dialogue. For example, Loth writes about the influence of being a Gamelan player in her music therapy practice (2006).

Digital music

In recent years some trainees have come from a digital music background such as a production or beat-making background. This has been achieved partly because of training institutions recognising and broadening entry requirements and audition processes. A music therapist working with young people in particular with digital, cultural and practical competence is likely to be able to reach more clients (Pizzute 2023). Accessing a musically diverse cohort of students who engage regularly in group improvisation and peer learning, and who share their autobiographies with each other can promote cultural learning within a programme. For example, attempts are being made to encourage all trainees to become more comfortable with digital sensory or beat-making technologies in workshops. These may be particularly relevant for people with limited mobility or to help scaffold songwriting, Rap or Hip-Hop and can sometimes be the only way to engage a young person.

> Trainees are all sent free online software packages and they have to try them out before the seminar, and then present them and say what worked and what didn't. The facilitator has tables full of kit, that they all get to play on (Trainer).

Keeping the client in the centre of the music making

For trainers there is a balance to be struck between empowering trainees to access deep musical resources within themselves, and to be able to suspend musical wishes and expectations in the service of a client. Placement educators (supervisors) in particular were keen to ensure that the trainee was able to focus on the client.

> I want students to recognise when what they are trying to do musically is getting in the way of the attention they are giving the client/s. For example, if a student trying to harmonise a song at the piano requires so much focus that they are not able to attend to the client/s I encourage them to simplify what they are playing. Where a student is using particular songs each week (e.g. in a nursery group) I expect them to make sure they can accompany these fluently in whatever way they choose. I encourage students to prioritise flexibility of musical response (placement educator).

Most importantly, a culturally sensitive approach promotes putting the client's music and culture in the centre of the work.

> [A trainee may have] got to this place where they're feeling really pleased with themselves and content because there's been a song or something that's been pleasing [in their placement work] and that's really telling. I would encourage them to ask 'is it the client's song? And how much is it from them?' Helping students to hold it lightly, their own culture (Trainer).

How much this kind of reflexivity is possible has been the subject of much debate. Stige (2016:550) argues that 'we engage the lens of our own culture when thinking about our role and place in culture' and therefore the way we hear our clients' music is always mediated by our own musical cultural accumulation. Understanding this, and remaining focused on discovering new ways of recognising one's own cultural agendas is a lifelong commitment which the training courses aim to foster from the beginning.

Music therapy as a life change

Some graduates expressed how making music with clients had broadened their outlook in unexpected ways which felt life-changing.

> My clients have introduced me to so much music and so many different ways of being a musician in the world. Interestingly, I now also feel more comfortable identifying myself as a 'musician'; something that felt out of reach or perhaps a bit self-important before the training (Graduate).

Trainers spoke about how they had experienced the change a music therapy training brings about personally. Furthermore, their clinical experience then informed how they wanted to educate.

> My teaching has been informed by my practice. That's important for me. What I learned from working with young people has really informed how I teach. That's why to move into the person-centred practice framework, which is not just about what we're teaching but how we teach, and how we are with one another as a staff team; at all levels it's about seeing the work as co-learning rather than teaching. We're being encouraged to talk about students as co-learners, in the new framework. How I talk was informed by how I had been when I was a music therapist working with [school] students and teachers and staff; it really fits with that because I've always seen trainees as co-learners. I've always thought that they bring so much and we all share… moving away from the fact that we're somehow experts and we're going to tell you what to do, and then you'll be experts. That 'top-down' is where I've been keen to move away from (Trainer).

It is perhaps helpful to think of musical improvisation as a complex of life skills. It involves the capacity to be flexible, responsive, creative; staying in the moment and having the space to explore identity, or transform relationships through music. It can involve an accumulation of many small changes as well as significant moments, convey meaning and yet not mean anything specific.

Finally, here are the words of a graduate who felt that music therapy was what they had been looking for for a long time.

> The practical musical training sessions were, to me, a fulfilment of the promise of a kind of education that I had not known during my schooling or undergraduate studies but had always wanted. There was a freedom to the discussions that reinforced the importance of materiality and experience in the moment, while also respecting the particular expertise and refined thinking of the tutors. It felt like apprenticeship in the best way – learning by doing, reflecting, trying again. More than good music therapy training, it was the best and most effective kind of musical education I've taken part in (Graduate).

References

Adams, L., Huntley, H. J., Morris, S., Whittaker, S. and Robertson K. (2019) *Master's Loan Evaluation Research Report.* IFF Research: Department of Education ISBN: 978-1-83870-009-6

Aigen, K. (2013) *The Study of Music Therapy Current Issues and Concepts.* London: Routledge.

Alanne, S. (2023) *The Theory and Practice of Psychodynamic Music Psychotherapy.* Dallas: Barcelona Publishers LLC.

Annesley, L. (2014) 'The music therapist in school as outsider', *British Journal of Music Therapy*, 28 (2), 36–43. Available at: https://doi.org/10.1177/135945751402800207 (Accessed 12th January 2024).

Annesley, L. and Haire, N. (2021) 'Experiences of music therapists sharing improvisation remotely during lockdown', *Journal of Music, Health and Wellbeing*, autumn issue. Available at: www.musichealthandwellbeing.co.uk (Accessed 12th January 2024).

Baker, F. and Wigram, T. (2005) *Songwriting: Methods, Techniques and Clinical Applications for Music Therapy Clinicians, Educators and Students*. London: Jessica Kingsley Publishers.

Baker, F. et al. (2008) 'Therapeutic songwriting in music therapy: Part I: who are the therapists, who are the clients, and why is songwriting used?', *Nordic Journal of Music Therapy* [Online], 17 (2), pp. 105–123.

Bergstrøm-Nielsen, C. (2010) 'Graphic notation – the simple sketch and beyond', *Nordic Journal of Music Therapy*, 19 (2), 162–177.

Bruscia, K. (2011) *Dynamics of Music Psychotherapy*. Barcelona Publishers.

Bunt, L. (2015) 'The integration of art and science in music therapy training: some challenges in the UK' in Goodman, K.D. (ed.) *International Perspectives in Music Therapy Education and Training: Adapting to a Changing World*. Springfield, Illinois: Charles C Thomas, Publisher, Ltd.

Bunt, L. & Hoskyns, S. (2002) *The Handbook of Music Therapy*. Hove: Brunner/Routledge.

Bunt, L. & Stige, B. (2014) *Music Therapy: An Art Beyond Words*. Second edition. London: Routledge.

Cohen, S. & Bodner, E. (2021) 'Flow and music performance anxiety: The influence of contextual and background variables', *Musicae Scientiae* [Online], 25 (1), 25–44.

Csikszentmihalyi, M. (2014) *Flow and the Foundations of Positive Psychology: The Collected Works of Mihaly Csikszentmihalyi*. Dordrecht: Springer.

Darnley-Smith, R. (2013) What is the Music of Music Therapy? An Enquiry into the Aesthetics of Clinical Improvisation (Thesis). University of Durham. http://etheses.dur.ac.uk/6975/

Edwards, J. (ed.) (2016) *The Oxford Handbook of Music Therapy*. Oxford Library of Psychology (online edition, Oxford Academic, 4 March 2015). Available at: https://doi-org.ezproxy.uwe.ac.uk/10.1093/oxfordhb/9780199639755.001.0001 (Accessed 12th January 2024).

Eschen, J. et al. (2002) *Analytical Music Therapy*. London: Jessica Kingsley Publishers.

Hadley, S. (2013) Dominant narratives: complicity and the need for vigilance in the creative arts therapies. *The Arts in Psychotherapy* [Online], 40 (4), 373–381.

Haire, N. & MacDonald, R. (2021) 'Thinking through improvisation: how arts-based reflexivity can offer new knowing about music therapists' experiences of humour in music therapy', *Voices: A World Forum for Music Therapy*, 21 (2). Available at: https://doi.org/10.15845/voices.v21i2.3104 (Accessed 12th January 2024).

Heath, B. (2014) 'Hello it's me...why aren't you there?', *The Lancet* (British edition) [Online], 384 (9947), pp. 948–949.

LaCom, C. & Reed, R. (2014) 'Destabilising bodies, destabilising disciplines: practising liminality in music therapy', *Voices: A World Forum for Music Therapy*, 14 (3). Available at: https://doi.org/10.15845/voices.v14i3.797 (Accessed 12th January 2024).

Lee, C. (2015) in Goodman, K.D. (ed.) *International Perspectives in Music Therapy Education and Training: Adapting to a Changing World*. Springfield, Illinois: Charles

C Thomas Publisher, Ltd. Available at: https://search-ebscohost-com.ezproxy.uwe.ac.uk/login.aspx?direct=true&db=nlebk&AN=940980&site=ehost-live (Accessed 12th January 2024).

Lee, C.A. (2003) *The Architecture of Aesthetic Music Therapy*. Gilsum: Barcelona Publishers.

Lee, C.A. and Houde, M. (2011) *Improvising in Styles. A Workbook for Music Therapists, Educators and Musicians*. Gilsum, NH: Barcelona Publishers.

Levinge, A. (2015) *The Music of Being: Music Therapy, Winnicott and the School of Object Relations*. London: Jessica Kingsley Publishers.

Lindo, D. (2023) 'Examining the accessibility of MA music therapy training in the United Kingdom for ethnic minority communities', *British Journal of Music Therapy*, 37 (1), pp.5–16. doi https://doi.org/10.1177/13594575231154491 (Accessed 10th January 2024).

Lockett, B. (2023) Learning to Improvise: The Lived Experience of Music and Music Therapy Students (Thesis). University of the West of England. Retrieved from https://uwe-repository.worktribe.com/output/7840380 (Accessed 12th January 2024).

Loth, H. (2006) 'How Gamelan music has influenced me as a music therapist – a personal account', *Voices: A World Forum for Music Therapy*, 6 (1).

Malloch, S. & Trevarthen, C. (2009) *Communicative Musicality: Exploring the Basis of Human Companionship*. Oxford: Oxford University Press.

Nachmanovitch, S. (1991) *Free Play: Improvisation in Life and Art*. East Rutherford: Penguin Publishing Group.

Nachmanovitch, S. (2019) *The Art of Is: Improvising as a Way of Life*. Novato: New World Library.

Nordoff, P. and Robbins, C. (2007). *Creative Music Therapy: A Guide to Fostering Clinical Musicianship*. Gilsum, NH: Barcelona Publishers.

O'Callaghan, C. et al. (2009) 'Resounding attachment: cancer inpatients' song lyrics for their children in music therapy', *Supportive Care in Cancer* [Online], 17 (9), pp. 1149–1157.

Oldfield, A. (2015) 'Reflections' in Oldfield, A., Tomlinson, J. and Loombe, D (eds.) *Flute, Accordion or Clarinet? Using the Characteristics of Our Instruments in Music Therapy*'. London: Jessica Kingsley Publications.

Pavlicevic, M. (1997) *Music Therapy in Context: Music, Meaning and Relationship*. London: Jessica Kingsley Publishers.

Pizzute, C. (2023) 'Level up: gaming to a beat: a virtual music composition program putting video game culture at the forefront', *Voices: A World Forum for Music Therapy*, 23(2). Available at: https://voices.no/index.php/voices/article/view/3737 (Accessed 12th January 2024).

Priestley, M. (2011) *Essays on Analytical Music Therapy*. Gilsum NH: Barcelona Publishers.

RSL Awards (2024) 'About us'. Available at: www.rslawards.com/about-rsl/#:~:text=Rockschool%20began%20offering%20these%20exams,exam%20syllabus%20for%20popular%20music. (Accessed 25/07/2024).

Silverman, M.J. & Baker, F.A. (2018) 'Flow as a mechanism of change in music therapy: applications to clinical practice', *Approaches: Mousikotherapeia kai Eidikī Mousikī Paidagōgikī*, 10 (1), 43–51.

Stern, D.N. (2004) *The Present Moment in Psychotherapy and Everyday Life*. New York: W.W. Norton.

Stige, B. (2016) 'Culture-centred music therapy' in Edwards J. (ed.) *The Oxford Handbook of Music Therapy*. Oxford Library of Psychology. Available at: https://doi-org.ezproxy.uwe.ac.uk/10.1093/oxfordhb/9780199639755.013.1 (Accessed 12th January 2024).

Sutton, J.P. (2002) '"The pause that follows": silence, improvised music and music therapy', *Nordic Journal of Music Therapy* [Online], 11 (1), 27–38.

Thaut, M.H. et al. (2015) 'Neurobiological foundations of neurologic music therapy: rhythmic entrainment and the motor system', *Frontiers in Psychology* [Online], 51185–1185.

Trehub, S., Becker, J. and Morley, I. (2015) Cross-cultural perspectives on music and musicality. *Philosophical transactions of the Royal Society of London. Series B. Biological sciences*. [Online] 370 (1664), 20140096–20140096.

Van der Kolk, B.A. (2015) *The Body Keeps the Score: Mind, Brain and Body in the Transformation of Trauma*. UK: Penguin Books.

Watson, T. (2005) 'Steering a path through change: observations on the process of training', *British Journal of Music Therapy* (London, England: 1995) [Online], 19 (1), 9–15.

Wetherick, D. (2016). *The musical audition requirements of UK music therapy trainings*. Paper presented at Royal Musical Association Conference, London, United Kingdom.

Wigram, T. (2004) *Improvisation Methods and Techniques for Music Therapy: Clinicians, Educators, and Students*. London: Jessica Kingsley Publishers.

Wigram, T. et al. (2002) *A Comprehensive Guide to Music Therapy: Theory, Clinical Practice, Research, and Training*. London: Jessica Kingsley.

Winnicott, D. (1971) *Playing and Reality*. London: Penguin.

Wosch, T. & Wigram, T. (2007) *Microanalysis in Music Therapy: Methods, Techniques and Applications for Clinicians, Researchers, Educators and Students*. London: Jessica Kingsley.

Chapter 5

Work-based learning

Catherine Warner

Introduction

> Placement was where all the learnings came to life and made sense. I cannot imagine the training without placement (Graduate).

Clinical or work-based placements are significant learning environments, where trainees gain the opportunity to observe music therapists and other professionals at work, and, crucially, start their own practice with clients under supervision.

The scope of placements

All training courses aim to provide trainees with a range of experiences in different settings, and some of these run over a period of months. The arrangement and opportunity varies with each course; but generally there are two or three main placements in varied settings for each trainee over the period of training.

For part-time courses spread over three years of training, there may be a 6-month placement each year for one day a week, with an observational component included at the beginning for four–six weeks.

For full-time courses the balance of the week is important:

> They are two days at the University and two days on placement, so they're busy four days, and the fifth day they write their essays and go to therapy (Trainer).

Placement preparation

This will vary and can include short visits to different contexts to gain some understanding of the breadth of music therapy practice. On the course, statutory training such as safeguarding, GDPR and data protection, manual handling and infection control are provided, and these may also be required and provided on a site induction, as with other health or social care placements. For example, at some institutions trainees have to successfully complete a placement passport before going out on placement.

In the early weeks, it is common for programme teaching to focus on developing confidence in improvisation, the capacity to reflect and in developing observational and clinical note writing. These continue to be developed throughout the training, but initially help a trainee to function on site, and record what they are observing. If a course includes a mother-infant observation, again this is an opportunity to hone observation skills and a capacity to reflect on what they see.

Trainees will typically discuss placement choice with their programme team: it can be quite an involved process.

> We meet with them at the beginning of term, we look at what experience they have got, we look at how they feel about particular settings, and then we look at the placements we have available every year which you can never really tell until the last minute. And we work out, having discussed it with them, where we think they would best go in their first year placement. It could be somewhere that is familiar to them because they need somewhere that is a bit more familiar to start with, to feel safe and start doing music therapy. Or it could be something that is completely different to their experience because they are too familiar with what they have done and need a new challenge (Trainer).

Introductory or observational placements

The first placement can be an introductory observational placement where the trainee observes the work of a music therapist on site who is usually, but not always, identified as the placement educator or clinical supervisor. These tend to be four to six weeks long, often followed by a more extensive placement in the same setting; between three and six months, for one or two days per week.

An observational placement will typically involve the trainee:

> ..getting to know the setting, observing what the therapists are doing, or them showing you videos of their work if you can't observe, or them talking about their work, and then they might go into classrooms or wards, and understand the setting. Then they write a report about it... the social setting of it, the cultural issues, funding, and how the music therapy works in there and how the referrals work, so they get a really good understanding of it. And it's a kind mutual assessment for the supervisor, they can flag any issues [to the programme team] ... if they feel that the person is not going to work in that setting. And that's rare but it can happen. (Trainer)

Range of placements

All training courses aim to provide contrasting placements to broaden experience.

> And so part one runs from September to December, and that's a partly observational placement with a placement therapist who is a trained placement therapist

in the approach we train. The idea is that they will go from purely observational to having a small caseload at the end of the placement. ...Part two is a full year placement, and that's usually in a place where there hasn't been music therapy before (Trainer).

There are variations between the courses on their expectations of first and second placements. For example, Anglia Ruskin University trainers work with students individually to think about their particular strengths, needs and experience, then put a placement plan together that aims to take these into account alongside the practicalities of geography and placement availability. At the University of the West of England, Bristol, based on a lifespan model, trainees start working with children and move on to adult work in the second year, then the trainee's choice in the third placement. Courses may have particular requirements for the range of experience, for example, ensuring all trainees have run at least one group by the end of training, or have worked with both adults and children and have had experience within a multidisciplinary team. This may be mediated by the choice that is available in reality, however.

Well as much as possible, we expect them to be part of a Multidisciplinary Team, and that they meet with others that they can observe or even take part in other sessions like an art therapy session.... they go to team meetings and handovers and maybe group supervisions if it's appropriate. Anything to do with the client, if they're at a school that they should have parent meetings where appropriate, they should always be thinking about what the relationship is with the parent and the trainee as well. And they do that through the teacher or the SENDCO (Special Educational Needs Co-ordinator) or you know there are some parents that you just won't get to see and there are some that you really will get to see. That's a really good learning experience for them. They get terrified! (Trainer).

Terrified or not, being exposed to and surviving rich and varied workplaces can be useful for professional confidence.

I felt well prepared to work with other disciplines due to the variety of placements I had been on, particularly in my last placement where I shared an office with Occupational Therapists and Speech and Language Therapists. I felt confident to talk to them about the work and I believe that this is an important principle – being open about what we do and sharing work where appropriate and with consent. A lot of other professionals I come into contact with don't know what music therapy is, so I believe that it's really important to communicate what we do and why we do it, but also the value of our work for our clients (Graduate).

Placements later in the training may provide music therapy supervision externally or at the training base, with a practice mentor or placement manager based on the site where the trainee is working, to aid with induction, referrals and site-specific support. This 'long-arm' or 'role-emerging' model is particularly useful if the idea behind the placement is to set up music therapy work which has not existed before in the setting. This needs plenty of initial training and support from the training institution.

> We help them in setting up a music therapy placement in a place that they're interested in or that hasn't had music therapy before. And a similar sort of thing happens once the placement has been agreed in that they have a placement supporter and supervision is at base. The idea being that they go from being really really well looked after to being quite independent and entrepreneurial at the end (Trainer).

Alternatively, final placements may be in a particularly complex setting such as a prison, or they may take place abroad for trainees at the University of the West of England with an approved music therapy supervisor on site.

These rich learning experiences need careful monitoring and opportunities for debriefing during and after the placement.

On site supervision and support

Regular supervision of their clinical work from a music therapist is critical for the trainee. It provides a space for the trainee to try to make sense of their work, to put it into words or music, witnessed and heard by their supervisor. In early sessions, supervisors might even be present in the room whilst they are carrying out their clinical work. It can sometimes be a safeguarding requirement of the placement setting. However, the supervision space itself takes place outside the clinical work.

> The practical experience of working with patients was essential for building confidence in trusting my instinct, making clinical decisions, and managing conflict in groups. I was fortunate to have a very supportive placement manager as well as other trainees in my setting, with whom I could participate in peer supervision and discuss the institutional dynamics which emerged (Graduate).

What is needed for the trainee in their early supervision? Summer identifies the need for primary focus on therapeutic presence, musical skills and working with the resistance of the client in the first placement (2019). Feiner (2019) acknowledges the tension for the trainee, or intern, where the supervisor must be trusted, yet holds the dual role of supervisor and assessor of the trainee. Trainees early on are vulnerable to doubt and confusion, yet they are often asked to explain to other members of the team what approach they are taking. John (2009) is helpful in identifying how any theoretical knowledge must first make sense to the trainee; this is useful advice to the placement supervisor. Research shows that the first placement is especially formative (Warner 2016), and therefore placement supervision requires a high skill level, as the supervisor needs to balance the different roles they hold on placement; ultimately representing the clients' needs first, but also sensitive to the importance of the experience of the trainee, in a supportive yet evaluative way.

> There's a three way route of support in that the Placement Educator will see the person in situ from week two, we'll see them for supervision at base, and then the tutor is the person who will liaise with the Placement Therapist and the student and the context if necessary, so it feels like we would either be able to iron out some difficulties or if anything was really really a real challenge, then we'd be able to bring the student in quite quickly and discuss with them (Trainer).

It may be that it is useful to think of the trainee's evolving learning in terms of developmental stages of supervision (Goodman 2023; Brown 2009; Feiner 2019). The structure of placements within the training courses aids this, with changing expectations from one placement to the next, such as increasing independence and reflexivity. As assessment of placement must be linked with the HCPC Standards of Proficiency in the UK, appraisals which map the development of skills and competence in a range of areas from these standards can provide clear evidence of the trainee's growing readiness to practice. As the emphasis on reflective practice is so strong for arts therapies training, student self-appraisal, reflective logs or journals and response to feedback are all documented and provided as evidence. Placement portfolios (now usually electronic) act as the repository for this evidence. Electronic portfolios are interesting in that they can accommodate many types of evidence including video and audio files. This allows for more innovative reflective practice, such as using 'response improvisation' recordings that trainees make as a way of reflecting through music their placement experiences including placement feedback.

Support of learning on placement at the training institution

All training institutions provide small group supervision, sometimes called reflective practice groups or clinical seminars. The purpose of this is to provide the trainees in the group the opportunity to see or hear work in different settings. Typically these groups have four to six trainees and meet regularly, usually weekly. If permission to record the trainee's clinical sessions has been granted by the client or their carer, these recordings can be shared in the group. The groups are led by trained music therapy supervisors.

> In the first term, we have what's called 'learning from placement' which is first of all a whole group and then smaller groups... Within that there's a lot of thinking about context, person, how you fit into this, what's going on for you, as well as seminars at the beginning thinking about you as a person, how you fit into the world, I guess trying to think about power, so there's a learning outcome in

terms of thinking about diversity and power relations, but also trying to focus it through them, as a person (Trainer).

Bunt, in 2015, was concerned that the survival of small practice supervision groups was in danger as a result of the business model most universities were adopting, and requirements to streamline and cut back on arts therapies training (Bunt 2015). Eight years on, budgets have been reduced in some institutions, yet all nine current training courses provide supervision groups with the same ratios as previously. It is one of the factors that is most consistent across training. During the pandemic lockdown periods, online versions of these groups were identified by trainees as being the main lifeline for their practice learning. This was apparent through our interviews with course leaders and material submitted by recent graduates.

> The regular supervision each week was crucial for developing my practice and skills as a music therapist. It encouraged and nurtured my self-reflection and 'inner supervisor' (Graduate).

The use of peer supervision, which needs to be carefully structured and thought through, is increasingly used, but not to replace the supervision group.

The analytic model developed by Heidi Ahonen (Ahonen-Eerikainen 2007) is particularly useful when adapted for peer supervision, as in a Balint supervision group (Rickwood and Storer, in press). This method can be taught to final year trainees effectively and uses musical improvisation, both group and individual, as a central process in this supervision method. Use of music in the supervision method is also discussed by Lee (2015).

Trainee voice

In preparation for this book a number of recent graduates were asked to reflect on their training experiences. Each graduate gave examples of placement experiences that had brought about learning. Here are some of them. These are all graduates who had at least one year of training affected by the pandemic.

> I feel honoured to have worked in two different areas; children and adults, verbal clients and non-verbal clients, and education and medicine. The whole process was thoroughly supported. Not only the on-site experience, but also the on-campus experience was useful; to write case study essays and to give a presentation.
>
> *What would I say to people studying music therapy now? Be open, interested, and engaged in asking what work people are currently doing, and be enthusiastic when you get the opportunity to find a parallel or overlap in an approach.*
>
> During my first clinical placement, running a group at a special needs school, one child was vocalising anxiously, and I started to sing with his sounds, thinking about attuning to the intensity of his voice, aiming to help him feel contained,

while accompanying on piano. I felt that there came a point where he realised that I was responding vocally to his anxious feelings. I had developed an interactive structure chart using symbols for our sessions, and he now pointed to the 'playing' symbol, suggesting that he understood that we were playing together with our voices. This was the first experience I had of a meaningful vocal, rather than verbal, dialogue, and I feel this has had a lasting influence on how I work vocally with clients who have limited or no words.

What would I say to current trainees? Realising things like: it's okay for work with a client to go nowhere profoundly beneficial, that onward referral is an important tool in the toolkit, that you will make mistakes in and over the course of several session(s) with singular clients. Survive this. Breaking Strings (Gilboa 2022) is an interesting book on my reading list that starts addressing this issue, opening up about unsuccess in Music Therapy, and how it is still a success with the right reflection.

If there is anything I would have appreciated, it would have made it easier if I could learn about the education and medical system in the UK prior to the placements. The education and medical system are considerably different compared to the ones in my home country (e.g. my home country does not have the GP system, it has only a small amount of charity organisations, let alone education charity). It was confusing to be in an environment without knowing it.

Placement educators' voice

We asked placement educators (often known as placement supervisors) who had hosted student placements from various training courses in the UK to reflect anonymously on a number of areas and share their thoughts. The main themes follow.

Motivation for hosting a placement

Placement educators were motivated to support trainees on placement for a number of reasons; some altruistic, such as wanting to pass on knowledge that comes from experience, and also for the pleasure that comes from seeing a trainee develop into a therapist. Validating one's own practice was also identified.

> My learning from the placement experience would be that I am able to justify my way of working and therefore I am hopefully doing a good enough job in my role as a music therapist.

A common motivation that was identified involved how the trainee brought energy, influencing the educator's own thinking about their practice, keeping it 'fresh and alive'. There were various ways in which they did this: Examples from five different educators.

I have learnt from them and their different approaches about different ways of being – musically and other. ...the braveness of trying out new ways of being with a child.

My student was able to identify that a recurring character in a young child's role play was taken from a series of films classified for adult viewing. This gave context to the child's play that would have been unknown to me as therapist and led to exploration of where the child was having access to adult material that was causing her distress.

I am aware of being in a state of flow with a client while making music during particularly good sessions. And this is a state that might be more difficult to review objectively while working in the moment. Considering the student's perspective allows for this.

Some very good students will discuss different topics they are learning on their course with you which widens your learning also. Information sharing is good to practise both ways from student to placement leader and placement leader to student. This can also include new musical practices, approaches to technology and cultural issues.

Enhancing the workplace

Most educators who contributed to this book identified areas in which the music therapy service was enhanced by trainee placements, for example: adding extra therapy slots, enabling a group to be offered and increasing the visibility of music therapy and generating new referrals.

> The trainee's tasks can include spending time in a waiting area or talking to other professionals about their work. The conversations that take place around these observations can encourage people who would not have thought about MT in their setting to become curious and find out more about it, perhaps referring to the service.

Challenges to hosting a placement

Placement educators at times were required to contribute considerable resources when supporting a student.

> Basically one day a week revolves around a student, offering discussions, observations, clinical supervision and giving time for them to observe my work and discuss it (Educator).

This can also be tiring. Educators wanted to do a good job, and sometimes put in extra time on the paperwork required for appraisal monitoring and organising interesting experiences for the trainee. Lack of office space since the pandemic was also a growing problem. Some educators had to work overtime and were not paid, depending on their employment contract. It was acknowledged that some trainees generated much more work than others, depending on their capacity to work autonomously, or where they were in the training journey. Balancing the learning needs of the trainee and the organisation could be tricky. Organisations who brought in a music therapy service were not always willing for sessions to be delivered by a student, so finding someone to work with could entail quite a lot of work.

In addition, trainees could sometimes be at a difficult stage in their training, having an interpersonal impact on their presence on placement. Two placement educators reflect here:

> Often MT training is a time when students are working through some personal issues, as they have their own therapy and are challenged by the training and the placement. It can be an intense time of self-reflection so people's resilience as they process this can vary hugely.
>
> *It is challenging for me when a student seems unable or unwilling to hear thoughts or reflections that I may offer that would be useful in their session and work around the sessions.*

This is addressed in detail in Feiner's book chapter (Feiner 2019). A couple of educators had been bruised by particularly difficult situations:

> Students with unresolved issues of their own, could potentially cause harm to myself or clients or patients.
>
> *I was threatened by a student.*

In both cases, immediate dialogue with the training institutions was essential. Some educators felt course teams had not been responsive enough.

In general, to mitigate the challenges of supervising on placement, course teams provide training days or events for placement educators each year, and there is usually a link person identified at the institution for each placement as well as a placement office, team or individual overseeing placements in the programme. But with growing numbers of students in each intake, and the pressure of finding and managing more placements placing increasing pressure on trainers, and consequently, placement educators.

The contemporary practice of setting up access meetings for trainees who have identified needs which might impact placement is a welcome contemporary development and reduces the risk of placement breakdown and suffering on behalf of the trainee and educator. However, this will not apply to many trainees but only to those who self-identify as differently able.

Giving formal and informal feedback

Educators made clear distinctions between formal and informal feedback on the trainee's progress in practice. There are parallels with the distinction made between formative and summative assessment at training institutions. However, how those types of feedback were made available to trainees varied:

> Office conversations for informal feedback, using the end of placement report for a more formal review.
> *Feedback is generally given verbally in a continuous, rolling form of supervision throughout the day the student spends each week on placement. There are college appraisals to be done at the various stages of the placement, and this is a time when we might approach things in a more formal manner.*
> Both are given at the same time – during supervision. I aim to provide a very relaxed atmosphere for our hour of supervision and take the lead from the student. Generally, they have been very receptive to feedback as I hope I give it in an 'easy to accept' manner.

Placement supervision style varied as well.

> The informal feedback tends to be more general observations, whereas specific points for students to consider are saved for supervision.
> *I meet issues head on if possible – this seems to be helpful for students.*

Educators considered how they needed to adapt their style according to the responses and emotional capacity of different trainees.

> I have had one experience where the student was unable to hear feedback and seemed to protest about it.
> *I usually find students eager to learn, and keen to engage in supervision. They vary as to how vulnerable they allow themselves to be.*

Expectations of trainees

Placement educators expected trainees to have a professional attitude, dress appropriately and safely (such as no hanging jewellery which might get pulled off), take responsibility for their actions and to be responsive to feedback. Curiosity, the capacity to seek out experiences and confidence to talk to other professionals were all identified as important, as was the ability to manage time, administration and managing their external demands. Educators found that trainees tended to vary considerably in the amount they prepared for supervision and how much research they had done about the client group before starting placement. Some educators asked to interview trainees before confirming the placement, and an 'interview' is often a requirement from the training institutions themselves.

> I now give them an interview similar to a job interview, to assess if we can work together and they will be safe for the clients.

The interview can be a place for the educator to pick up if the trainee is not ready, and they can recommend more preparation time. It also allows the trainee to identify early on if they do not feel ready for the placement. Expectations might be raised for later placements, again identified in the interview.

> I expected more of trainees on second or third placement; an ability to think about the child within the context of the family or institution and how that might resonate with the trainee's own experience.

In terms of managing resilience, educators identified that trainees needed to recognise when they need support and to know where to access this, for example, through supervision, personal therapy or student services, as appropriate. This was not always as straightforward as it seemed in placements where the institution itself was under great pressure or where the people needing therapy had particularly complex situations. A recent graduate shared this experience:

> The experience of my second year placement was deeply informative. I was on an adult mental-health placement in a semi-secure environment, and my supervisor was a visiting music therapist once a week to the ward to facilitate an open group. [Relationships between] the team and the patients and the environment were packed with transference and unresolved projections which I let go unnoticed and unmanaged for months on end, which led to a quite profound depression in me and sense of disillusionment in the work and the discipline as a whole. It wasn't until this was picked up on in personal therapy, and then academic supervision, and finally in placement supervision, that I could reconcile my feelings about the experience. I engaged with the placement over the last 2–3 weeks in a healthier way, and thankfully continued my training. As someone that struggles to ask for help at the best of times, allowing that habit to continue almost cost my health and potential career. (Graduate)

This honest account shows how a trainee's struggle can be hidden even from themselves. The educator supervisor was employed by the organisation but was not embedded within this particular team, and in this case, left the trainee in the position of containing the despair experienced by the people on the ward, both patients and staff. Another educator said:

> I would need to know that the student's own mental health is in a secure place prior to starting the placement; that they have personal therapy in place or good support around them. This is regardless of whether it is a first or second placement. They would need to be able to cope with the severity of presentations likely to be exhibited from our clients. Although I would not choose a client for a student that was likely to hurt them physically, it is likely they would see this around the site (Educator).

Another mentioned 'some willingness to work on building inner resilience where necessary'.

The centrality of the placement experience

It made a difference to the success of placements if trainees and their training institutions saw placements as central to their learning. This appeared to be understood as a moral stance as a clinician.

> The importance with which the course views placements will affect how the students engage with placements. I've usually found that students value their placement hugely as this exposes them to the work they wish to do (Educator).

Recent graduates in retrospect acknowledged just how formative placement learning was.

> As a means of experiencing the texture and shape of the working life, placement was invaluable. On paper, music therapy is one thing – and it is that thing – but in reality it is other things too. It is a lonely job, and can be an anxious one. Getting the whole picture, I suspect, takes a long time, and I am still learning, but without the experience of placements I wouldn't have had any realistic picture of the working life to come, and thus wouldn't have been able to commit to it (Graduate).

There were several comments from educators about how things go awry when placement does not take priority. Here are three examples:

> I'm not sure it is necessarily to do with the culture of the courses, but I do notice students looking for examples in their placement work that correspond with particular course subjects that might have come up that particular week. No doubt this happened to me as a student myself, but this is obviously not an authentic way of working as a music therapist.
>
> *Sometimes students have seemed to focus only on the work that is required for assessment as part of their training course (i.e. a client/group they will be presenting as a case study) and sometimes a student's focus on their research project/dissertation has appeared to take priority over their clinical.*
>
> When having other students that do a lot of theory first their practical skills are a little behind. A lot of work to link the two is needed when this happens.

Theoretical stance for practice and supervision

Educators discussed taking trainees from courses who hold different theoretical stances to the music therapist educator. Although most felt their stances fitted well with the training institution, some said that if a stance was different, 'I encourage a student to explore both approaches'. Others said that the training leaders knew their stance and how it was likely to inform their supervision: 'Although I am flexible when thinking about different approaches, psychoanalytic theory will inform any supervision I give'. Others had developed their practice since training: 'It's a good fit with possibly more emphasis at my work place on systemic thinking and use of play materials as well as musical play'.

This is interesting to think about, as the trainee has two sources of supervision generally; from the placement educator and the group supervision at the training institution. Trainees therefore have the opportunity to explore differences in supervision, stance or outlook in particular. Any tensions, if managed well so as not to cause splitting between the placement institution and the training institution, can allow trainees to think more about where they naturally lean towards. It's also modelling of how differences in approach can be managed, which is in itself a valuable training experience for a trainee therapist.

Communication is essential in this situation, particularly when it means the trainee finds the differences in supervision difficult to understand or feel 'split' or misunderstood. 'I feel that closer liaison would make for a more integrated experience for students' said one placement educator.

The impact of the Covid 19 pandemic

During lockdown, access to learning on placement was the most significant concern trainees and trainers faced. It was difficult, if not impossible, to access any kind of placement experience online.

Many placement educators were furloughed and could not work.

Workplaces responded to the Covid 19 situation in various ways:

> During the first year, all student placements were cancelled in order to lower foot fall on the site. And as things began to recover and new ways of working virtually became available, some placements were reintroduced. However, I did not feel virtual platforms were a positive experience for music therapy students generally (Educator).

Opportunities opened up more when music therapy educators returned to in person work. This was particularly difficult for trainees in their first year of practice as lockdowns started in March, just as many trainees were either about to start their first clinical work, or when they were only a few weeks in. There were exceptions:

> I was able to offer two placements on the inpatient wards for people living with dementia, as these were open throughout lockdown.

In this case, trainees needed to work using PPE (Personal Protective Equipment); a challenging way to learn as spoken and musical communication was so difficult behind masks, and use of wind instruments or singing were not considered safe.

The British Association of Music Therapists offered resources and advice based on what research was available, and an international forum of trainers was set up to share videos of good practice and resources for working online or with PPE.

Online placements were the most common, with placement providers and training institutions providing equipment in some cases to assist with this. Occasionally trainees worked with clients on the phone, which was considered a very unusual practice before the pandemic. This severely restricted what was possible, with receptive methods the most common, such as the client choosing a song, then trainee and client listening together and reflecting on it. Some trainees benefitted from online placements if they were clinically vulnerable or did not have access to a placement because of lack of opportunities in their area. Usually, observation sessions were possible with trainees using their own devices or those provided by the training institution. However, graduates were well aware of the limitations of their learning experiences at the time. One said:

> Watching recordings of people's work really isn't the same as being with a music therapist for a whole session or a whole day to see, for instance, how they transition between ideas and achieve balance across a session (Graduate).

As a result of the compromise to placement learning experience during the pandemic, the BAMT in 2022 instigated a mentoring scheme for new graduates to provide extra support for those who lack confidence in their practice as a result of limitations to placement learning (see Chapter 8). It will be interesting to see an evaluation of how successful this has been in supporting new graduates in the workplace in the future.

Educator views on how placements have changed

Placement educators identified that they used their own student placement experiences as a model to facilitate placements. This is consistent with experiential training practices and shows how the culture of practice is passed on rather like apprenticeship. However, when reflecting on how placements have changed since they trained, the general feeling was that modern placements have more to offer in terms of supervision.

> When I trained we were expected to see clients from day one of week one! There was little formal clinical supervision, general chats were the most we could hope for. The profession has moved on enormously since I trained in the 80s, as has the training.

Educators felt that trainees nowadays are more empowered in general.

> I hope that placements I am involved in have an approach to trainees that respects them as part of the team and values the experiences they bring, rather

than the more autocratic style of placement supervision that was not unusual at the time I trained.

Nowadays particular skills are more closely monitored and supported, such as clinical note writing and online working 'which was never considered a viable option at the time I trained' (Educator).

Inclusion in the multidisciplinary team and exposure to the realities of working were seen as more modern advantages by educators in the survey:

> I like the fact that the student is expected to do far more than just the music therapy session. My own placement experience [when I trained as a music therapist] was to arrive, do the session, have supervision, and leave. Today, the student gets a far better feeling for the whole workplace and I would encourage them to shadow me for as much of their day as possible originally. I organise for them to spend time in all the different classrooms so they have an idea of different client needs and how these are met by various teaching styles and therapies. I also like them to be around at lunch time so they can get a feel for how people manage this time (don't have one/grab 10 minutes, etc) and how we as therapists find the time to speak with colleagues about our clients when often teachers have so little time to spare.

As the most motivated educators are likely to be the ones who took part in the survey, it is not surprising to read many examples of how educators have striven to develop, practice and improve experiences for their trainees. However, the authors, who trained in the 1990s, also recognise that the qualities identified were present in some placement opportunities then, and also that the quality and opportunity of experience still varies considerably depending on the employment status of the educator and how embedded they are in the organisation.

Ongoing issues for placement

It is still difficult for educators who work freelance to support a trainee on placement, particularly because they are not paid for the time, and may lack sufficient time to work closely with other professionals in the workplace before moving on to their next clinical venue. Working as a freelance therapist can be beneficial: one educator said 'I work autonomously so I am able to decide how I oversee and supervise students'. However, the educators who received more support from their institutions for their placement work were given time to oversee and supervise trainees. At times, in institutionalised settings, barriers were put in place to actively prevent trainee placements even if the educators wanted to host students:

> One manager has been very reluctant for the service to support placements with the lack of office space cited as a reason why students could not go there and a reluctance to consider possible solutions to this.

This means that music therapy course teams need to nurture and develop their relationships with educators who are sufficiently supported to offer good quality training experiences over the years, and to communicate and offer resources to those where the support is not so readily available from the workplace. From the survey, it was clear that in some instances, educators did not feel this happened enough, particularly when trainees were having difficulty accepting feedback, despite some examples of when the educator and the training institution worked well together to support difficult situations.

Examples of best practice on placement

Educators were keen to identify examples for useful practice for enhancing a trainee placement. One example involved trainees in a professional development day at the workplace, where a trainee worked with two newly qualified members of the team to deliver a session on equity and diversity issues encountered during their training. Another described 'case study and cake' sessions where trainees were invited to share a case study, practicing for their college assessments, with team members giving feedback. This had benefits for the team as themes arising gave opportunity for group discussion and reflection on case material.

Enhancement extended into introducing a type of 'role-emerging' opportunity.

> A student who had been running groups with me in a children's centre then had the opportunity to independently set up and run groups in a children's centre that had not previously had music therapy.

Some training institutions go beyond this and require trainees to set up their own placements in final year, with the support of a clinical supervisor and also some training first on running workshops and explaining music therapy. In this case, music therapy clinical supervision is usually given externally, offering trainees the opportunity to learn job creation skills and managing external supervision in the way they will post-qualification. Clearly this is useful experience for a trainee, although potentially daunting, but if handled sensitively could contribute to growth of confidence.

Dilemmas relating to placement work

Educators spoke about particular challenges they had faced, and how they learned from this. Communication was a key theme:

> I had a situation when the student's client died at the beginning of a break and it had particularly personal resonances for them. They actually did find out about the death before they went on leave but I wasn't aware of this. The student learned that it is healthy and appropriate to ask for emotional support when they need it and that it would have been better to discuss how they were feeling with

> me before they went on leave. I learned some of the difficulties with managing placements when they are not in my personal work setting. That closer liaison was needed between the ward and myself.

Other educators were aware of what they inherited from trainee's previous placement experiences.

> I have found it challenging when hosting students who present as 'knowing it all', or are haunted by past failed placements and almost hijacking the new one with ghosts from the past. Keeping as linked as possible with uni seems the best way forward.

Views on equity and diversity in music therapy training

In the survey, educators were asked for their thoughts about having differently able students on placement. Responses about their experiences varied but educators were keen to work on a case by case basis, to find ways for differently able students to access varied learning experiences.

> By meeting a student with unconditional positive regard, this might not be a huge issue.
> *A student [I hosted] who has a disability felt that the placement offered did not fully engage with, nor meet, her needs. The Higher Education Institution (HEI) involved were extremely supportive of both the student and the placement setting and valuable learning has come from this experience, highlighting a need for there to be further guidelines on setting up placements for students with a disability.*
> There was a challenge in finding suitable clients at suitable times for a trainee who had specific travel needs/physical limitations and strength.

Communication problems with the HEI came up again.

> The student assumes that the placement educator has been given information about them which, in fact, has not been shared (for example, a student who assumed the setting had been informed of adjustments available to them due to a mental health condition). I understand from HEIs that course staff are not always made aware of mental/physical health issues or specific learning needs unless the student tells them.

Some HEIs have introduced detailed planning with the trainee to prepare the placement setting for their needs, through 'Access to Placement' meetings, where information can be shared. This is now a widespread practice. As there is often a manual handling expectation on placement involving moving instruments for example, or working with a particular mobile client, this can be challenging for a trainee with, for example, fatigue, being pregnant or having physical limitations of some kind. But hidden disabilities must also be taken into account. In many cases, a trainee with a disability makes their lived experience useful for their clinical work. For example, a client may trust them more because they can see their own vulnerability. This is a complex area and can helpfully be reflected on in supervision, therefore needing educators who are highly reflexive. This is explored in more depth in Chapter 7.

Race was also identified by all respondents as an area that needed addressing in their placement practice, and there was a strong level of awareness of the lack of ethnic diversity in the trainee population.

> I think every student I have had on placement has been a white, middle class female.
>
> *I would hope that the opportunities for a diverse range of individuals to have access to music making at a young age is now more available than it was when I was young. Music lessons in my day were for the privileged few, and this was reflected in the non-diverse cohort I trained with. I'm not sure how the music therapy profession can change this as I feel it is something that needs to be put in place at the earliest stages of education.*
>
> I welcome the new Apprenticeship schemes as this may invite people with differing backgrounds and experiences to train.
>
> *I think it is time for us to wake up and to really question the perceived Euro-Centric wisdom....there are many healing musical traditions which have simply been ignored. As a placement educator I feel I need to be aware of and honour these and to honour the cultures from which they came.*

One educator discussed how difficult it was to change attitudes at their workplace, being torn between the needs of her colleagues and the young people they supported.

> Sometimes, I fear we are not as tolerant of colleagues as we ought to be. For example, someone who needs to have a lot of breaks in the day – difficult to be patient when staff work 8.5 hour days with a 20 minute unpaid break. Another member of staff does not take part in a school initiative which involves yoga based stretches in the mornings as this conflicts with her religious beliefs; staff find this hard when the ethos is about leading by example, especially when our young people have autism and need to see all staff signing/entering in to the group activity. So I think it is a massive issue and each situation needs to be thought about carefully. There also has to be an element of realism .... it would not be safe for music therapy students with some types of disability to work with my client group for example.

Another felt that it was themselves who had to change.

> My own practice has been challenged through listening to people who have spoken out about some of the assumptions and attitudes they encountered on music therapy placements. I recognise the importance of acknowledging my own privilege and being alert to attitudes and assumptions that can arise from this.

Educators were on the whole strongly receptive to their own learning from trainees, and most were dedicated to making the client journey and perspective central to the training experience.

Service user voice feedback for trainees

The HCPC Standards of Education and Training require that for every music therapy course accredited by the HCPC: *Service users and carers must be involved in the programme* (HCPC 2023: S.E.T. 3.7)

This includes feedback and evaluation of trainees wherever possible. On placement, the opportunities for capturing this kind of feedback are most obvious. Educators had various ideas and strategies.

> Where possible, the student [young person] will be asked directly via the communication means available to them.
>
> *Clients here are able to give feedback directly to students on placement and this anecdotal evidence is always well received.*
>
> Children are invited to reflect on their experience of music therapy in a variety of ways (to allow expression through a medium chosen by them) and giving feedback about the student is part of this.
>
> *Many clients are able to understand that the student, like them, is on a learning journey and are able to identify and share where they feel the student is doing well and how things could be different.*
>
> I have a service user/carer questionnaire for students to use.

To aid this relationship from the outset, one educator suggested it would be useful if trainees could provide an accessible social story prior to their arrival so the placement therapist could send this out to staff, sharing it with the young people who might be offered therapy. This way the service users would be empowered to know the trainee in advance of the therapy.

What graduates need for employment

We asked placement educators 'if you were to employ music therapy graduates, what key attributes would you seek?' The responses are informative.

> Commitment; an enquiring mind and professional curiosity; authenticity in communication and relationship building.

I would want to see a professional approach to their work as well as evidence that they could build strong relationships with clients and colleagues alike.

To fit into our established team well, and be an independent practitioner with initiative and growing confidence.

Able to ask for help and able to implement their own ideas.

Someone who can stay thinking in the face of difficulty and has an obvious rapport with clients/patients.

Willingness to learn, a strong sense of self-awareness and psychological thinking, a sense of humour, an interest in people.

Ability to work collaboratively, to self-reflect and able to listen.

Strong work ethic – time keeping essential.

Articulate – especially about therapy.

There were new skills educators thought training institutions should be equipping trainees with. These reflected the contemporary pressures in music therapy practice and included competences in short-term working and time-limited sessions, working with measurable outcomes and understanding the importance of policy frameworks. The ability to think systemically was emphasised and one educator asked 'How else can they use their skills outside of clinical sessions?'

With the advent of online working, the importance and relevance of receptive music therapy was felt to be more important, and educators wanted there to be more depth in training on this musical approach.

Continuing Professional Development

This chapter concludes with the thought of how practice development can and should be sustained through Continuous Personal Development following training, and is further developed in Chapter 8. CPD courses are provided by HEIs and the BAMT for music therapists as well as other arts therapies organisations. The mentoring scheme already mentioned provides much needed support for the transition from trainee to practitioner, particularly when graduates lack confidence to practice. Graduates also told us about other initiatives they took in terms of volunteering and reflecting on how long development into a confident professional might take.

They have the final words in this chapter.

Having completed my final year, I went on to undertake further clinical work on a voluntary basis, to gain more experience before starting employed work as a music therapist. I found this additional experience invaluable once I had completed training.

I was 100% on board from the start with what I understood as the basic premise of music therapy – that music can often be helpful and sometimes transformative for people – but it's taken me two years of training and almost two years of practising to feel like I really get what music therapy is... It's something I know and feel now, but is hard to explain. That intangible quality of music therapy!

References

Ahonen-Eerikäinen, H. (2007) *Group Analytic Music Therapy*. Gilsum, NH: Barcelona Publishers.

Brown, S. (2009) 'Supervision in context: a balancing act', in *Supervision of Music Therapy*. eds Odell Miller H. and Richards, E. 1st edition [Online]. United Kingdom: Routledge. pp. 119–134.

Bunt, L. (2015) 'The integration of art and science in music therapy training: some challenges in the UK' in Goodman, K.D. (ed.) *International Perspectives in Music Therapy Education and Training: Adapting to a Changing World*. Springfield, Illinois: Charles C Thomas, Publisher, Ltd.

Feiner, S. (2019) 'A journey through internship revisited; roles, dynamics and phases of the supervisory relationship' in Forinash, M. (ed.) *Music Therapy Supervision*. Second edition. Gilsum, NH: Barcelona.

Gilboa, A. & Hakvoort, L. (eds.) (2022) *Breaking Strings: Explorations of Mistakes in Music Therapy*. Arnhem, Netherlands: Artez Press.

Goodman, K. (2023) The music therapy supervisor: developmental perspectives. A qualitative study including systematic reviews and interview study utilising interpretative phenomenological analysis. PhD Thesis, Aalborg University. [Thesis not yet available in repository yet has been successfully defended – likely to be available before the end of the year].

Health and Care Professions Council (2023) Standards Relevant to Education and Training. Available at: www.hcpc-uk.org/standards/standards-relevant-to-education-and-training/ Accessed 25/07/24.

John, D. (2009) 'Getting better: some thoughts on the growth of the therapist' in Odell-Miller, H. & Richards, E. (eds.) *Supervision of Music Therapy: A Theoretical and Practical Handbook*. London: Routledge.

Rickwood, J., Storer, H. and Warner, C. (2025 - in press) 'Large group peer supervision: working online with the unthought known' in Warner, C and Sloboda, A. (Eds) Music therapy supervision: diverse perspectives. London: Jessica Kingsley.

Summer, L. (2019) 'Supervision of first-time practica' in Forinash, M. (ed.) *Music Therapy Supervision*. Second edition. Gilsum, NH: Barcelona.

Warner, C. (2016) 'Student perspectives on working with assistants on placement during vocational music therapy training' in Strange, J., Odell-Miller, H. and Richards, E. (eds.) *Collaboration and Assistance in Music Therapy Practice: Roles, Relationships, Challenges*. London: Jessica Kingsley Publishers.

Chapter 6

The trainee experience

Catherine Warner

In this chapter the experience of the trainee is explored throughout the course of their training journey, including examples from recent graduates and ending with two recent training case studies. Perspectives of trainers and placement educators also contribute to different aspects.

Preparation for training

Training as a music therapist, although it can be rich and joyful, is intense and challenging, whether undertaking a part time or full time route. Therefore, trainers tend to look for applicants who show resource and determination to train, and who have researched their decision thoroughly, as is evident from the accounts of these recent graduates.

> To prepare for training I did some community projects and outreach work that was music and wellbeing-centred. I read quite a lot of books when I was preparing to apply for a course. I also met with some people who were currently training or had completed.
>
> *I undertook some voluntary work experience in a college for young adults with learning disabilities and school for people with profound learning disabilities, to gain experience of working with relevant client groups. These experiences were invaluable in gaining knowledge and insight into these client groups. I also attended a few music therapy sessions myself, to gain some understanding of the client experience and learn more about working as a Music Therapist.*
>
> I began preparing to train by researching music therapy online, and then set up a meeting with a music therapy charity to find out about a career as a Music Therapist. I contacted Music Therapists who were friends of friends to ask about their experiences. I shadowed Music Therapists working at a charity and a hospital. I went on Introductory courses at Roehampton and Nordoff and Robbins, and a Musical Improvisation course at Nordoff and Robbins. I also took piano and jazz singing lessons.
>
> *I asked some Music Therapists to let me visit their workplaces, such as hospitals and day centres. It was a great opportunity for me not only to deepen my*

DOI: 10.4324/9781003517962-7

understanding of the real music therapy work, but also to connect with people who have the same interests and passion. Another great experience was at the World Congress of Music Therapy in Tsukuba, Japan. It was encouraging and reassuring to see such a big group of people talking about something I truly care about.

(International graduate)

Readiness to train

A well prepared applicant has engaged thoroughly with the question of whether they are ready to train. However, readiness to become a therapist is something that can be difficult for a potential applicant to gauge. For some people, this question is only answered fully through the process of applying to train; from writing the personal statement to undertaking the detailed interview and audition. The interview may be a place to have discussion and feedback from the interviewers about their perceptions of the applicant's readiness, and to have an honest discussion about what else is needed. It may be helpful to think about the selection process as being one of co-production where the applicant and the training team explore together whether the applicant is the best fit and if this is the best time to train. It is not uncommon for applicants to be successful second time around having undertaken the advice received.

An unpublished study by Halford (2021) identified a useful checklist of questions for prospective applicants to ascertain readiness. These involved ensuring sufficient finance and time to study, sufficient social support, including childcare where appropriate, mental health readiness, having maturity and self-awareness, personal warmth, a growth mindset (Aird 2017), a capacity for critical and analytical thinking, sufficient work experience, musical confidence, musical ability, openness to improvisation and sufficient English skills. Halford writes 'If trainees can be resilient enough to manage the complex emotions associated with failure and be reflexive and willing to learn from experience, this will enable them to be a *good enough trainee Music Therapist*' (Halford, 2021: 33). Cozolino supports this: 'The best therapists are fully human and engage in the struggles of life. Our own failures help us to remain open to the struggles of others; our personal victories give us the optimism and courage to inspire those struggling with their lives' (Cozolino, 2004: 6–7).

In the following sections, trainers' views of the key attributes of a prospective music therapist are explored, and how they might explore this potential during selection.

Musical readiness

From the graduate quotations above, it is clear that musical preparation is important, and the selection process has already been discussed in Chapter 3. Being open to develop and interrogate one's musicianship requires a particular state of readiness.

Bunt and Hoskyns identified as essential 'an ability to project any musical utterance in a convincing way and to understand the basis of music as a feeling experience' and as a musician 'to relate sensitively and to be acutely aware of the [musical] impact on others' (Bunt and Hoskyns, 2002: 25). They specified the need for acute awareness of the details of music in a structural and analytical way, and the possession of keen aural and observational skills. These qualities and skills are still relevant today. If an applicant is not engaged in regular music making with others, but is rather solitary in their musicianship, they may struggle with the community of trainees and the expectation of working in small groups with their music for much of the training process.

One trainer described the small improvisation group that they ran at the beginning of the interview day for the applicants, where they participated musically, as 'an ice breaker. This allows the applicants to have a model of how they might be both supported and challenged in music during the teaching.' Another trainer gave an example of how in the audition, the applicant was asked to improvise with the person who was auditioning them. "We'd say, 'we're going to improvise together' but we might give them a theme, something like 'what's your journey been like getting here? And you can treat that as your psychological journey, your emotional journey, or your physical journey, or however you want to think about it; just improvise together.' Even if an applicant has never improvised, this allows for the applicant to show their openness to experiment and express themselves through music."

This trainer explains the process in more detail and relates it to the need to be able to respond to different people who need music therapy.

> People might struggle to take risks in the music, so in the improvisation we do one where it's just 2 pianos, but it's not about testing harmony necessarily. It's more about, can you be atonal, can you thump around on the piano, what can you do? Can you follow, can you lead? Similarly with the voice, we do a little vocal improvisation… Sometimes you might come across people [music therapy clients] who need you to be loud, they need you to be bouncing around; likewise sometimes you come across people who need you to be really quiet and you need to taper that.

Pre-pandemic, and for overseas applicants, this process of assessing improvisational potential online was more difficult to determine. One trainer explained 'Those who really couldn't travel were interviewed by skype but with the audition recorded materials uploaded in advance. The audition materials were the same tasks as in the face-to-face auditions, but it was sometimes obvious that they'd prepared a themed improvisation in advance rather than doing it spontaneously. To compensate we would talk more about improvisation in the interview'. During the pandemic more complex musical processes were devised online; 'we asked candidates to respond live to a single recorded line of saxophone improvisation by improvising on their own alongside, and then send us the audio recording of this duet. Although this could be 'rehearsed' in advance it gave a good sense of people's musical creativity and how well they heard the musical line and implicit harmonies.' (Trainer)

Trainers were clear that the audition processes allowed applicants to gain a sense of how learning might be experienced on the course. "We frame it as 'this is for us to see what sort of potential you have for working in this way, and it's also for *you* to see how comfortable you feel with learning in this way'." (Trainer)

Some auditions require applicants to undertake leadership activities within the small group improvisation, and leadership skills are increasingly being promoted during training as necessary employment skills. All auditions involve both prepared and spontaneous elements, giving the applicant some sense of control over the process, but also a sense of exploring the unknown.

The ability to engage with people

One trainer was keen to identify applicants who were 'curious and interested and empathetic to people who have different needs'. Another said, 'you want to pick up on some lovely warmth in them and interest [in others]'. This can be explored both in music and talking. Group improvisation during selection can help the interviewers, as the applicants' responses to each other can be observed. One trainer was impressed by an applicant who showed a strong musical and professional track record, only to express reservations, as 'once he started improvising in a small group, he started to dominate the music, showing scant regard for others who may have been more nervous, to the point where he was only one who was audible'. This capacity to engage (or not) will be felt relationally during the interview and audition process by the trainers and will contribute to the ultimate decision-making. It may allow trainers who have improvised with the applicants to give useful feedback on the spot, such as 'I felt you were able to listen empathically when I played hesitantly, but I did not feel you joined me strongly enough when my music became more chaotic'.

The ability to reflect on self in relation to others

One trainer said of an applicant "If they say, 'I hadn't thought of that' and then expand, that to me is a really good sign, because what they are saying is 'you've given me a new idea and now I'm thinking about it'." Another explained, "In interviews I've often stopped the role plays, and said 'what are you attending to? Can you think of it like this?' When somebody responds, 'I've never thought about people and music this way', you think 'aha, you're the type of person I want', because you're willing to take on board an idea, and it's changed you".

Trainers looked to ensure that applicants were aware of the challenge of training to be a therapist. A future trainee needs to understand 'why certain experiences on the training might trigger all sorts of things, but also how *not* knowing about things narrows and limits and restricts what you might be able to do and understand. A glimpse for people about what they might need to think about. And it's not for everyone.'

Emotional maturity

Music therapy trainers will be looking for authenticity, honesty and emotional courage to find potential therapists who will be able to take the necessary therapeutic risks for their clients. This might involve using searching interview questions and looking for the capacity to admit to vulnerability. "I would say 'tell me the last time you were really angry about something, and what you did about that anger'. One applicant said 'actually it's something that I might shy away from. Maybe that's something for me to work on'. I thought that was promising" (Trainer).

In their practice, music therapists will need to interpret, manage and respond to challenges. There is no rulebook outlining responses to particular situations. For the trainee, the ambiguity of this can cause stress, particularly for trainees who have limited clinical experience to draw upon (Pica, 1998; Skovholt and Rønnestad, 2003; Warner, 2016). As will be discussed in Chapter 7, relational therapy practices such as music therapy can cause anxiety (Kumary and Baker, 2008; Truell, 2001) or even psychological damage (Halleck and Woods, 1962; Corey and Corey, 2010) if there is insufficient self-care. Stress may also come about as a result of the emotional toll from the work, as clients' emotions can be transferred and strongly felt by the music therapist through the music, or through verbal exchange, and the therapist's own emotions can also be triggered (Skovholt and Rønnestad, 2003). Whilst these aspects become understood and more manageable through training, it is not particularly responsible for trainers to accept a new trainee who they feel is at particular risk of becoming depressed or stressed through their training experience. One trainer said 'in some ways, it is like a parent expecting their first child; they may feel prepared to parent, but it is impossible to understand just how much their life will be changed until it happens. That's so for a therapy trainee.'

Therefore, trainers when interviewing applicants need to consider the potential harm a trainee may face, and identify those who might be less able to exercise self-care, or who are already in particularly challenging life situations.

One trainer gave an example of the interview process: a person where, over the last two generations there had been family trauma. The trainer reflected to the interviewee what she was hearing from her about the trauma, and the interviewee started to realise that the training was likely to bring up some challenging realisations for her. However, from exploring this together, the trainer recognised potential: 'what I felt was that they were somebody who did think about things deeply; and was also feeling that there were many other things they wanted to be in touch with. ... I could see why they wanted to train, and that they had a capacity to begin to recognise things below the surface'.

In this case it was ultimately for the applicant to decide whether they were ready. The trainer had seen their promise and had been honest with them about what training might bring up for them.

Attitude to and understanding of personal therapy

Linked to emotional maturity is the applicant's capacity to understand why personal therapy is an essential part of training as a therapist, and to demonstrate openness and commitment to this. At the present time in the UK, trainees are required to fund their own personal therapy throughout the training as an additional cost and they need to understand why this commitment is crucial. Seeking therapy may have shame or stigma attached to it (Vogel and Wade, 2022) and this is something that trainees will need to be aware of and work with. However, it is common for an applicant to have undergone some kind of therapy in the past when it was needed for them, and have since countered any experience of shame to some extent, also recognising the benefit that it has brought. It may be useful to have some kind of conversation around the stigma of therapy during the interview to help gauge the maturity and commitment of the candidate in relation to this question. One trainer said 'quite often people will not have had therapy. If they haven't we will ask if they can think of a time in their life when they *might* have wanted therapy and sometimes that opens stuff that is useful to talk about in the interview.'

An understanding and knowledge of the music therapy field

As the four examples at the beginning of the chapter show, successful applicants have put in considerable preparation before training. Sustained work experience is recommended, often beyond what can be achieved in a first degree with a single music therapy module. Trainers expect direct work experience of some kind in a social or health setting, but they also expect that applicants will have read about music therapy specifically, ideally through case studies. It is sometimes challenging to gain access to observation of a music therapy session, and for good reasons: The presence of an observer in the room can adversely affect the therapy.

One trainer remarked: 'It's surprising how many people come to interview and they've read absolutely nothing about music therapy.' Trainers interviewed for this book all agreed on this, although they gave examples of when applicants had sought videos to watch online. Relying on this can be problematic, as in many cases, examples online do not represent the best ethical practice, especially if the client is not able to give informed consent due to a lack of capacity. In these cases, carers or relatives may have given assent instead. Videos have often been made for marketing reasons to paint a particularly rosy picture or give examples with incomplete evidence of process. Examples also may not be culturally relevant to music therapy practice in the country the applicant wants to train in. Despite this, there are some excellent examples online where there is evident collaboration between the client and therapist about the making of the material. Written case studies can give a particularly useful insight into the therapist's process, providing a sense of how therapy contributed to change over time. *Music Therapy: Intimate Notes* (Pavlicevic, 1999) is a common recommendation from trainers; other introductory texts also include a number of clinical examples (Darnley-Smith and Patey, 2003; Nordoff and Robbins, 2007; Bunt and Stige, 2014).

When applicants have lived experience of a person with a disability in their family, or a disability of their own, this gives valuable insight, although some trainers expect more experience than within the family: 'Family experience is very intense and is just one experience, rather than when you're volunteering somewhere and you're meeting lots of different people'.

The appropriate time to train

Music therapy is a profession that is often taken up as a second or third career (Health Education England, 2021; All-Party Parliamentary Group on Arts, Health and Wellbeing, 2017). Applicants commonly state that they had wanted to train for some years but not had the opportunity. During and following the pandemic, there was a surge in applications for all UK based training courses. This was interesting, and trainers asked themselves whether this was to do with shrinking opportunities to work as professional performing musicians, or whether the enforced career break which affected many during lockdowns gave time for contemplation of a different career direction. Again, trainers identified that this was an area worth exploring at interview. One trainer put it like this: "I would ask 'why *now* do you want to become a Music Therapist?' especially if they've got a very successful arts and health or teaching practice; why change?" It is helpful to think about whether this is a relatively stable time emotionally and financially, given the investment and resources needed to train.

Barriers to training

Financial barriers

In the UK, UK and Irish nationals and people with 'settled status' under the age of 60 can gain a postgraduate loan towards a masters training, unless they already hold a masters degree (Student Finance England, 2023). In terms of readiness to practice, an applicant needs a clear plan of how they are to finance their training to avoid the worrying scenario of having to defer or leave the training due to insufficient funds.

Part time courses may help with this, as trainees then maintain paid employment alongside what may be a single day at their training institution and a single day of placement per week. Flexible working can also help if the trainee is able to do this, such as private instrumental tuition. Often trainees undertake care work alongside the training as they feel it compliments what they are learning, yet care work is notoriously under paid and trainees undertaking night shifts may become too fatigued to give their best to the training.

Until bursaries for training become available to all arts therapies trainees, as they are to other pre-registration courses within the allied health professions, and when apprenticeships become available, only those who have sufficient financial security can usefully embark on the training. A graduate of a full time course said this:

> As with many degrees, the cost is a huge barrier. I had to continue working whilst training for financial reasons, and one and half days a week was the maximum I could manage alongside the full-time course. This could be quite stressful to balance considering the headspace required to process the training. The part time option may help ease this pressure but then extends the time commitment.

International students have to deal with even more substantial training expenses. This international student who travelled from their home country to the UK to study candidly explained 'It does require a considerable amount of money. Indeed, the financial commitment was a huge part of the training (e.g. international student fee, visa application fee, moving fee). It was something I considered carefully before the training'.

This may explain why so often music therapy training is a second career choice, because applicants may have amassed sufficient finance from their first career. However, this brings its own problems. Whilst the financial cost of training is such a heavy burden, the challenges people face from lower income backgrounds, also single parents and those who have had little access to a detailed musical training will be disadvantaged, despite the diversity and richness they will bring from their life experiences.

Music education barriers

Lack of opportunity for state school educated people in primary and secondary music education was cited by trainees and trainers alike as a real concern for reducing diversity of intake. One graduate said:

> I've had conversations with people who are curious about a music therapy career but have voiced concerns about not having good enough harmony and improvisation skills, or not having had any formal musical training or being able to read music. There must be a lot of people who are interested in the work and would make brilliant therapists, but who lack the confidence and reassurance that the career is for them.

This suggests that there is work for trainers to do to ensure that course websites emphasise the diversity they seek, mentioning that reading music or grades are not essential, and that a broader range of musicianship is being considered. One trainer raised the 'decimation of music in state schools' saying that it is 'a task for the wider music profession, to encourage people at all levels to not give up on music either'. Various sources support this analysis; the All-Party Parliamentary group for Music Education identifies music education in state schools as being 'in crisis' (APPG for Music Education, 2019: 2), the Musician's Union describes 'a perilous state' (Savage and Barnard, 2019: 3) and in primary schools a 'dramatic decline' of music (Cooper, 2018: 4). Part of this is due to the rise of academies and free schools which are not required to follow the National Curriculum which makes music a compulsory subject (Bath, 2020).

The same trainer also discussed the undervaluing of formal music education in society:

> At school level, people generally don't encourage their sons and daughters to pursue music because they think it's not going to earn them any money and it's not a relevant subject; even people who are very good at it don't do it at A level and so they are then not so equipped to do it in Higher Education and so it just sort of gets dropped. So I think it's a wider problem in society that's quite a narrow group, a demographic of people who think that music is really important as a subject to study, it's worth studying, it's worth doing it at that level (Trainer).

Another trainer said 'The fact that it's a Masters degree is excluding people who would be brilliant practitioners but just can't write to Masters' level, can't think critically in that way'. Arguably, therapists do need the capacity to think critically, having the capacity to both analyse their work and to explain it accessibly and coherently to others. But a trainer cannot assume that an applicant cannot do this when they have not had an opportunity to undertake a degree and so must determine some capacity for critical thinking when interviewing the applicant.

What is interesting is the rise in self-taught musicianship. Although self-taught musicians do not necessarily have the same auditory processing advantages as those who have been trained through a conservatoire or with music lessons (Zendel and Alexander, 2020) they may experience more vivid mental imagery when conceptualising music (Talamini et al 2023) than those who read music. This may also be the case for those who listen to music very regularly, which could be valuable as a music therapist. With increasing availability and sophistication of compositional software and beat making digital music, it may be that future music therapy trainees will be increasingly represented by self-taught musicians. Younger clients may increasingly expect beat making technology as part of a music therapy intervention or find that it reduces the stigma of being in therapy.

One trainer describes: 'A trainee who has a background in Rap and Hip-Hop has found that young people in an inner-city school have been engaging in music therapy but not anywhere else in school. This trainee is inspired to think of how she might be able to support victims of knife crime and those pulled into gangs in her future work'. Hip-Hop is often portrayed as linked to violence, yet it has great potential to be aspirational and bring together those from minoritised backgrounds (Viega et al., 2022).

Mental health barriers

Before, during and after the Covid 19 pandemic, mental health issues for trainees have been of primary concern during music therapy training. Despite access to personal therapy during the training, trainees can still find study challenging due to mental health difficulties.

> I had a difficult time with my mental health at the start of the second year of training, struggling with depression and with it, low confidence. I'm not sure how much of this was to do with the pressure I was putting on myself in the training and how much to do with personal circumstances and things coming to a head in personal therapy. It was when I received some clear feedback that I was doing ok and was valued on my second placement that I seemed to become more stable. Although this wasn't the easiest time on the course, it did give me richer life experience to take with me into the work and an experience of the importance of looking after ourselves in order to best serve our clients (Graduate).

The HCPC Standards of Proficiency require a practitioner to be aware of their self-care needs and to know how to seek help when needed (HCPC: Standard 3). For therapy trainees prone to anxiety, there are many stressors during training. Trainees are not only assessed on their clinical work, but usually their examiner is their supervisor, with whom they share their vulnerabilities (Richards 2009). This may generate further pressure and a feeling of unease if not managed sensitively (Pica, 1998; Skovholt and Rønnestad, 2003). They may also experience feelings of inadequacy if they do not meet high personal expectations, particularly in relation to solving the situations faced by their clients (Skovholt and Rønnestad, 2003; Truell, 2001). The idea of being 'good enough' is important for trainers to promote here: to have high expectations but realism about what can be managed in time-limited therapy work, and the importance of valuing small changes. Clinical seminars or reflective practice groups can be very important here for reality checking, and for the value of seeing other trainees working in challenging circumstances (Pederson 2023).

Trainees may not always use the support systems available to them early enough; this was particularly notable during pandemic lockdowns when teaching was all online. This influences the entire student group.

> [Trainees] were breaking down, but not saying. So we needed to name-drop [trainees who were struggling]. That's how dire the scene was. [...] After talking with the course leader, she talked to [trainees] who needed extra support, which created positive changes in the atmosphere of the lectures. [Trainees] need to use the opportunities for feedback, via course reps and questionnaires. If you're

unhappy about something, it's not fair to just expect course leaders to magically know.

(Myerscough and Wong, 2022)

Challenges for international trainees

Trainees who move abroad to study are likely to be disadvantaged if they do not have a cultural background in the health and social care systems of that country. Furthermore, the training approach may be culturally alien.

> Cultural adjustment was a huge part of the training for me. The view that the culture is based around individualism in the West and collectivism in East Asia is largely true. I found it challenging to participate in classroom discussion because that is not something students normally do in classrooms in my home country. In a more broader picture, the individual's opinion is less valued than groups. It was also challenging not to have cultural references of the UK (e.g. slang, old sayings, customs, understanding of how the society works). I am from a culture which stigmatises "asking for help". It took me some time to realise I am influenced by this culture and cultivate how to do it.
>
> (Graduate)

In an interview it may be difficult for the applicant to understand 'that people just want you to be yourself in these auditions when you've not had that sort of education' (Myerscough and Wong, 2022:139). However, once on the training, the change in culture may be enriching: 'The lecturers would give lots of questions, but not many answers. I'd argue it's an interesting way of teaching. It makes us think more' (Graduate).

Diversity in training

Curriculum and diversity

Because of the diversity amongst the people who access music therapy, there is a strong focus in the debate about what and how music therapists are taught. Gelbert, writing within the context of music therapy in the US, puts this well:

> 'I saw—and continue to see—the necessity of therapists adapting to the highly divergent communication styles people from various backgrounds may have. Music-based modalities often have a way of transcending such differences, but as an ethnomusicologist, I know music is not a universal language ... and as a Roma person, I know that even two people from the same small country may interpret the same melody in contrasting ways.'
>
> (Gelbert, 2021)

Consideration of indigenous psychology and ethnomusicology in music therapy practice teaches us first that mental health and music is thought about differently across the world. This is the case for clients within native, first nation and immigrant populations (Hämäläinen et al 2021; Hodgson, 2018; Morales-Hernandez and Urrego-Mendoza, 2017). These three authors show that music therapy practice can incorporate both indigenous and traditional music therapy practices if the therapist has cultural humility (Hook, 2017) and cultural awareness (Hadley and Norris, 2016).

Recent graduates we consulted when writing this book were aware of the need for a more culturally aware and diverse curriculum, but also a change to teaching approaches was needed, suggesting the curriculum 'can introduce students to the founders of the approach along with their insights and resources without placing too much value on one musical tradition'.

Another graduate's experience was this: 'the theoretical foundations upon which the practice sits – anthroposophy, the western classical tradition, alternative education models – are all traditionally white and middle class, and the gender balance tips heavily towards female. These facts give the working culture an overall tone and flavour that some might find more foreign than others.'

Savneet Talmar, introducing a book on intersectionality in arts therapies education wrote: 'intersectionality demands that we examine the social construction of the art therapies and the historical discourses that have shaped our professions and reinforced the normative versus the deviant body. By doing so, arts therapists will be better equipped to help clients understand mental health stigma and the cultural forces that produce emotions of shame, guilt and fear' (Talwar, 2022: 15).

Whiteness, and in particular, colonialist stances have been discussed in Chapter 2, alongside some of the work that is being undertaken to address this in UK music therapy training. However, training needs to actively introduce trainees to the contextualisation of any traditional approaches that are used, and to present alternatives.

If a curriculum includes, for example, how to work with difference in groups, mechanisms of 'othering' and how to challenge these, what cultural competency involves, indigenous psychology, intergenerational trauma and client led approaches, these all support trainees in developing their own reflexivity, critique current training approaches and bring culturally informed approaches to their own practice. Diversity amongst staff teams helps this immeasurably, yet it can take some time to develop. There is a tension between diminishing lecturer budgets and the need to introduce lecturers with diverse experiences, including race, disability, neurodiversity, gender, class and indigenous experience. Trainees are trainers of the future, and if their access to training is compromised because of barriers, then the future workforce is impacted.

If understanding diversity, equity and inclusion is placed at the heart of the curriculum, this is likely to be most effective if all stages of the training journey are impacted. Therefore, it is important to identify an intersectional approach on course webpages, discuss this actively during the admissions processes and during induction when the cohort gets together for the first time: 'Wording on the website, making it really clear that we're all ages, all backgrounds welcome, all musical experience, not having to read notation, not having to have a degree...we did remove reference to grades in music [therefore] not making that the benchmark' (Trainer).

Diversity can and must also be taken into account when designing and undertaking assessments, with trainers recognising when an assessment is likely to impact adversely on the trainee. The aim should be to cultivate a training environment which allows trainees who experience a significant difference to feel that it is possible to talk about and reflect on their experience without fear of stigma if they wish, for example, in terms of disability, sexuality, class, gender, age, spirituality, mental health, neurodiversity or attachment experience.

Building culturally competent therapists

Culturally competent assessments of clients or service users is something that trainers are keen to introduce in the UK, building on some helpful work in North America (Whitehead-Pleaux, Brink and Tan, 2017; Hadley, 2021). Trainees can be encouraged to attend for questions about musical heritage, socio-economic situation, generational consideration (particularly relevant in relation to exposure to music technology), the impact of ableism on those with disability, and the culture of their location. If the client is a trauma survivor, a displaced person or from a subculture where therapy is viewed with suspicion, it is helpful that the trainee therapist can take this into account from early on in their work.

A useful place to start is by sharing musical autobiographies within the training peer group, as differences between trainees in all these areas will become more obvious. Trainers are advised to be mindful of the sensitive facilitation of this sharing. The risk of opening trauma through revisiting it in the autobiography is higher the earlier this is introduced into training, because the trainees have less experience to make judgements about disclosure, therefore some trainers choose to introduce this in the second year. Trainers are well placed to support trainees in navigating the balance between self-disclosure and self-care, developing reflexivity and providing safe or braver spaces for these differences in identity to be explored. However, centering an intersectional approach can also be challenging for those in a minority within the trainee cohort. Myerscough and Wong (2022:137) discuss stereotyped mass grouping, where the trainee representing a 'difference' such as race or LGBTQ+ status can end up doing excessive emotional labour within the training in terms of representing the perceived group, or becoming an expert: 'I could've got more involved in student politics, campaigning for gender-neutral toilets, etc. I've done that a lot in previous institutions, but it's very tiring to do it everywhere and you can't do it all the time'.

Furthermore, stereotyping can happen on placement: Wong describes how she was given a client from Hong Kong who shared her heritage and language. 'It wasn't offensive, but are the [placement educators] judging me by colour or by abilities? If I was not from Hong Kong, would they have referred this client?' (Myerscough and Wong, 2022:134). It may be argued that Denise's client's recovery was enhanced by his capacity to communicate in his native tongue if needed, and that the choice was based on client need, yet it is important that the trainee is aware of this and is able to raise these questions with educators freely.

Interviewer and assessor subjectivity

All trainers who contributed to this book made it clear that their intention and focus during selection was to find *potential* in people rather than to find reasons for them not to train. However, there may be unconscious reasons for a trainer to select one applicant over another; therefore interviewers need reflexivity in this situation. There is some agreement between trainers about the key principles in seeking a suitable candidate to train: the challenge is to apply an intersectional approach in order to ensure the interviewers are continually interrogating their own cultural biases when deciding on suitability to train.

This includes the importance of having more than one perspective and a thorough and accountable approach to interview practice. As one trainer puts it: 'We always have at least two on the panel. We use forms and give marks so that we can really feedback clearly and transparently; areas they didn't score highly enough on and so on'. This is not the case for all courses, given the cost of having two interviewers, and in this case the course team needs to be inventive.

Good practice in both interviewing and assessment arguably includes opportunities for different interviewers to work in varied combinations, as in assessments, allowing for debate between interviewers, and therefore refreshing reflexive challenge of their own assumptions. Those interviewers who have substantially different lived experience are likely to bring fresh viewpoints and help seasoned interviewers identify their own limitations. If an applicant is 'promising' in some ways but shows vulnerabilities in others, this may not necessarily be a barrier to training, especially if support could be put in place within the training or by the applicant. For example, people who identify as trans may be more prone to profound anxiety and interviewers need to take this into consideration (Myerscough and Wong, 2022). Applicants need the opportunity to show what they may be able to make of the training, hence the focused and sometimes lengthy interviewing process.

Similarly, for assignments, effort needs to be made to ensure marking teams are carefully moderated. The purpose of moderation, which is carried out both internally (usually by the module leader) and externally (by the External Examiner for the programme) is to look at a broad sample of the same assignment, with marks and feedback, to ensure that different markers are marking along the same lines and at a similar level. In turn, the marking criteria for each assignment needs to be clear so that trainees can be confident there is a transparent process in marking against the criteria. One way an assessment team can promote good marking practice is for everyone to mark the same assignment and share their feedback with one another transparently. When trainees are disappointed in a mark for other assignments, they should have the opportunity to discuss this with their tutors and receive clear feedback in order to improve next time.

Diversity in gender and sexuality

The importance of clients having access to diverse therapists cannot be overstated. Rowe, when considering LGBTQ+ clients considers how the therapeutic alliance can be compromised, considering the higher likelihood of trauma and health problems experienced, by this broad community: 'a client may not be eager to form an alliance with a therapist who looks like other medical professionals and may represent a field that has harmed them in the past and does not share a lived experience' (Rowe, 2022: 214). Spencer Hardy (2021) identifies the kinds of questions around self-disclosure that a therapist who is from the LGBTQ+ community may face. 'How is it that my queer, transgender identity plays such an incredibly important role in my personal life, my sense of community and my professional career and yet it is often completely hidden in my clinical work? I feel it is my responsibility as a clinician to present my genuine, authentic self to my clients, but how do I do this with a part of me that is unseen?' (Hardy, 2021). This raises the question of how trainers can help support trainees to navigate these queries around disclosure, genuineness and trust in the therapeutic relationship from early on in the training journey.

Lived experience of trainees with disabilities

Traditionally, the music therapy profession has been particularly sensitive to the needs of clients with disabilities, but not necessarily for trainees and trainers who themselves have disabilities. Ableism within the profession has been discussed by Pickard (2022) and critical disability studies advocated for in training approaches. It is impressive that a number of music therapists practice despite physical and sensory disabilities, neurodiversity or fatigue (Cole and Warner, 2020; Pickard, 2022).

> As a disabled person and especially since I became a wheelchair user, every single element of my life has barriers. Everything has to be preplanned and thought out because the world just isn't an accessible place. Little tasks require far more effort and thought which can be exhausting. I think the training was really well geared to remove these barriers as much as possible, and help me think about my rights, but it's impossible to make those barriers completely go away (Graduate).

In this case, some critical thinking about disability as part of the core curriculum in music therapy training supported this trainee wheelchair user to find ways of accessing work. Reasonable adjustments and a dedicated disability service provided by a higher education institution should provide each trainee registered with the service equipment, mentoring, extra time for assessments and access to placement preparation, to ensure trainees can reach their potential.

There are particular challenges for trainees who experience chronic fatigue in returning to campus after the Covid 19 pandemic.

> One of the biggest challenges for me coming back to university during a pandemic was that I felt marginalised as a student with a health condition. If the university had promoted an awareness and acknowledgement that some people are immunocompromised, with the government COVID-19 guidelines being rejected as ableist and so a continued retention of mask wearing and testing, I would not have been made to feel that I didn't fully belong (Graduate).

Flexibility within a training course, allowing suspension of studies, to recover from adverse circumstances can be especially helpful to those with chronic health conditions who nevertheless have much to offer to music therapy practice.

> As my fatigue was present throughout the training, I found getting to placements incredibly difficult, especially in my final year. I was extra sensitive and more prone to overstimulation, so there were limits as to how much I could give to placement settings, how many sessions I could run and how many clients I could see, but this is the reality of working as a Music Therapist (Graduate).

In this case, having an 'access to placement' assessment before starting placement did help manage educator expectations (also see Chapter 5), and also having a supervisor who, themselves, had lived experience of managing a health condition allowed the trainee to feel that it was possible to work and contribute as a music therapist. The BAMT provides guidelines for accessibility and inclusivity for disabled students on placement (BAMT, 2024).

Learning needs and access

One important principle of higher education learning is to ensure preparation of learning materials well in advance. If students with different learning needs, such as dyslexia or dyspraxia can access a teaching document in advance, they can edit the background or font size, allowing them to follow the content more easily during the seminar for which it has been prepared. Lectures and seminars are usually recorded, and assessment staggered throughout the year to allow for pacing for all trainees.

Barrington, in her interview for this book mentioned that neurodiversity is one of the protected characteristics of the workforce that is more strongly represented in music therapy than in many other work environments. For teaching, environments where trainees feel able to make requests about the lighting or other sensory input can be helpful not only for those trainees, but others who have not realised what an overstimulating environment they are in. Involving lecturers who are neurodiverse can have a positive influence and can promote a neurodiverse-affirmative model of music therapy (Davies, 2022). Choosing creative assessments that promote the medium of artistic expression and don't duplicate learning outcomes can also work towards a more inclusive and achievable curriculum.

When things go wrong

Placements are unpredictable and complex environments, and although they bring about some of the richest and most central learning experiences, can bring about difficulties from time to time. Due to the asymmetry of the supervisory relationship, where the supervisor is also the assessor, this can cause anxieties in the trainee and result in unconscious defensive strategies that trainees employ, such as: over-intellectual discourse, expressing shame or feeling not good enough, excessive preparation of notes allowing no room for discussion in supervision or lack of initiative in sessions (John, 2009). Most of these aspects can be addressed in supervision and in reflective practice groups. However, when a relationship breaks down on placement it does sometimes take a three-way meeting with a course representative, the trainer and the supervisor to find a way through. If a trainee does fail a placement, it should not be a surprise to them, if feedback has been regular and systematic, allowing them the opportunity to develop their practice for the placement. A placement contract clearly stating expectations for the trainee and educator from the outset can be helpful.

At times, students paired on placement work well together and support each other. They can explore the exchange of roles in a shared facilitated group, for example. But sometimes these pairings can cause strife or anxiety and it is important for the students to be able to express and explore this. Risks include being made to feel shame for complaining about a fellow trainee, or causing splits where other trainees are encouraged to take sides. Supervision allocation can be helpful in this case. If the trainees are supervised together on site with their placement supervisor, they can sit in different supervision groups at college. The supervisors of these groups also need to communicate with each other to ensure splits do not occur. Ideally the differences can be held together in the same space through careful supervision, potentially resulting in considerable growth for both parties.

There are formal 'professional suitability' or 'fitness to practise' processes in place at Higher Education Institutions, only be instigated if there were serious concerns, such as falsifying records or persistent failures in safeguarding which would have been raised but not addressed by the trainee. If a trainee has poor mental health and is not practicing self-care, the trainer may need to intervene and delay the placement start or cancel due to fear of harm to clients. A trainer explained: "On one occasion I actually had to say 'I'm really sorry, I can't put you out on placement; you're not well enough'. And she was almost pressuring me to do it, and I had to say 'if you do that, I will have to put in the *cause for concern*'. If a cause for concern process is instigated, the trainee will have representation and an opportunity to plead their case, as they would also do in a professional suitability hearing. Nearly all concerns can be addressed at programme level, well before the problem escalates, but there does need to be a robust process in place for seriously concerning behaviour because of the responsibility to the public (the service users with whom the trainee is working). All music therapy programmes are run by music therapists registered with the HCPC and therefore as registrants their first responsibility is to protect the public.

Placement educators will be involved in these decisions and may be the person that raises a cause for concern after talking with the trainee. Good communication between placement educators and trainers is critical here. HEIs have discretion as to whether they allow a trainee to undertake a placement if the first has broken down or is incomplete, unlike other assignments where the right to re-sit is automatic. However, the decision is generally favourable to the trainee. In most training courses, trainees are asked to complete a self-assessment of how they developed on placement as well as receiving feedback from supervisors and service users on placement, and reflective practice group leaders. These multiple perspectives cultivate a great sense of reflexivity and help the trainee recognise where things can be different in the future.

When the training is not right

Sometimes ending the training early can be the best outcome for a trainee. As one trainer put it: 'We have to be open to allowing people to self-select and leave. In therapeutic training people can fail, and that's in some ways sometimes the best outcome.' Circumstances change, or the trainee has had different expectations of what training to be a music therapist was going to entail. In music therapy training, which involves so much discussion and consultation, it is most likely that it is the trainee's decision to leave rather than that of the trainer. Those reasons are likely to have been discussed and the decision supported by the training team. As seen above, the training team will be open to the training journey taking much longer if necessary for the trainee. Good therapists are not necessarily made in just two or three years. Leaving the course early or taking longer to train may bring about personal and professional developments that are still beneficial, as the second case study at the end of the chapter illustrates.

The impact of student satisfaction surveys

Most HEIs require trainees to complete an anonymous Postgraduate Taught Experience Survey (PTES) once a year which allows trainees to complete both qualitative and qualitative feedback on their experience of the training course. The results are publicly available. A key part of this is the way that trainers are able to give feedback to trainees each year on what they have been able to do to turn around areas of dissatisfaction. This should encourage a healthy sense that there is always capacity for improvement and development. Module evaluations and verbal feedback from student representatives and individual trainees during the year also contribute to the continuous improvement and development of the training course.

Alongside the rigid teaching situations explored in Chapter 1, the PTES survey can be a stressor for the trainers as the hosting HEI will place importance on the overall satisfaction result and applicants can compare satisfaction rates between institutions. One trainer said, 'Although I think it is important to gain detailed qualitative and quantitative feedback about the experience of the training, I wish more students filled it in, because the results can be skewed otherwise' and another expressed that 'it feels reductive to bring things down to overall satisfaction; another example of how the business model predominates in higher education'.

This chapter ends with two anonymised stories. The first is from a recent graduate representing different experiences and challenges.

Case study: Music therapy as a first career

My first experience of study was at music college. Once I started on the music therapy course I started to appreciate music for what it was more. I was less focused on the performance aspect; instead I was more interested in the experience of the music. It's almost like before, music was a 2D experience but during the training it became more of a 3D experience. There were suddenly so many different elements and sides to it that, although I wasn't consciously thinking about them, they were there in how I was experiencing music. Going into the training I was in a place of having a slightly negative relationship with music. I absolutely loved it but this love also had elements of trauma from the classical world sewn in. As I went through the training it was like I rediscovered my passion for music; I found that initial excitement that I once had again.

Now I am qualified, I have been continuing to develop my music by no longer mentally limiting myself or being so judgemental of my own music making. This has freed me to be able to explore different ways of playing music and allowed me to push the boundaries of how I play in both music therapy and as a string player.

It's hard to say what was the single most helpful element of training. I wouldn't have been able to find placement so helpful without reflective practice and supervision. I wouldn't have been able to engage in reflective practice or supervision without therapy. I suppose placement was the most helpful as that's when the theories and techniques you learn about in class suddenly start to click and make sense. I think peer support is a hugely important part of the training experience too. I feel so connected with my peers from the training and I feel very grateful to have had them throughout the training and that they continue to be an important part of my working life.

One theory that I always come back to in my clinical work is a secure base. I've also found that stopping and considering all the different elements of music as written in *Music Therapy: An Art Beyond Words* (Bunt and Stige, 2014) a very useful thing to explore in my work and I loved doing a micro-analysis of some of my practice.

The personal development that the training requires is hugely intense. Everyone said to me before the course 'you won't believe how much you'll change during the course' and I nodded politely but they couldn't have been more right! It's hard though to be truly honest with yourself and to do the work needed to make those personal growths.

Although I did have some incredible placement experiences, I also had one that was challenging. I will definitely carry the lessons learnt from that experience with me and try to grow from it but it has taken a while. I was lucky to get a good amount of experience working with other disciplines during my placements. I think the most important principle for me is to constantly think about a holistic approach that has the clients' needs at the centre.

A pivotal moment came somewhere through my final year when I felt like I was drowning in the workload but also working hard to make progress in my placement. I suddenly realised that my world felt a lot bigger. I just started to notice that the way I had been experiencing life and approaching work before was very tunnel-visioned. When my world opened up, I could experience everything so much more and this really allowed me to make the most progress in my training.

The second case study is from a trainee who undertook training as a music therapist as a second career.

Case study: Music therapy as a second career

Having first thought about becoming a music therapist in 1986, I began my training 32 years later. It marked a new phase in my life and one that I was eager to begin. However, within three weeks of having started the course, I was diagnosed with cancer. It was my intention to carry on, but wise lecturers advised that treatment would be exhausting, and it might not be in my best interests to continue. So, after approximately six weeks of study, I suspended my studies. Whilst at the time, it was a huge disappointment, it was the right decision.

Following successful treatment, I returned and found myself presented with a whole other set of problems. It was COVID and much of the course had moved online. In a short time, I had felt established in my first cohort which had been smaller, and so I found this new, larger, online cohort harder to settle into. I remember thinking, how do I get round explaining why I am starting again – am I even ready to be open about why? I was also bothered about being such a mature student!

The cancer journey is complex but simply put, it felt that I had 'crossed a line' which somehow set me apart. I am aware that I may have appeared remote, even insular and there were times when I found it hard to navigate the group dynamic. I had lost some confidence and was maybe a little shut down too; this resulted in me being less open to new connections and friendships which I regret. I completed the first year but early on in the second year, my mum, who I had been caring for, died. The demands of the course, family, a teaching role, and a significant bereavement became too much. I did not complete the year. Another false start. The saving grace was that I completed my second placement. I was fortunate to be in an established Learning Developmental Disabilities Arts Therapies Team who 'held' me during that time. My placement was such a positive experience that I knew, whilst full of regret that another year would be incomplete, I was in the right place with 'my kind of people'.

Another year on and I did not immediately return to my studies. Why further delay? On a purely practical level, I had to earn a living and that was as a teacher. Trying to balance the role of teacher and therapist had left me feeling increasingly conflicted and frustrated. I knew I needed to leave teaching before I could embrace the role of therapist.

Having now left teaching, I have made a determined effort to seek out work in therapy related areas; leading singing groups for people living with a dementia, assisting a music therapist in a therapy group for people with early onset dementia, working in a school for children with complex needs in a flexible 1:1 music 'teaching' role and I have collaborated on a piece of research with my second placement team around the use of Virtual Reality headsets in a clinical setting. I am not sure these opportunities would have presented themselves or I would have been open to them had I been training. This experience is proving to be invaluable learning leaving me well placed for when I pick up my studies again.

My journey through the training so far has been rich with some complex and difficult life experiences which have taken me time to process. Should I have pushed harder and finished earlier? I am not sure I would still be on the journey to becoming a therapist if I had.

References

Aird, R. (2017) From impostership to mastersness: Experiences of a postgraduate student's transition to higher education reflected through poetry. *Journal of Research in Nursing*, 22 (6–7), 522–532. (Accessed 10 December 2023).

All-Party Parliamentary Group on Arts, Health and Wellbeing (2017) *Creative Health: The Arts for Health and Wellbeing*. Available at: www.culturehealthandwellbeing.org.uk/appg-inquiry/ (Accessed 9 December 2023).

All-Party Parliamentary Group on Education (2019) Music Education: state of the nation Available at: www.musiceducationappg.org/publications.html (Accessed 25 July 2024).

Bath, N. et al. (2020) The declining place of music education in schools in England. *Children & Society*, 34 (5), 443–457.

British Association for Music Therapy (2024) BAMT Guidelines for Accessibility and Inclusivity for Disabled Students on Placement, Available from: www.bamt.org/resources/guidelines-for-accessibility-and-inclusivity-for-d accessed 22/7/24

Bunt, L. & Hoskyns, S. (2002) *The Handbook of Music Therapy*. Hove: Brunner/Routledge.

Bunt, L. and Stige, B. (2014) *Music Therapy: An Art beyond Words*. Second edition. [Online]. United Kingdom: Routledge.

Cole, S. & Warner, C. (2020) 'It's just a different dimension': Music therapists' experiences of hearing loss. *Approaches: Mousikotherapeia kai Eidikī Mousikī Paidagōgikī*. [Online] 14 (2).

Cooper, B. (2018) *Primary Schools: The Decline of Arts Education in Primary Schools and How It Can Be Reversed*. London, UK: Fabian Society, Children & the Arts, Musicians' Union.

Corey, M. and Corey, G., 2010. *Becoming a Helper*. Toronto: Nelson Education.

Cozolino, L. (2004) *The Making of a Therapist: A Practical Guide for the Inner Journey*. New York: W.W. Norton and Company.

Darnley-Smith, R. and Patey, H. (2003) *Music Therapy*. London: Sage Publications.

Davies, H. (2022) 'Autism is a way of being': An 'insider perspective' on neurodiversity, music therapy and social justice. *British Journal of Music Therapy*, 36 (1), 16–26. https://doi-org.ezproxy.uwe.ac.uk/10.1177/13594575221090182.

Gelbert, P. (2021) A skeptic in the land of music therapy: Evaluating evidence at the beginnings of practice. In Hadley, S. J. (ed.), *Sociocultural Identities in Music Therapy*. Dallas, TX: Barcelona Publishers.

Hadley, S. and Norris, M. S. (2016) Musical multicultural competency in music therapy: The first step. *Music Therapy Perspectives* [Online], 34 (2), 129–137.

Hadley, S. (2021) *Sociocultural Identities in Music Therapy*. 1st edition. Dallas, TX: Barcelona Publishers.

Halford, E. (2021) *'Am I good enough?': An exploration of music therapist and trainee understanding of the term 'readiness to study' in relation to music therapy*. Unpublished dissertation. University of the West of England.

Halleck, S.L. and Woods, S.M., 1962. Emotional problems of psychiatric residents. *Psychiatry*, 25 (4), pp.339–346.

Hämäläinen, S. P. et al. (2021) Yoik in Sami elderly and dementia care – A potential for a culture sensitive music therapy? *Nordic Journal of Music Therapy* [Online], 30 (5), 404–423, DOI: 10.1080/08098131.2020.1849364

Hardy, S. (ed.) (2021) The long journey toward self-acceptance: Living as a queer transgender music therapist. In *Sociocultural Identities in Music Therapy*. Dallas, TX: Barcelona Publishers.

Health Education England (2021) *Art, Drama and Music Therapy Career Choice Factsheet*. Available at: Allied Health Professions (AHP) Careers Awareness Toolkit. (Accessed 10th January 2024).

Hodgson, N. (2018) He oro waiora: Music therapy and well-being in adolescent mental health. *New Zealand Journal of Music Therapy*, 16 (16), 71–94.

Hook, J. N. et al. (2017) *Cultural Humility: Engaging Diverse Identities in Therapy*. First edition. Washington, District of Columbia: American Psychological Association.

John, D. (2009) Getting better: Some thoughts on the growth of the therapist. In Odell-Miller, H. and Richards, E. (eds.), *Supervision of Music Therapy: A Theoretical and Practical Handbook*. Sussex: Routledge.

Kumary, A. and Baker, M. (2008). Stressors reported by UK trainee counselling psychologists. *Counselling Psychology Quarterly* [Online], 21 (1), 19–28. (Accessed 10 December 2023).

Morales-Hernández, L. A. and Urrego-Mendoza, Z. C. (2017) Health, mental health, music and music therapy in a Colombian indigenous community from Cota, 2012–2014. *Revista de la Facultad de Medicina, Universidad Nacional de Colombia* [Online], 65 (3), 461–465.

Myerscough, F. and Wong, D. (2022) (Un)learning from experience: An Exposition of minoritized voices on music therapy training. *Music Therapy Perspectives* [Online], 40(2), 132–142.

Nordoff, P and Robbins, C. (2007) *Creative Music Therapy: A Guide to Fostering Clinical Musicianship*. Gilsum, N.H: Barcelona.

Pavlicevic, M. (1991) *Music Therapy: Intimate Notes*. London: Jessica Kingsley Publications.

Pedersen, I. N. et al. (eds.) (2023) *Resonant Learning in Music Therapy: A Training Model to Tune the Therapist*. London: Jessica Kingsley Publishers.

Pica, M. (1998) The ambiguous nature of clinical training and its impact on the development of student clinicians. *American Psychological Association* [Online], 35 (Fall), 361–365. (Accessed 29 July 2021).

Pickard, B. (2022) Anti-oppressive pedagogy as an opportunity for consciousness raising in the music therapy profession: A critical disability studies perspective, *British Journal of Music Therapy*, 36 (1), 3–64.

Richards, E. (2009) 'Whose handicap? Issues arising in the supervision of trainee music therapists in their first experience of working with adults with learning disabilities. In Odell-Miller, H. and Richards, E. (eds.), *Supervision of Music Therapy: A Theoretical and Practical Handbook*. Sussex: Routledge.

Rowe, N. (2022) Disabled and LGBTQ+: A music therapy perspective. In Collier, J. & Eastwood, C. (eds.), *Intersectionality in the Arts Psychotherapies*. London: Jessica Kingsley.

Savage, J. and Barnard, D. (2019). *The State of Play: A Review of Music Education in England 2019*. Musicians' Union, Music Industries Association, Music for All, UK Music.

Skovholt, T. and Rønnestad, M. (2003) Struggles of the novice counsellor and therapist. *Journal of Career Development* [Online], 30 (1), 45–58. (Accessed 10 December 2023).

Student Finance England (2023) Eligibility – Postgraduate Loan – Postgraduate Education – Products – SFE, Practitioners. www.practitioners.slc.co.uk/products/postgraduate-educat ion/postgraduate-masters-loan/eligibility/ (Accessed 25 July 2024).

Talamini, F. et al. (2023) Auditory and visual mental imagery in musicians and non-musicians. *Musicae scientiae*. [Online] 27 (2), 428–441.

Talwar, S. (2022) Foreword. In Collier, J. and Eastwood, C. (eds.), *Intersectionality in The Arts Psychotherapies*. London: Jessica Kingsley.

Truell, R. (2001). The stresses of learning counselling: Six recent graduates comment on their personal experiences of learning counselling and what can be done to reduce associated harm. *Counselling Psychology Quarterly*,14 (1), 67–89. https://web-p-ebscoh ost-com.ezproxy.uwe.ac.uk/ehost/pdfviewer/pdfviewer?vid=0&sid=199829cd-56fc-45ca-a113-c30fc64e123e%40redis (Accessed 10 December 2023).

Viega, M., Blackman, T., and Pharoh, D. (2022) The agency of HipHop as a force of liberation and healing in music therapy. In The Colonialism and Music Therapy Interlocutor's (CAMTI) Collective (Eds) (2022) *Colonialism and Music Therapy*. Dallas, Texas: Barcelona Publishers. Available at: https://search-ebscohost-com.ezproxy.uwe.ac.uk/login.aspx?direct=true&db=nlebk&AN=3396188&site=ehost-live (Accessed: 25 July 2024).

Vogel, D. L. and Wade, N. G. (2022) Introduction to the Handbook of Stigma and Mental Health. In Vogel, D. L. and Wade, N. G. (eds.), *The Cambridge Handbook of Stigma and Mental Health*. Cambridge: Cambridge University Press (Cambridge Handbooks in Psychology), 1–8. doi: 10.1017/9781108920995.001.

Warner, C. (2016) Student perspectives on working with assistants on placement during vocational music therapy training. In Strange, J., Odell Miller, H. and Richards, E. (eds.), *Collaboration and Assistance in Music Therapy Practice: Roles, Relationships, Challenges*. London: Jessica Kingsley Publishers.

Whitehead-Pleaux, A., Brink, S. and Tan, X. (2017) Culturally competent music therapy assessments. In Whitehead-Pleaux, A. and Tan, X. (eds.), *Cultural Intersections in Music Therapy*. Gilsum: Barcelona Publishers.

Zendel, B. R. and Alexander, E. J. (2020) Autodidacticism and music: Do self-taught musicians exhibit the same auditory processing advantages as formally trained musicians? *Frontiers in Neuroscience* [Online], 2020-07, 14, 752–752, Article 752. (Accessed 21st December 2023).

Chapter 7

The reflective practitioner

Tessa Watson

Introduction

Reflective practice is a stance or approach taken to the role of music therapist that will be adjusted and developed throughout the career of the music therapist. It is important for the provision of a high quality service but also for sustainability, for both individual practitioners and the profession. Reflective practice is central to a music therapist's practice, supporting a developmental, sustainable and satisfying work life.

Music therapists' job satisfaction has been linked by various authors with the following factors: An ability to support service users, to work with music therapist colleagues and other members of the health and care team, and the availability of supportive networks in the workplace (Stewart (2000), Hills et al (2000) and Vega (2010)), all factors which have links with reflective practice. Recent studies into music therapists' job satisfaction in the US (Branson (2023), Eyre et al. (2023) and Meadows et al. (2022)) present a complex picture, including concerns about the sustainability of and advocacy for the profession. Eyre et al. make an inevitable link between low job satisfaction and the decision to leave the profession (2023).

This chapter will consider different elements of reflective practice with a focus on the trainee's learning about self-care and the centrality of music as part of this. Early encouragement to develop a reflective practice stance during training helps to minimise training risks such as trauma and secondary trauma, health issues or failure to progress due to these experiences. In professional practice a reflective practice stance assists in maintaining a sustainable and satisfying career.

Reflective practice

The idea of reflective practice is embedded from the start of a training programme and links to all learning and teaching experiences, supporting trainees to make the most of their learning. Being able to reflect upon and analyse learning, gain personal insights, and consider issues from multiple perspectives brings deeper understanding, flexibility and resourcefulness in all aspects of the work role. Trainees need teaching opportunities to explore the importance of self-reflection, to link their personal background to their training, and to know where to take issues for further exploration. I have developed a workshop that is delivered at the start of training which presents and explores the central position of reflective thinking and learning for training and professional practice. The workshop includes an explanation of the importance of reflective thinking throughout learning and teaching, the reasons for personal therapy and experiential work, and engages trainees in a consideration of their experiences of culture, play, education and approaches to reflecting on and managing mental experience. It includes discussion about how to reflect, the idea of a position of curiosity, of self-care and advice about 'what goes where' (a phrase often heard when interviewing trainers for this book).

Sobey, an experienced trainer, wrote about the central place of reflection within music therapy training thus:

> 'The underlying issue for students throughout training is their capacity for change. Initially this may focus on how they will acquire so much new information and develop skills on so many fronts. However, beneath this is something more fundamental as students realise the extent to which they are required to reflect on their own process and to use their own feelings and responses as a primary factor in the therapy. This is often exemplified in the changes in musical identity which is immediately challenged in their music studies: here they may experience feelings of loss as habitual ways of playing seem to be less valued and new ways of being with someone musically are not yet developed. Linked with this is the fear of not being 'good enough' in time for embarking on work with their first clients'.
>
> (Sobey in Sutton, 2003: 43)

The sections that follow explore the different aspects of self-reflection and the challenges that can arise for music therapists within their careers.

The use of music in reflective practice and self-care

> 'Improvising is central to my self-care and emotional regulation as a practising music therapist.' (Graduate)

The trainee's exploration and development of their relationship with music is central to their training, and their use of music is central within reflective practice and self-care. Woodcock refers to the pleasure and pain relating to the trainee's relationship with music during the training journey: 'Change is inherently painful, as well as joyful, even the change in one's concepts of what music itself is' (Woodcock, 1996: 24). Training programmes draw personal music practice and reflection into learning and teaching in various ways. For example, trainees might be required to write about their relationship with music or their instrument/s as part of an assignment, or to keep a listening diary that is shared and discussed within the peer group (see Chapter 4). Assignments may involve creative responses to learning, using live improvisation, performance and discussion, or recorded musical representations of learning. Individual and group independent study time is designated for music practice appropriate to individual trainees' development. This independent time embeds the habit of using and engaging with music both actively and passively, in order to develop professional practice and to support self-care.

Engagement in music is encouraged as a nurturing habit during training. This supports graduates to meet the HCPC standard of proficiency to 'recognise that the obligation to maintain fitness to practise includes engagement in their own arts-based process' (2023: standard 2.13). Trainees and new graduates can find it hard to continue with regular musical engagement or find that their musical energy is depleted by clinical work. Trondalen writes that 'it might be terrifying when the joy of music making or listening to the music is decreasing due to feeling emotionally and mentally drained' (2016: 942). Regular opportunities to use music in a developmental and self-nurturing way during training help to keep music a creative source of personal support for the trainee once they are in professional practice.

The physical impact of music within professional practice

An issue that is often overlooked in relation to self-care is the physical impact of the music therapist's work and it is suggested that this should be considered during training. This typically falls into two areas, that of hearing and physical impact. Having hearing loss is not a barrier to working as a music therapist; Cole and Warner's article presents some of the challenges and strategies that music therapists with hearing loss experience in their work (2022). In their work music therapists may be impacted by loud music over a sustained period of time (MacMahon and Page, 2015). In the UK this experience is included in the Control of Noise at Work legislation (Health and Safety Executive, 2008, 2021). Music therapists can usefully adopt the habit of making a risk assessment regarding music volume at the beginning of each new engagement with a service user. It may be necessary to dampen loud instruments (such as drum kits) or use equipment such as ear plugs (potentially custom made), ear defenders or acoustic screens. The Musicians' Union suggest that the use of such equipment should be considered when daily or weekly exposure levels exceed 80dB (Musicians' Union, 2023). Music therapists who are concerned about their hearing should seek an audiometry appointment, as prevention is an essential step to take in relation to hearing loss.

Another physical impact of the work can come from the requirement to frequently move and set up instruments, and where room set up means that the music therapist is adopting inappropriate working positions. For example, twisting their upper body whilst playing the piano/keyboard, or holding instruments for long periods of time to facilitate playing. Trainees and music therapists frequently need to transport instruments to different wards or settings. Where this is the case, appropriate moving equipment such as trolleys or wheels should be provided, and assistance may be required from colleagues. Where room set up or a particular piece of work involves physical stress that is impacting the music therapist, a risk assessment should be undertaken and a plan put in place to manage the impacts.

Personal development

> 'Through the process of learning to help other people to change, student therapists must also be helped, and change, themselves'.
>
> (Watson, 2005: 9)

Whilst music therapy training is an academic programme of study, all therapeutic trainings also involve considerable personal development. Within current MA Music Therapy training courses this is likely to involve taught content to support the trainee's understanding of reflective practice and their stance as a practitioner, reflective practice groups and supervision on placement and engagement in experiential work such as an experiential group and individual personal therapy. Trainers work to support the links and transitions between these different experiences. In this sense the role of trainers in their relational support of trainees may be performed differently to other programmes of study in a university. For example, they may meet with trainees more frequently and talk about more personal issues given the nature of music therapy training.

Therapy and the 'wounded healer'

The concept of the wounded healer is one of Jung's archetypes, now referred to within many therapeutic disciplines (Klayman-Farber, 2017). Pavlicevic's chapter reminds us that motives for working as music therapists are 'complex and multi-layered' and explores the idea of power and the different poles of the healer-patient archetype (1997: 176). Through the authors' own personal work they are aware of the impact of personal experience in motivating a wish to train as a therapist. Trainees will have a variety of ideas about who and what a healer might be. They may be motivated by spiritual or religious principles, their own experience of therapy, experiences of trauma or intergenerational trauma, and a range of other reasons and wounds (see also Chapter 6 in this volume). Frequently, trainees are not fully aware of their motivations to train, as Adams suggests, asking two questions: 'Why did you train to become a therapist, and why did you *really* train to become a therapist' (2014: 10). Deepening trainee understanding of the impact and motivations of their past experiences and wounds can provide deep personal awareness and challenges during the process of training. Trainees may become aware of issues they are avoiding, patterns they are repeating, or wounds they are re-opening by engaging in work with clients. Pavlicevic writes about keeping her own wounds 'tightly stitched' and allowing herself to understand this and explore vulnerabilities (1997: 180). Reflection upon motivations to train can support learning and development and assist the trainee in identifying the role service users might take for them, including understanding when engagement in the development of others is meeting their own needs. As Shaw et al. consider, some of this work may enable the building of a sense of pride and strengthened voices around trainees' experiences of disability and ableism (Shaw et al., 2022). All this reflection assists the trainee in knowing when they might need to seek additional support in order to look after their own self-care.

Personal therapy

Personal therapy supports the trainee in their journey through training, in developing their music therapy stance and in understanding and managing their self-care. Trainees may choose to use psychotherapy, music therapy or another of the arts therapies disciplines. This is usually required through the majority of the training. It is noted that the cost of personal therapy presents a barrier to training for potential trainees and this is an issue currently in discussion between trainers.

The purpose of personal therapy and development in a therapeutic training is 'to help trainees increase their awareness of how their personality, behaviour, personal and cultural beliefs might impact on, and influence, their clients' (Spencer, 2006: 109). This is supported by the HCPC Standards of Proficiency for Arts Therapists which state that practitioners must 'recognise the potential impact of their own values, beliefs and personal biases (which may be unconscious) on practice' (2023: standard 5.3) and 'understand the value of therapy in developing insight and self-awareness through their own personal experience' (2023: standard 1.4). Personal reflection at the depth required in a therapeutic training is demanding. It requires an ability to reflect upon personal challenges past and present including areas of difficulty and barriers to development. Personal therapy will also usefully include reflection upon the motivations for training. The experience of approaching, beginning, engaging in and ending a period of personal therapy – and reflecting deeply upon this – is a central element of music therapy training.

Experiential training groups

The experiential training group is an additional support for trainees to develop their reflective capacities as they form an identity as a music therapist. Experiential groups are used in music therapy training in the UK and across Europe, and have a variety of names, including, music therapy groups, process groups, experiential groups, interpersonal learning groups or self-experience groups. This group opportunity provides a focused and safe container for exploration of themes in training, the trainee's own identity and impact, and allows, as Streeter describes, trainees to 'fall apart safely', even questioning 'why they have chosen to do this work and whether or not they want to continue' (Streeter, 2002: 270). These groups are likely to include both music and talking (see examples in Davies, 2009). Not essentially a therapy group nor a teaching experience, the question 'what is this group for' is likely to be ubiquitous.

One graduate explained that 'the process group was incredibly helpful both professionally and personally. Without it, all the other learning would not have been as meaningful. It was helpful not only to have the experiential group and personal therapy, but also to write about it as an assignment. Once I wrote my learning experience down, what seemed chaotic was more manageable to understand'. This quotation conveys the importance of the group in assisting trainees to move towards deeper understanding of their own processes, particularly within a group.

The experiential group can be experienced as a stormy journey (Davies, 2009: 150). Common themes in literature about experiential groups include relatedness, connection and transference, individual trainee progress and issues (including musical identity), identification with the profession and the role of music therapist, the receiving of empathic support or experiencing a lack of support, and ideas of competition, rivalry, boundaries and containment. To support engagement, an introduction to the group and the centrality of reflective practice is usefully provided for trainees prior to the group beginning. This might usefully be delivered by a member of the staff team (not the group facilitator), linking the group purpose with learning outcomes for the training and providing a safe harbour from which to embark upon the journey. Issues of communication and confidentiality around the group are useful to address directly. The group facilitator may meet with the course leader occasionally to ensure any urgent issues are managed, rather than discussing content. Issues of serious concern are shared, with the knowledge of the trainee, between the group facilitator and course leader in order to provide appropriate support for trainees. Part time programmes may experience challenges in delivering these groups given the length of the training and the resource needed to deliver such a group throughout the training. This has led to trainers being resourceful about when the group is introduced, and in providing other points for review and reflection throughout the training.

These groups and the experiences of group leaders are described in various chapters and it is clear that the facilitation role demands experience and resilience (Streeter, 2002, Davies and Greenland, 2002, Davies et al., 2009 and 2014, Bonde et al., 2019). Streeter writes that 'testing out the group convenor is more or less an essential part of a training group experience and anxieties may run extremely high from time to time. This means that projections are likely to be strong and therefore will require the time and space for refection and understanding on the part of the music therapist who is running the group' (2002: 273). Supervision that includes consideration of issues of power and vulnerability are important for facilitators.

Supervision and reflective practice

Clinical or practice supervision is a central and crucial feature in both training and continuing practice as a music therapist. During the training journey, trainees must learn the importance of the supervision space to interrogate and understand their own work more deeply. Michelle Forinash puts this well:

'Supervision is a relationship, one in which both supervisor and supervisee actively participate and interact. It is a process of unfolding – not simply following a recipe, but engaging in a rich and dynamic relationship. Supervision is then a journey, or odyssey of sorts, in which supervisor and supervisee learn and grow and from which both will very likely leave transformed in some way'.
(Forinash 2001: 1)

There are few publications about music therapy supervision (Odell-Miller and Richards 2009; Forinash, 2001, 2019) and about creative supervision in the arts therapies (Lahad, 1999) despite the significance of this practice.

Practice supervision during training will take the form of regular, usually weekly, supervision on site when on training placement with a music therapist. These music therapist supervisors are known as practice educators by the HCPC. There are some exceptions where more experienced trainees may be supervised on site by another arts therapist, psychologist, or an allied health professional, particularly in the case of emergent placements where no music therapist is yet employed. This arrangement varies between training courses. However, all courses, in addition to individual supervision, also offer regular reflective practice groups, or clinical seminars, where small groups of trainees share their work in turn led by an experienced music therapist. These groups allow trainees to follow the journey of several different music therapy participants or music therapy groups from different placements, but within the confidential setting of the reflective practice group.

Bager-Charleson notes that 'The therapist's task is difficult. He has to feel affected without acting upon his own feelings: to feel, but to use his own feeling in the service of the patient' (2010: 48). Thus, adequate and appropriate supervision for trainee music therapists is important to allow for the processing of clinical work, an ability to experience closure once the work is done and to reflect on self-care strategies.

Music therapy supervision typically takes the shape of dialogue between supervisee and supervisor in a private uninterrupted space. If the music therapy work can be audio or video recorded, listening back to parts of the session for in depth exploration and reflective dialogue with the supervisor can be an important part of the process. Creating live music in the supervision session can be another way of helping to reflect on the work.

One example of the use of musical processes in supervision is explored in depth by Heidi Ahonen-Eerikainen, using a supervision group based on principles from Balint reflective practice groups and group analytic therapy (Ahonen-Eerikainen 2003). As part of the supervision experience, the person bringing the case for exploration talks about it but then moves into musical improvisation, joined later by the rest of the group. This allows for reflection on the embodied experience that the free musical association has brought about. Various people in this supervision group will experience different aspects of the client work so the collective thinking brings about more insight. Some training courses make use of this method, or other ways of using musical improvisation in clinical seminar/reflective practice groups. One trainer explained that 'teaching the Ahonen method to final year trainees has allowed them to conduct their own peer supervision groups once a month, in addition to their regular supervision. Some of these peer groups continue beyond training, not as a substitute but as an additional supervisory practice; to share difficult felt aspects of their work and think together with others about the complex therapeutic situations they are dealing with'.

Placement supervisors may also use improvisation within a supervision session or encourage a trainee to create their own reflective improvisations to help process their own feelings following a session.

Trainees on all courses are expected to write reflections on their own supervisory experiences as well as their experiences in their music therapy work. Casement's idea of the development of the 'internal supervisor' is one of the main learning and teaching aims of supervision and reflective practice groups. Casement writes about this as the ability to 'draw upon our thinking more readily when we are with a patient' (2006: 132). Subsequently the new graduate will have the capacity to understand their own changing supervisory needs, acknowledge the importance of pursuing this throughout their working life and have the ability to make use of their developing sense of the 'internal supervisor'. Although the HCPC do not provide specific advice on what form supervision should take for their music therapy trainees, they do provide a statement on student supervision relevant to all disciplines registered by this body (HCPC, 2023).

Disruptions to the training journey

Trainees can experience interruptions to their training for a variety of reasons. They may need to lengthen their training journey due to health issues, maternity leave or struggles in financing their training. Whilst there is high continuation through to qualification, some trainees choose to leave the training, finding that it is not right for them. This can be a difficult experience given the amount of preparation required prior to embarking upon a training.

Some experiences of disruptions to the training journey are powerfully conveyed below through the voices of graduates, beginning with a music therapist whose training took two years longer than planned.

> In my first year I became very unwell due to an undiagnosed condition which took a long time to recover from. I was also grieving a friend who passed away unexpectedly. The nature of this training highlights your own life experiences and you develop a lot of self-awareness. It became apparent that I had other support needs – I was diagnosed with dyspraxia during my training and received initial assessments for ASD and ADHD. This was quite a mentally draining process, so I needed to slow down my studies to manage this as well. It was hard seeing the cohort I started with move on without me; I wanted to experience the

journey from start to finish with them, but ultimately this was the best decision for me. I needed the time to process everything as well as being fully healthy and present for clients on placement. It was like I had a 5-year course because even in the time I took away, I was still connected to the training, reading, and actively thinking about it even without that lecture time and my assignments being deferred.

Another graduate writes about their challenging experience of managing a health condition during Covid, and the impact that this had upon their training:

Halfway through my second year blood tests revealed that I had blood cancer, and that this was a likely reason for the fatigue that I was having to manage. The week after my diagnosis the country went into lockdown because of the COVID-19 pandemic, and I was advised to shield, given the label "clinically extremely vulnerable". I struggled emotionally with my diagnosis and the isolation that shielding brought but managed to complete my second year with the help of personal therapy and thoughtful educational and emotional support from University. At the end of my 2nd year, I made the difficult decision to take a year away from the training due to the anxiety and isolation that being advised continually to shield had and was causing. Leaving my cohort, with whom I had made strong bonds was difficult, but I remained a part of their journey, being present for their final research presentations, and their farewell meet on campus at the end of their studies in October 2021. I resumed my studies in October 2021, but felt it necessary to spread my final year over two academic years. One of the biggest challenges for me coming back to university during a pandemic was that I felt marginalised as a student with a health condition. Ongoing questioning by the university of where privileging exists would have been helpful to promote inclusion and equality. Taking a year out allowed me some valuable processing time. It also allowed me time to notice the attitudes of our society towards clinically vulnerable people. I now experienced othering and ableism at first hand. This changed me and shaped me as a therapist. I now more acutely saw the effects of our society; one driven by productivity and dominated by the medical model and recognised the need to cultivate interdependence and social responsibility.

Lastly, a graduate who took a period of maternity leave reflects upon their experience:

During my first year, I fell pregnant with my first child. This resulted in me taking a whole year break from the course. This experience was both positive and slightly difficult. During the whole course of training, I found the shared experience with my peers to be an important factor that enhanced my learning. I had a strong bond with my initial cohort and found leaving the group, along with the knowledge that they would continue on their journey without me, to be quite painful. On the other hand, I was able to pause my training, focus on my family and new role as a mum, returning to the course at a time that felt manageable. Becoming a mother during the course was quite a unique experience. On the one hand, it supported my learning, such as increasing my understanding and appreciation of mother-infant interactions and early child development. I experienced some challenges where I found professional skill development and my own personal experience to be conflicting. This was particularly prominent during the infant observation. I was able to reflect on these challenges with my tutor and unpick it further during personal therapy. In hindsight, this was a valuable learning experience that I have since continued to reflect on during my time in the profession. My experience of taking longer to train felt hugely positive and I felt very grateful for the support I received during my studies. My tutors were open and receptive to my concerns, and they supported me to create a realistic plan for my return.

Each of these accounts demonstrates the complex experience of taking longer to train. Each account shares one factor: The challenges of leaving their cohort and missing these strong bonds. Despite the challenges, it is clear that each graduate felt the experience provided insights that they were able to use in their future practice, including relating to their own self-care.

Sustainable practice

The work that music therapists undertake often brings positive experiences and developments in their lives. Trondalen writes about music therapists being vitalized in the therapeutic relationship and quotes an experienced colleague who states 'I am trying to be really present in every meeting with the client. If I should rush from one to another, I would never experience and gain the profit of being a fellow traveller' (2016: 942). I have written myself of the privilege and learning that I have gained in my work with adults with learning disabilities; 'the work it has been my privilege to have undertaken in music therapy with people with learning disabilities has been transformative for my own understanding of what a good life can be' (Watson 2024). These experiences can contribute to job satisfaction and sustainable practice, however, negative impacts can also arise due to the nature of the work. For example, burnout, secondary trauma and compassion fatigue (see also Chapter 6 in this volume).

An understanding of the relationship between the impact of clinical work and self-care develops through the training. This understanding is usually deepened once the trainee begins their placement work. One placement educator suggested that placements 'teach the student something about the expectations of the work and the resilience necessary to undertake the work.' A second placement educator spoke about the importance of trainees being able 'to recognise when they need support and to know where to access this eg supervision, personal therapy, student services as appropriate'. Research about resilience in psychotherapy suggests that the four characteristics of highly resilient therapists are a) being drawn to interpersonal relationships, b) a desire to grow and learn, c) possessing a core values and beliefs framework and d) actively engaging with self (Hou and Skovholt, 2020 and Cronin et al., 2023). Rather than considering resilience to be a quality a music therapist either does or does not have, it is considered within this chapter as an ability to learn skills and self-care for sustainable practice.

Negative impacts arising from the nature of music therapy work can be burnout, secondary trauma and compassion fatigue. Authors differ in their consideration of the relationship between these three experiences, with some literature suggesting that burnout and secondary trauma can lead to, or are components of compassion fatigue (Pellegrini et al., 2022). The impact of all three components on health and care professionals has been written about in recent years and is considered in the paragraphs that follow.

Burnout

Burnout, included in the ICD-11 as an occupational condition, is often defined as a psychological response to ongoing personal stress in work (Maslach and Leiter, 2016, World Health Organisation 2021). It is experienced as exhaustion and challenges in completing cognitive tasks. Personal traits, the nature of the work and the quality of professional support are all factors within burnout. For those working in the health and care professions, the constant requirement to be emotionally available and empathic, and to support people at the most challenging times in their lives, are likely to be two of the specific factors that lead to burnout. Brooks (2013) writes from the perspective of a music therapist providing therapy for a person with burnout, describing symptoms of anger, frustration, boredom and helplessness, alongside behaviours which could be compulsive or addictive (over/under working, substance reliance), and associated physical symptoms. For music therapists, burnout may come from being asked to, or deciding to take on more work or to extend their role in ways that are challenging to manage. The pressure of the requirement to demonstrate that music therapy works, to persuade sceptical colleagues, and to continually push open doors for the profession without adequate support can be an added stress (Brooks, 2013, Vega, 2010). These issues are present for music therapists both in training and in professional practice.

Secondary trauma and compassion fatigue

Indirect and prolonged exposure to traumatic events through therapeutic work can lead to secondary trauma, with self-care and workplace support again recommended to mitigate against this (Pellegrini et al., 2022). Some writers consider that those working in mental health services are greater at risk of secondary trauma. During training an awareness of the trainee's own trauma map is helpful in thinking about appropriate areas of work and self-care. Personal responses to secondary trauma include avoidant, passive or active coping mechanisms (Vukčević Marković and Živanović, 2022).

Lastly compassion fatigue, which can arise suddenly and is sometimes likened to post traumatic stress disorder. Compassion fatigue is usually described as physical and emotional exhaustion, a decline in the ability to feel empathy and a sense of dread in relation to work (Trondalen, 2016). Some writing suggests that given the nature of a therapist's work, it is more helpful to develop robust and responsive self-monitoring, self-care and workplace support rather than trying to eliminate compassion fatigue (Brooks, 2013, Bentley, 2022).

Music therapists may experience these three components as related to direct therapeutic contact, as well as through the burden of over work through additional hours, roles or projects. Self-care, prevention and sustainability has two imperatives: The preservation of a healthy and enjoyable work life for the music therapist, and the ability to provide a high quality service for the people in the care of the music therapist. Learning how to maintain and replenish self-care and professional energy is an essential part of training, to enable a sustainable career. Supervision, supportive peer relationships and work initiatives, for example, mindfulness or exercise opportunities, can help in reflecting upon work, finding a supportive community and noticing emerging symptoms (Vivolo et al., 2022). Specific resources for those who experience burnout or compassion fatigue suggested in Brook's chapter include; adjusting expectations about their work/life balance and capacity, developing enjoyable aspects of work, a support network and developing self-care (Brooks, 2013: 771). These are usefully explored in tutorial discussion when trainees are considering their preferred settings for professional practice.

Self-care

All the writing in this chapter points to the importance of self-care, the focus of this concluding section. Trondalen writes about self-care as 'giving to yourself and also receiving care and support from others, not least through the means of music' (2016: 937). Three areas for self-care are suggested: Biological, psychological and contextual (Ibid 2016). In the UK the HCPC Standards of Proficiency support self-care in the requirement that music therapists should both 'understand the importance of their own mental and physical health and wellbeing strategies in maintaining fitness to practice' (2023, standard 3.2) and 'develop and adopt clear strategies for physical and mental self-care and self-awareness, to maintain a high standard of professional effectiveness and a safe working environment' (2023, standard 3.4). As part of this, Trondalen notes the importance of keeping an eye on one's personal context, by being alert to any significant events or experiences at work, home and community (Trondalen, 2016). Actively engaging in music and other arts media during training and finding playful ways to attend to self-care is a central aspect of training. Trainers, placement educators and graduates involved in this book talked about a wide variety of self-care activities such as physical activity (including walking, biking, running, yoga), cooking, meditation, religion and spiritual practices, journaling, photography, poetry and gardening as supporting their self-care.

One graduate said, 'I've definitely become aware of a feeling among people working in helping professions that you need to be extra strong and resilient in order to carry out the work and be of reliable service to others, which can lead to a neglect of self-care and difficulty in sharing vulnerability and expressing needs at work.' This underlines the importance of embedding self-care as a regular practice within training, and supporting trainees to balance their need to progress with the need to reflect upon self-care, ask for help when needed and to consider where their professional practice might begin. Running alongside the centrality of self-care is the valuing of the use of lived experience in music therapy practice, and in supporting trainees (and trainers) in being able to do this in a way that is safe for the music therapy and effective for the service user (Davies, 2022, Shaw, 2022).

Trainers also spoke about their self-care, with most support being informally developed within staff teams. One trainer described a good experience of management and support, sharing that '…we're quite a tight team. We have formal meetings, which have a focus on CPD but there is always a focus on thinking about what's happening for people, processing, and then we also have a focus on something related to CPD and that often brings up sort of ways of dealing with certain situations depending upon how people are. We also have a buddy system for new tutors. So everybody gets assigned somebody who's experienced in the team.' Another trainer talked about the importance of their team having a balanced workload and of continual reflective discussion about their work within the team 'Well, we make time after every day; even if it's just quickly after say, supervision, to try and go over things'. Other trainers spoke about meaningful support as coming from the team, rather than the institution, 'there is no formal mechanism: there's just nothing. I think we try to be good team players and we try to spend time valuing each other as a team. We tend to have weekly team meetings. We consciously are aware that we need to support each other. People bring food and treats. And we'll go out, once a term for a meal or to someone's house or something.' Where formal support for trainers such as management support, reflective groups or supervision was not available to trainers a range of self-care rituals and activities were developed individually and within teams.

To conclude: Using creativity and music

To end this chapter, ideas from two poets are used, which have been of use in thinking about the richness of reflective music therapy practice and the nurturing qualities of our art form. Firstly, the English poet Keats and his idea of negative capability. This idea was introduced to the me in reflective practice in my training at Roehampton. It explores the idea of working therapeutically without always knowing the direction nor conclusion of the work. Keats expresses negative capability beautifully as the capacity to be 'in uncertainties, mysteries, doubts, without any irritable reaching after fact and reason' (Keats and Colvin, 2011: 60). A belief in the process of therapeutic work and of a 'human-with-human' therapeutic relationship (Fansler et al., 2019) may be part of the framework for sustainable reflective practice. Secondly, the Irish poet Seamus Heaney, to whose poetry I referred in framing the BAMT 2021 conference (Cousins-Booth et al., 2021). Heaney credits poetry for 'being itself and being a help.' (Heaney, 1998: 450). To borrow from Heaney, music therapists can likewise credit music in their self-care, for being itself and for being a help.

References

Adams, M. (2014) *The Myth of the Untroubled Therapist.* London: Routledge.
Ahonen-Eerikainen, H. (2003) 'Using Group–Analytic Supervision Approach When Supervising Music Therapists', *Nordic Journal of Music Therapy,* 12 (2), pp. 173–182.
Bager-Charleston, S. (2010) *Reflective Practice in Counselling and Psychotherapy.* Poole: Learning Matters.
Bentley, P. (2022) 'Compassion practice as an antidote for compassion fatigue in the era of COVID-19', *The Journal of Humanistic Counseling,* 61 (1), pp. 58–73.
Bonde, L.O., Jacobsen, S.L., Pederson, I.N. and Wigram, T. (2019) 'Experiential and resonant learning processes: Music therapy self experience', in Jacobsen, S.L., Pederson, I.N. and Bonde, L.O. (eds.) *A Comprehensive Guide to Music Therapy. Theory, Clinical Practice, Research and Training.* London: Jessica Kingsley Publishers, pp. 461–466.
Branson, J.L. (2023) 'Leaving the profession: A grounded theory exploration of Music Therapists' decisions', *Voices A World Forum for Music Therapy,* 23 (1), pp. 1–22. https://voices.no/index.php/voices/article/view/3259.
Brooks, D.M. (2013) 'Professional burnout', in Eyre, L. (ed.) *Guidelines for Music Therapy Practice in Mental Health of Adolescents and Adults.* Gilsum NH: Barcelona, pp. 767–796.
Casement, P. (2006) *Learning from Life, Becoming a Psychoanalyst.* London: Routledge.
Cole, S. and Warner, C. (2022) '"It's just a different dimension": Music therapists' experiences of hearing loss', *Approaches: An Interdisciplinary Journal of Music Therapy,* 14 (2). Available at: https://approaches.gr/cole-a20201005/ (Accessed 24 November 2023).
Cousins-Booth, J., Partridge, L. and Watson, T. (2021) *Book of Abstracts. Open Ground: Music Therapy in Collaborative and Exchange. Fourth BAMT Conference 9–11th April 2021.* London: British Association for Music Therapy.
Cronin, S., Allen, T., Hou, J-M. and Walker, L. (2023) 'Therapist resilience in an ever-changing world: A systematic review', *Journal of Prevention and Health Promotion,* 4 (1), pp. 60–86.
Davies, A. (2009) 'Experiential groups on music therapy trainings', in Davies, A., Richards, E. and Barwick, N. (eds.) *Group Music Therapy: A Group Analytic Approach.* London: Routledge, pp. 149–162.
Davies, A., and Greenland, S. (2002) 'A group analytic look at experiential training groups. How can music earn its keep', in Davies, A. and Richards, E. (eds.) *Music Therapy and Groupwork: Sound Company.* London: Jessica Kingsley Publishers, pp. 274–287.
Davies, A., Richards, E. and Barwick, N. (2009) *Group Music Therapy: A Group Analytic Approach.* London: Routledge.
Davies, A., Richards, E. and Barwick, N. (2014) *Group Music Therapy: A Group Analytical Approach.* London: Routledge.

Davies, H. (2022) 'Autism is a way of being': An 'insider perspective' on neurodiversity, music therapy and social justice', *British Journal of Music Therapy,* 36 (1), pp. 16–26.

Eyre, L., Meadows, A. and Gollenberg, A. (2023) 'Music Therapists' thoughts about their future and the direction of the profession: An explanatory sequential mixed method study', in *Voices A World Forum for Music Therapy,* 23 (3), pp.1–24. Available at: https://voices.no/index.php/voices/article/view/3912 (Accessed 3 November 2023).

Fansler, V., Reed, R., Bautista, E. Taylor-Arnett, A., Perkins, F. and Hadley, S. (2019) 'Playing in the borderlands: The transformative possibilities of queering music therapy pedagogy', *Voices A World Forum for Music Therapy,* 19 (3), pp. 1–19.

Forinash, M. (2001) *Music Therapy Supervision.* Gilsum: Barcelona Publishers.

Forinash, M. (2019) *Music Therapy Supervision.* Gilsum: Barcelona Publishers.

Health and Safety Executive (2008) *Sound Advice. Control of Noise at Work in Music and Entertainment.* London: Crown Copyright.

Health and Safety Executive (2021) *Controlling Noise at Work. The Control of Noise at Work Regulations 2005. Guidance on Regulations.* Norwich: The Stationery Office.

HCPC (2023) *Standards of Proficiency Arts Therapists.* Available at: https://www.hcpc-uk.org/globalassets/standards/standards-of-proficiency/reviewing/arts-therapists---new-standards.pdf (Accessed: 20 February 2023).

Heaney, S. (1998) *Opened Ground.* London: Faber and Faber Limited.

Hills, B., Norman, I. and Forster, L. (2000) 'A study of burnout and multidisciplinary team-working amongst professional Music Therapists', *British Journal of Music Therapy,* 14 (1), pp. 32–40.

Hou, J.M. and Skovholt, T.M. (2020) 'Characteristics of highly resilient therapists', *Journal of Counseling Psychology,* 67 (3), pp. 386–400.

Keats, J. and Colvin, S. (ed.) (2011) *Letters of John Keats to His Family and Friends.* New York: Barnes and Noble Digital Library, p. 60.

Klayman-Farber, S. (2017) *Celebrating the Wounded Healer Psychotherapist.* London: Routledge.

Lahad, M. (1999) *Creative Supervision; The Use of Expressive Arts Methods in Supervision and Self- Supervision.* London: Jessica Kingsley Publishers.

MacMahon, L. and Page, A. (2015). 'Noise induced hearing loss in music therapists: A case study', *Journal of Environmental Health Research,* 15 (1), pp. 57–70.

Maslach C. and Leiter M.P. (2016) 'Understanding the burnout experience: recent research and its implications for psychiatry', *World Psychiatry,* 15 (2), pp. 103–11.

Meadows, A., Eyre, L. and Gollenberg, A. (2022) 'Workforce characteristics, workplace and job satisfaction, stress, burnout, and happiness of music therapists in the United States', *Voices A World Forum for Music Therapy,* 22 (1), pp. 1–19. Available at: https://voices.no/index.php/voices/article/view/3366/3398 (Accessed 3 November 2023).

Musicians' Union (2023) *The Importance of Hearing Damage Prevention in Musicians' Work.* Available at: https://musiciansunion.org.uk/news/the-importance-of-hearing-damage-prevention-in-musicians-work#:~:text=There%20are%20two%20so%2Dcalled,level%20exceeds%2080dB(A) (Accessed 20 October 2023).

Odell-Miller, H. and Richards, E. (2009) *Supervision of Music Therapy: a Theoretical and Practical Handbook.* London: Routledge.

Pellegrini, S., Moore, P. and Murphy, M. (2022) 'Secondary trauma and related concepts in psychologists: A systematic review', *Journal of Aggression, Maltreatment and Trauma,* 31 (3), pp. 370–391.

Shaw, C., Churchill, V., Curtain, S., Davies, A., Davis, D., Kalenderidis, Z., Langlois Hunt, E., McKenzie, B., Murray, M. and Thompson, G.A. (2022) 'Lived experience perspectives on ableism within and beyond music therapists' professional identities', *Music Therapy Perspectives*, 40 (2), pp. 143–151. https://doi.org/10.1093/mtp/miac001.

Spencer, L (2006) 'Tutors' stories of personal development training – attempting to maximize the learning potential' in *Counselling and Psychotherapy Research,* 6 (2), pp. 108–114.

Stewart, D. (2000) 'The State of the UK Music Therapy Profession: Personal Qualities, Working Models, Support Networks and Job Satisfaction' in *British Journal of Music Therapy,* 14 (1), pp. 13–31.

Streeter, E. (2002) 'Some observations on music therapy training groups', in Davies, A. and Richards, E. (eds.) *Music Therapy and Groupwork: Sound Company.* London: Jessica Kingsley Publishers, pp. 262–273.

Sutton, J. (2004) 'International Interview Series', *British Journal of Music Therapy*, 18 (2), pp. 41–44.

Trondalen, G. (2016) 'Self-care in music therapy: the art of balancing', in Edwards, J. (ed.) *The Oxford Handbook of Music Therapy.* Oxford: Oxford University Press, pp. 936–956.

Vega, V.P. (2010) 'Personality, burnout, and longevity among professional music therapists', *Journal of Music Therapy*, 47, pp. 155–179.

Vivolo, M., Owen, J. and Fisher, P. (2022) 'Psychological therapists' experiences of burnout: A qualitative systemic review and meta-analysis', *Mental Health and Prevention,* 33. https://doi.org/10.1016/j.mhp.2022.200253.

Vukčević Marković M. and Živanović M. (2022) 'Coping with secondary traumatic stress', *International Journal of Environmental Research and Public Health,* (19) 19. Available at: https://www.ncbi.nlm.nih.gov/pmc/articles/PMC9564895/pdf/ijerph-19-12881.pdf (Accessed 9 November 2023).

Watson, T. (2005) 'Steering a path through change; observations on the process of training', *British Journal of Music Therapy*, 19 (1), pp. 9–15.

Watson, T. (2024) 'Music therapy with adults with learning disabilities – a view from the United Kingdom' in Bunt, L., Hoskyns, S. and Swamy, S. (Eds) *The Handbook of Music Therapy,* Oxon: Routledge, 114–140.

Woodcock, J. (1996) 'Stretto. Meet them where they are', *British Journal of Music Therapy*, 6 (2), pp. 24–25.

World Health Organisation (2021) *Burn-out an "occupational phenomenon": International Classification of Diseases.* Available at: www.who.int/news/item/28-05-2019-burn-out-an-occupational-phenomenon-international-classification-of-diseases (Accessed 13 October 2023).

Chapter 8

The career of a music therapist

Catherine Warner

This chapter is concerned with the transition into a music career following graduation, the challenges and opportunities that graduates face and the direction they may choose.

Policy and context shaping career paths of the music therapist

Following the accreditation of first music therapy training courses in the late twentieth century, the professions of art and music therapy joined the Council for Professions Supplementary to Medicine (CPSM) in 1990, followed in 1991 by dramatherapy. After the 2000 Health Act, the CPSM was replaced by the Health Professions Council (later the Health and Care Professions Council when social work joined the group in 2012) as the body of registration, and by doing so, brought about numerous changes such as greater visibility of the profession, better work prospects, increased professional status and greater alignment with the work of the medical professions. This generally benefitted music therapists despite some difficulties aligning with medicine (Barrington, 2015). This enabled accreditation for training courses and the development of Standards of Proficiencies both specific to music therapy and some generic to all accredited professions of the HCPC (to which reference is made throughout this book). All qualified music therapists in the UK must abide by these Standards and also the HCPC Code of Conduct, Performance and Ethics. Music therapy also joined the Allied Health Professionals Federation (http://www.ahpf.org.uk/), and is aiming to join the Psychological Professions Network (https://ppn.nhs.uk/).

As a result of being part of the HCPC, the job title *Music Therapist* is protected by law and the only route to becoming a music therapist in the UK is to qualify at Masters level from an HCPC accredited training, of which there are eight presently. These accredited training courses in turn must follow the HCPC Standards of Education and Training, available here:

www.hcpc-uk.org/globalassets/resources/standards/standards-of-education-and-training.pdf

European standards

As mentioned in Chapter 3, at present the European Music Therapy Confederation has been working to develop standards as competencies across the various European countries, in order to provide guidance for emerging music therapy professions in particular countries. This is a work in progress (European Music Therapy Confederation, 2023). Additionally, the European Consortium of Arts Therapists Trainers, in collaboration with other European arts therapies associations, is undertaking a project to identify best practice in arts therapies trainings and establish useful standards in arts therapies training and arts therapies education research. This project is called The State of the Arts Therapies Training in Europe (SATTIE: www.ecarte.info/sattie). Therefore in the next few years it is likely that there will be greater clarity and guidance on common approaches for emerging new arts therapies training, and perhaps better mapping and recognition of the wide range of theoretical and practical approaches within this across Europe. It is recognised that the UK perspective has much to offer these consultations due to the extended experience of the strengths and limitations of working with the HCPC standards in terms of training and practice.

Role of the HCPC

One important aspect of HCPC registration is that the primary role of the HCPC is protection of the public. Any member of the public can raise a concern about any registrant and there are processes by which an HCPC registrant can be struck off if found unfit to practice (www.hcpc-uk.org/concerns/). The HCPC also identifies its role as maintaining public confidence in the professions by regulating them and requiring standards to be met. There is a requirement that each registrant maintains a level of continuing professional development which can be audited by the HCPC, therefore maintaining a level of currency in their practice.

There has been plenty of discussion as to the pros and cons of HCPC registration (Procter, 2008; Barrington, 2008, 2015). HCPC registration may support work in the NHS, but it does not necessarily help address status, pay and accountability in other settings such as education and the voluntary sectors. Therefore there remain many challenges to music therapists finding and sustaining work despite the protected title. There are concerns that registration may support professionalism for its own sake rather than the sake of the client, and that standards may lead to rigid practice (Ansdell and Pavlicevic, 2008). There will always be a need to find a balance between maintaining public credibility of the profession and the freedom and flexibility to practise in a responsive way where the power dynamic between the person in therapy and the therapist is reflexively considered.

Arts and health context

A music therapist needs to be able to think about where their work may sit within the broader umbrella of arts and health. The value of arts in health is becoming more clearly recognised at a governmental level (Gordon-Nesbitt and Howarth, 2020). Challenges to the relationship between music therapy and other health musicing practices can come from professional insecurity, lack of definition of different practices and, particularly, competition in funding between different types of music and health. It seems important to encourage respect and understanding between practitioners and Moss (2016) proposes thinking of all music and health practices in terms of a continuum which can range from music in building design to music psychotherapy.

Community musicians will work with musical and artistic aims as well as some therapeutic focus, and these aims may be conceptualised differently (O'Grady, 2004). Community music practice itself is varied, often involving great skill and careful preparation (Aasgaard, 2023) and there have been many creative collaborations between music therapists and community musicians (Bonde, 2011). Music therapy is not always the approach that is needed: 'Need is often interdependent with other social, cultural and political factors, such as those concerning where and how people live, and how music can help them' (Ansdell and Pavlicevic, 2008). Some music therapists choose to work both as music therapists and alternate as community musicians, or teachers or performers within their working week. This may allow continuation of a previous profession, provide a creative mix of professional practice and support self-care within the intensity of therapeutic work.

Jobs and employability: The landscape

The most recent survey of the UK music therapy workforce commissioned by the BAMT (Carr et al., 2017) found that of survey respondents, 28% were fully self-employed, 41% held only contracted employment and 27% had a mixture of both. Although the limitations of the survey must be considered (44% of BAMT members fitting the survey criteria responded), the proportions of employment and make-up were largely similar to the previous BAMT survey (Stewart, 2000). An important statistic for graduates was that 89% of respondents had found work within 6 months of qualifying, a high figure, but still showing that in some areas there are difficulties. It is worth noting the proportion of self "employed therapists, as this indicates the need for many new graduates to have the skills and capacity to set up their own work.

The impact of the pandemic: challenges and opportunities for employment

A worldwide study of music therapists' adaptations in the workplace in the early months of the pandemic showed in many cases and increase in the valuing of music therapy: 'Music therapists who were working as part of a health care team proved the profession's adaptability and functionality, and as part of the crisis-response mentality of "all hands on deck", demonstrated their ability to work in an agile and improvisational way outside the boundaries of their role. Family members of clients who had to assume the role of therapy assistants were able to witness firsthand progress made towards clinical aims' (Leandertz et al., 2021). One trainer in Scotland described one graduate developing: *'whole YouTube channels of accessible material. One graduate in Aberdeen set up a huge business as well as her music therapy work. It's all Open Access; so she's made a really big shift. And she's not the only one posting, promoting music therapy. Other music therapists are sharing what they do well online, making it accessible to families. We've seen a lot more of that since Covid but it wasn't a new thing'*. This shows how the pandemic may have assisted music therapy visibility. Similarly, for school businesses in the USA, music therapists led organisational change by recognising the importance of collaborative structures, transparent communication and flexibility (Meadows et al., 2023). However, in the same report, the music therapists who had transitioned to a virtual practice 'reported reported limitations to their approaches and use of specific interventions'.

Preparing for gaining employment in training

Articulating theoretical stance and underlying philosophy in a job interview allows the interview panel to gain a sense of how the applicant's approach will fit with their organisation's mission. Having the capacity to explain what it is that a music therapist does, and how they work and think is a crucial part of the working music therapist's skill. It is not enough just to be able to 'do'. John explores an example of a trainee therapist competently carrying out some clinical work, yet when confronted by a manager asking what music therapy is about, becoming tongue-tied (John, 2009). John argues that theoretical thinking can only be fully embedded within a trainee's practice if the theory makes sense to them; conversations on placement with the music therapist supervisor will help with this. Other placement activities can contribute to the trainee experience of explaining and framing their work to others. Presentations to a professional team allows for developing the use of language. Trainees may also help enhance an existing provision when on placement: 'Having a student in a setting can help to increase the visibility of music therapy' (Placement Educator).

In some work environments, there is a tendency to undervalue music therapy compared to more established disciplines. This can impact not just the perception of the discipline but also practical aspects like justifying the work, approach and fees associated with music therapy. Barrington (2015) identifies how important it is that music therapists are able to use language that is understood across professions in order to make the case for music therapy and explain how it embeds within a team. This is a skill that graduates will need to be prepared for in training. One graduate wrote: 'I have learned that each discipline possesses its unique approach to therapy and methodology for reporting outcomes. One of the critical realisations has been the inherent competitive and structural dynamics within organisations, particularly in positioning music therapy among other disciplines. Gaining recognition and validation for music therapy at senior levels of an organisation can be challenging, especially in contexts where music therapy might be perceived, rightly or wrongly, as a "last resort" option for challenging cases.'

Career direction

The career direction the music therapist takes is often related to the philosophical and theoretical drivers of their original music therapy training. It may make sense to seek a team or organisation which shares a recent graduate's training values or culture. Alternatively, work after qualification can be an opportunity to broaden one's approach and seek new supervisory or work experiences.

Career choices may be related to the opportunities available locally and a particularly creative approach is needed if music therapy practice is not known. A capacity for self-reflection and a willingness to learn from others is usefully balanced by the knowledge and confidence of what the music therapist can offer. Trainees often talk about experiencing imposter syndrome, and lack of confidence in graduates is common, especially in environments where music therapy is not fully appreciated. In these cases it is useful to be able to provide a narrative that presents core principles in music therapy practice, whatever the theoretical orientation of their training. One common factor from all accredited music therapy training approaches in the UK is the importance of centring or empowering the person who seeks or receives therapy. This is found in different ways in different music therapy programmes; for example from the Nordoff and Robbins focus on empowerment and social context to the person-centred care philosophy of Queen Margaret University, from the work of co-production with service users at Roehampton University to the anti-oppressive practices promoted at the University of South Wales. Linked to this, sometimes the use of the word 'therapy' can induce stigma in communities where the concept of therapeutic support is challenging to accept. In this situation using labels and medicalised language may present a barrier to building trust within the relationship. There is considerable range in the use of language around music therapy: some approaches eschew 'clinical' and 'treatment' for example, whereas in some multi-disciplinary settings, use of these words align with other team members to allow clear communication to assist in a complex team understanding of a person's health and social needs. Stige's point that music therapy needs to be context sensitive is an important one (Stige, 2002).

More recently, the importance of understanding music and health from an indigenous perspective has been foregrounded (Kalsi, 2023), where music may be heard differently, used differently and where spiritual beliefs form a major part in the understanding of health. The newly qualified music therapist who can practise with cultural sensitivity is perhaps better equipped to recognise how to value co-production, diversity and value of lived experience in their work, which can inform the direction they take in terms of new and innovative practice. Or, more radically, as one recent graduate put it: 'Exploring different ways to frame training could align more closely with the modes of healing and support sought in environments like churches and community settings or through musical genres such as rap music.' Furthermore, a training course that has provided frameworks for understanding institutional dynamics may equip a therapist to think carefully about how they can understand and survive in an environment under great pressure, and how they might be able to influence change.

Career direction can also be shaped by the music therapist's own personality, strengths and interests. Some people thrive in community settings, and others in work settings where there is a structured career progression. Placement experience during training can determine awareness of a particular area of interest, or passion. Furthermore, a therapist who has the strength to advocate for themselves and others, and manages their self-care well is likely to have a positive influence in a team affected by low morale or unsafe practices.

Music therapists have enormous adaptability and can seek varied employment choices across the lifespan. Music therapy is not necessarily a profession to join to become financially wealthy, and it is important to recognise the deep emotional labour that can be involved in being a music therapist. However, the wealth is found within the meaning of the work. As in music, music therapists may benefit from understanding the value of structures and of freedom; how they are bound by professional structures and when it is helpful to loosen those structures or boundaries.

Needs of practitioners in early practice

Supervision

In early practice a graduate can miss the structure and support of a training curriculum, although also many feel relieved to be away from an assessing gaze. However little practice they may start off with, regular supervision for their work is vital. Trainers recommend that it takes place *at least* once a fortnight, a step down from the weekly supervision whilst training, but still frequent enough to engage with the challenges of transitioning into new work. It is important to consider supervision before practice has begun, so that the new therapist has support in planning caseloads. It is essential to negotiate the costs of supervision within a freelance or new employment contract.

Some supervisors offer a sliding scale and if a graduate has very little therapy income initially, they may find a supervisor who will adapt their costs until they are engaged in an organisation fully committed to supervision of practice. Avoiding mixing managerial and clinical supervision is not always possible, but this is recommended in terms of good practice. It is very easy to compromise the focus on practice if a therapist is supervised by a manager who has other concerns and pressures in relation to employment.

Staying engaged as a musician

Continuing musical engagement is crucial in order to continue to develop skills in the workplace and to retain a fresh focus on creativity. Just because a music therapist is creating music in sessions does not mean they should neglect their own enjoyment and appetite for music making outside therapy. Following training, graduates often reconnect with their own music in new ways and this can flourish alongside their music therapy practice.

Staying creative within music therapy practice

Staying creative with the music therapy role, working collaboratively and communicating clearly about music therapy practice are all essential to developing a burgeoning practice, whether in self-employment or in a post.

> You do see graduates developing their roles quite creatively and adapting to quite different contexts. Working with the need and adapting to meet that need. And to work with the team. For example, there are a lot more open groups. And working with local partners as well; the model of skill sharing. I think online working too, sharing, and making resources available (Trainer).

Understanding institutional dynamics

A focus on institutional dynamics during training may help to prepare graduates to navigate challenging team situations, and to assess what is needed at any one time. During the Covid 19 pandemic, it became clear that music therapists had a strong role in supporting teams beyond their clinical practice because of skills in understanding the emotional needs of groups under extreme stress. A good understanding of institutional dynamics frameworks and having the knowledge to critique power structures will equip a therapist not only to navigate their own employment situation and help make decisions about where they want to work, but may assist them in developing excellent collaborations.

Building on employment skills

Training courses do provide introductions to setting up social enterprises, freelance work, managing tax and interviewing skills. However new graduates will need to build upon these skills using continuing professional development. Two examples of how this could happen follow: using service evaluation and using mentorship.

Service evaluation and innovation

One skillset essential for job creation and securing employment involves capacity to communicate the benefits of music therapy with clarity and using supporting evidence. Music therapy literature has discussed service evaluation in terms of its practice (Tsiris et al., 2020; Moss, 2003), importance (Wood, 2016) and with service users (Bradt, 2018). New services will particularly benefit from service evaluations or pilot studies to promote sustainable funding but all services benefit from regular improvement through evaluation, involving all stakeholders, in terms of good practice. There is a strong case for promoting service evaluation proficiency during training so that practitioners graduating recognise how it contributes to service quality and sustainability, and have the confidence to be involved in evaluation, or to design the evaluation themselves. There is also a case for professional associations to provide Continuing Professional Development courses that will promote confidence and competence in different ways of evaluating services and presenting that evidence effectively and accessibly.

Mentoring for early career music therapists

Clare Maddocks, the Education and Research Officer for the BAMT has been tasked with continuing the BAMT pilot mentoring scheme for Newly Qualified Therapists, initially developed by Jonathan Cousins-Booth. This is a new initiative within the wider umbrella of Allied Health Professions, where mentoring practice is only found 'in pockets'. The scheme was conceived out of concern for music therapists who trained during the pandemic and had compromised placement experiences. Course leaders, through the BAMT Training and Education Committee, had been raising concerns about how lockdowns had resulted in fewer session hours for trainees, reducing confidence in practice. Graduates themselves and supervisors of early career therapists also identified the need for a mentoring role, in addition to the supervision needed to focus on the details of music therapy practice. Mentoring was needed for the transition into a music therapy career, for the confidence to be professionally assertive, and to recognise what was reasonable to be asked of a newly qualified therapist.

Recent graduates benefit from sustained peer support from those they trained with, and many have retained transferable skills from a previous career or work experience. However, in a conversation for this book, Maddocks acknowledged that workplaces themselves had changed in many ways as a result of the pandemic and therefore extra mentoring support would be helpful in addition to any practice supervision newly qualified therapists were accessing for their work. As the latest BAMT workforce survey showed, a substantial proportion of the music therapy workforce (28%) is employed solely on a freelance basis with plenty of lone working and isolation for some early career music therapists. The mentoring scheme places two mentees with a single mentor: 'We group people together who are going through similar experiences, or we feel could complement one another. We've got people in a mentoring pair, for example, who are keen to set up services in a rural area. If there's someone experienced in freelancing from a previous career and there's someone new and they seem like a good personality fit, then that could work out well. Or the mentees paired together might be doing very different things in the work, but emotionally they're in a similar place'.

There is also concern that newly qualified music therapists are regularly asked to undertake duties in their new employment that are not appropriate for their role. Mentoring support can help address this.

One pilot scheme mentor explained: 'One mentee used the early sessions to process some of the relational challenges they experienced in training, having felt scapegoated by their cohort and having a lonely ending to their training. They valued being heard and having their feelings validated. The other mentee spent most of the time exploring the pros and cons of being a poorly paid music therapist in contrast with a successful, secure career as a gigging musician. Together we thought about personal identity, motivation, practical financial issues and career progression providing an opportunity for the mentees to respond to their peer, share their perspective and acknowledge commonalities in their experience.'

A mentee explained: 'Within my mentoring relationship I have been able to gain clarity around practical issues such as discussing the types of private and public organisations I should be looking at contacting regarding future work, understanding how to build a business to support my work and how to set my fees at a standard that is appropriate. My mentor supported me by talking through the issues I faced as they arose; whether these were business, personal or practice based. This supported me to shake off the imposter syndrome feeling that almost stopped me entering practice. I have now designed and set up my own branded business, have signed up three large pieces of contractual, well paid, pieces of music therapy work and I am currently considering plans to develop a Creative Arts Therapy agency. If somebody had suggested this when I qualified, I would never have believed that it was possible.'

Although this scheme is in its infancy, there will be valuable lessons to be learned from this for all AHPs about the value of mentoring structures. A similar approach can already be seen for Nurses, Midwives and Nursing Associates in the form of Preceptorship schemes (Nursing and Midwifery Council, 2023).

A career in the NHS

In 2022 to 2023 Alison Barrington completed a year as Health Education England's National Allied Health Professional Education and Transformation Lead (Art, Drama and Music Therapies). The report of her findings will be published in accessible form by NHS England (not available at the time of this book going to press). From her extensive consultation Barrington identified five main areas for critical development of the arts therapies workforce in the NHS.

Recommendation 1: A more diverse workforce

The most substantial challenge to diversity in all forms is that training is self-funded, creating barriers to training and therefore new accessible routes are needed into the profession. In some countries pre-registration training is at undergraduate level (for example in the USA) whereas it is at Master level in the UK. Barrington asks, 'How collaborative can we be in terms of thinking creatively about this?', recommending that more thought could be put into the undergraduate route leading to a Master level music therapy training without preventing entry level being at Master level.

Schools career advice about music therapy is underdeveloped and this is partly because the qualification route to practising as an arts therapist is through a Master's degree; school career advice is more focused on undergraduate courses. A recent HEE commissioned survey showed that most music, drama or art therapists in England decide to train during their undergraduate study, and 44% choose it as a second career. In terms of barriers to this choice of profession, 63.4% agreed that a 'lack of understanding from career advisors contributed; challenges in accessing information about the profession (44%) and limited amounts of information about the profession were also barriers (51%)'. Additionally, 'poor access to work shadowing' was experienced as a barrier by 49% of the sample (Health Education England, 2021).

Recommendation 2: Reimagining the workforce

Barrington said 'Only 5% of MTs work in the NHS (although some of these also work in the third sector) so to help people understand and value what MTs do we need to be speaking the NHS language and for people to be listening and hear us. Some charitable organisations I spoke with during the year (third sector employers) said the NHS employs them to do small pieces of work but then those projects go away. We need the NHS to give us substantive posts. Geographically there are some deserts yet there are many vacancies within the NHS, so where a Trust is looking for an OT, why not consider Music, Drama or Arts Therapy? Bear in mind that we may be a small profession but we're very skilled and experienced. Put us into senior jobs. Don't try and limit who we are. I've seen that happen'.

Recommendation 3: Introduce apprenticeships and alternative career progressions

When considering degree apprenticeships as a new entry route to music therapy, Barrington mentioned that when the relatively small prosthetics and orthotics profession had started an apprentice degree route this did aid in swelling the professional workforce, despite taking a few years before this was felt. At the time of writing, the first year of the first Arts Therapy Apprenticeship (Art) has begun at Teesside University, and there are plans to extend this to music therapy at the University of Roehampton.

In the NHS in particular there is a small range of truncated pay scales available to the qualified music therapist; usually bands six to eight. Barrington says 'People get stuck by this narrow bandwidth. What about developing different kinds of music therapy assistant at bands four and five? Perhaps MTs can be training and developing support workers to think longer term about their career structure and progression? They may find that apprenticeship routes are a good way forward. We already work with Teaching Assistants and Mental Health nurses. So as a profession can we consider what we offer to the NHS, not just Music Therapy but a greater umbrella?' This may also promote greater access to music therapy as a career thus promoting diversity (NHS Digital 2021).

Recommendation 4. Levelling up the student experience

In terms of student experience in training, having good quality placement experiences were crucial, as Barrington described; 'HEIs who had someone specifically looking after the clinical placements: there was a flourishing quality to that. The lack of a placement tariff for Arts Therapies (unlike other AHPs where entry level to the profession is through an undergraduate route) means that placement educators are not paid for their time in the NHS. Other AHPs have a clinical tariff, only Osteopaths and Arts therapists don't'.

Role emerging placements, where there is not a music therapist on site but a different supervisor, but with additional music therapy support from the training institution, was seen to be a way of developing more varied placement opportunities, as long as this was supported properly, for example by putting more experienced trainees into these placements. Barrington said 'Everything is context dependent; making sure role-emerging placements during training have adequate support may well lead to more NHS jobs'.

Barrington identified that course leaders were already working collaboratively in the UK and Ireland: 'I would praise the profession of Music Therapy for having the Training and Education Committee of the BAMT. There's a collegiality to Music Therapy; HEIs that are talking to each other, collaborating and sharing practice, rather than being precious about "this is ours and we're not going to share it". It feels healthier.'

Recommendation 5: A clearer sense of the workforce

Barrington reported that presently any data on what is happening in the NHS with regard to the Arts Therapies is 'woefully inadequate. Any kind of workforce development with any useful strategy is going to need a clearer picture of the state of these professions, and also the geographical inconsistencies across the four countries of the UK. Being aware of gaps in provision can be helped by Music Therapists being clear about their unique strengths. The long-term workforce plan for the NHS identifies key areas for change which fit very well with the strengths of Music Therapy practice: working with the marginalised, illness prevention, "upstreaming" (how can we impact the economic, social and environment causes of ill health) and changes in health inequalities. And, for example, forming an alliance with the small but powerful group within the NHS advocating for stopping overmedication of people with autism and learning disabilities, STOMP, (NHS England, 2018) can show how strong we are in that area.'

She recommends 'picking up rumblings in social media about gaps in provision where we can say "we are your guy" – and knowing how to speak NHS speak. On an individual level we need to know our own limits and skills. For example, my passion is dementia care and I know that in the long-term workforce plan dementia is one of six main areas for development. If you can match it with your geographical area, you can make a stronger business case. Don't be ashamed to be entrepreneurial, not to elevate yourself, but to be passionate about the work.'

Placement educator views on the workforce

Placement educator views on what is needed specifically in the workforce have been discussed in Chapter 5, and emphasised flexibility in approach, awareness of diversity and institutional dynamic thinking and agile, reflexive use of language to explain Music Therapy. Placement educators also emphasised the importance of working with service users to improve services.

The rise of the service user voice

Historical discussions clustered around the Community Music Therapy discourse (Barrington, 2008; Ansdell and Pavlicevic, 2008; Procter, 2008 for example) highlighted the lack of voice of the person in therapy in Music Therapy Practice. This debate happened alongside other drivers such as the promotion of participatory action practices in Music Therapy (Stige, 2002; Warner, 2014). The general movement in health to focus more on service users (or 'the consumer' of health services) has resulted in more unity in the present narratives. The revised HCPC Standards of Proficiency of 2023 require all registrants to demonstrate competence in consultation and co-production with the people who engage in music therapy (HCPC 2023), and the Standards of Education and Training require each training course to demonstrate how they involve clients and carers in their delivery and curriculum design. This is a significant policy shift. There are varied examples of this. People with lived experience of music therapy have more recently been foregrounded in BAMT conferences, employed as visiting or associate lecturers on training courses (although this practice has been common for some years), as Trustees on Charitable Boards and employed as an integral part of a multi-disciplinary team at East London NHS Foundation Trust. One contemporary question for all Music Therapists is how well we collaborate with people with lived experience and integrate these views, and mediate influence so this involvement is not tokenistic but drives real change.

International graduates: current employment challenges

The UK government is discussing proposals from April 2024 to reduce the graduate visa from two years to six months. Although this is not yet policy, it demonstrates some of the pressures international trainees face. If the plans are implemented, those applying for a Skilled Worker Visa will need to be earning >£38,700, a significant rise from >£26,200. Whilst music therapy is classed as a skilled worker occupation, it is not classed as a profession that is difficult to recruit for so there are no special exemptions. The biggest issue is that even if an organisation is able to sponsor the international worker, the MT would need to be earning a minimum of £38,700 and this needs to be within one contract, rather than multiple part-time contracts. BAMT reports this as being 'very concerning'.

A BAMT member put this eloquently: "This change in the visa ultimately means there is no career path for international Music Therapist trainees coming to study in the UK on a student and graduate visa".

On the other hand, for international trainees, returning to work in their country of origin may be extremely challenging if there is not a developed infrastructure. One graduate put it like this:

> Working in my home country has been challenging. People might assume international students would find it easier to go back and work in their home countries, which is not how I found it. I needed to develop my ability to use my mother tongue in the work. I did not do my placement in my home country, meaning I needed to learn about the educational / medical / social welfare systems like I did in the UK. There is no HCPC or BAMT. There is a very small number of Music Therapists, perhaps none, who were trained in the UK.

It is clear that international graduates are facing unique situations which will need thought and advocacy from the training courses and BAMT in the future.

A career in research

Since 2006 the entry level to the profession has been at Master level; formerly it was a postgraduate diploma. One significant change in 2006 was the introduction in training curricula of an expectation for both research and service evaluation competency for all music therapists.

The trainee's research project: choosing the focus

All music therapy trainees undertake either a dissertation or major project in their final year of study, and often this involves undertaking a research project. A small research project during training gives the trainee the experience of identifying a gap in the research literature, justifying a project, undertaking research design, learning how to collect and analyse data, and learning how to write up a project. The critical engagement with this work can sound daunting to the trainee, yet feedback is often that trainees have enjoyed designing and implementing their own project much more than expected and feel a sense of achievement. This area of study relates to the HCPC standards relating to research, which include the requirement to demonstrates awareness of and ability to use research and evaluation methodologies and approaches, in co-production with service users as appropriate.

Range of methodologies

With the recent rise of the understanding of anti-oppressive practice, growing attention is given to how music therapy clients can be involved in research, so much so that HCPC standard 13.11 (HCPC, 2023) identifies this. However, this was explored as early as 2002 by introducing ethnography and participatory action research as a paradigm in music therapy research (Stige, 2002) followed by doctoral level participatory action research studies (Warner, 2014; Rickson, 2014).

Learning about research methodology during Master's study equips a trainee to understand and value a range of philosophical underpinnings. Qualitative research is often chosen by trainees for small projects, partly because it is more feasible to manage the smaller sample size acceptable for phenomenological projects based on phenomenological analysis, for example. However, international surveys are relatively straightforward to set up and yield much broader perspectives for a research question. Ethnographic and autoethnographic approaches are fast gaining currency as more music therapy trainers gain confidence in these approaches and ethnography is the main methodological approach in some training courses. Once a graduate has decided to pursue a research career there will be greater opportunity to embrace a wider range of research approaches such as the use of Big Data analysis and projects which involve international collaboration.

Although there are a number of publications that introduce research methods and present methodologies to the prospective music therapist (Jacobsen et al., 2019; Wheeler and Murphy, 2016; Meadows, 2005; Langenberg *et al.*, 1996) the field 'remains without a dedicated resource that assists students and professionals to read, process, and apply research in their practice and professional development' (Potvin, 2017). Furthermore, ideas about what areas of research would be most urgent or ethical to undertake are under debate. Sheri Robb (2023) suggests starting with these reflexive questions when considering where to focus music therapy research resource:

- Who is represented in our research?
- Who is receiving (has access to) our services?
- Where are services delivered and available?
- Are services congruent with the culture, identity, and values of recipients?

(Robb, 2023)

The 2020 BAMT Diversity report identified funding for research within BAME communities as a need (Langford, Rizkallah and Maddocks 2020). Health inequalities in relation to ethnicity have been widely debated since they were spotlighted during the pandemic, but there is scope for much more research to be done in relation to this in music therapy research. Further on music therapy training, supervision and research competency would also support development of the reach of the music therapist (Aafjes-van Doorn and Barber, 2023).

According to Li *et al.* (2021) there is an increasingly upward trend of published music therapy research studies worldwide. Three keywords predominate music therapy research citations internationally: *efficacy, health* and *older adults,* with improvisational music therapy as 'the current research frontier in the field' (Li *et al.*, 2021). The UK does not yet feature in the top ten countries in relation to highly rated music therapy research publications but does rate extremely highly in terms of collaboration with international research projects. This picture is fast-changing. The development of the Cambridge Institute of Music Therapy Research (CIMTR) in 2017 has enabled a concentration of music therapy researchers in the UK, promoting research and collaboration in areas such as dementia care, autism, brain injury and neuroscience in music therapy (see Helen Odell-Miller's case study in Chapter 9). Some music therapy training courses have established PhD programmes such as at the Nordoff and Robbins Centre, Anglia Ruskin University and Guildhall School of Music and Drama, and it is possible to undertake a PhD self-funded at any Higher Education Institution who will be able to provide a suitable supervision team and who will accept the project. A music therapy trainee aiming for a career in research has many options ahead of them.

Broadening practice: The development needs of experienced practitioners

Building experience through doing music therapy, particularly combined with consistent exploration in supervision and continuing professional development should ensure a highly skilled workforce with a range of competence. There are risks too: knowledge loss, and the danger of experience being used as a proxy for expertise. Therapy is complex and the over-stretched therapist may receive little feedback about what might have been effective. Complacency or being under-resourced will mean practitioners do not keep up with rapid changes in the profession or recognise potential biases such as racial and cultural prejudice. Roy and Liersch, when writing about psychotherapy practice, discuss the phenomenon of *illusory superiority*. They argue this is quite common: 'as, for example, most drivers believe that they are better than the average driver' (2013). If this is the case in music therapy practice also, and even if it is not, there is a compelling case for maintaining appropriate continuing development, and making clear decisions about what is best needed for each therapist.

Continuing professional development

For inexperienced and experienced therapists alike, the opportunity for discussion and practice-sharing with others who work in a similar setting or similar way can be a good way of staying in touch with current innovations, new ideas and reducing practice isolation. The BAMT offers a range of special interest groups, area groups and groups where people share similar lived experience. These can accommodate trainees, those new to the profession as well as people with long experience.

Geographically there will be part of the UK where there are gaps in provision and local therapists may need to be inventive or use online peer group supervision to break down isolation in practice. Peer group supervision can accommodate people with a range of different experiences and there are some useful practices developed which can allow for in-depth musical exploration of clinical issues (Ahonen-Eerikainen, 2003). When therapists move into new areas of work, for example changing clinical groups, then supervision and contact with those working in the new area of practice will be helpful.

Supervision for experienced therapists

There are some interesting questions about how seasoned therapists best use the supervision sessions. Is it most useful to focus on a particular dilemma in a particular piece of work, create a thorough musical case formulation, or gain wider therapeutic knowledge? Music therapists with a few years' experience could consider setting up a supervision practice, and joining the BAMT supervision register, guided by specific relevant CPD (see also discussions of supervision in Chapters 5 and 7). Following the rise in online supervision, there are several concerns to consider. Perhaps most importantly there is the question of whether supervisees and supervisors are picking up on embodied responses sufficiently within supervision (Koch and Fuchs, 2011). Another is security: even if an online system is GDPR compliant, it still may be susceptible to hacking or viruses so issues of confidentiality become more complex (Phillips et al., 2021).

Further extensive related training

In the development of their careers, some music therapists choose to undertake a psychotherapy or psychoanalytic training or undertake doctoral study. Development of specific practices such as Guided Imagery in Music (GIM), Vocal Psychotherapy (Austin, 2016), Neurologic Music Therapy or therapeutic songwriting represent ways of further broadening understanding and practice. Cohen (2017) identifies these as 'advanced practices'; generally undertaken following a first Master's degree; for reasons of expense and time, they may not be feasible for all. For example, to become a GIM Fellow a further three years of training to complete level three are required (Frohne-Hagemann, 2017). To become a Vocal Psychotherapist, two years of online training are required which results in a certificate in vocal psychotherapy and depth psychology from the Music Psychotherapy Center in New York City, USA (Austin, 2016). Neurologic Music Therapy training initially lasts four or five days and can be undertaken by trainee and qualified music therapists and those in other therapeutic disciplines such as speech and language therapists and occupational therapists. Becoming an NMT Fellow relies on considerably more practice experience, with the practitioner being required to show video evidence of their application of the practice to a peer group of other fellows before they are considered successful.

Consultancy work

Consultancy roles for allied health professionals are now available in the NHS, and generally involve managing and supervising other AHPs or whole services. There are few music therapists who fulfil these roles at present, but it is an opportunity for career progression. Similarly, music therapists can offer consultancy on a freelance basis in an area where they have excellent knowledge and experience or can set up a consultancy business.

Engaging with the next generation

Other than the meaningful aspects of clinical work, engaging with the next generations of therapists can also be helpful and rewarding to develop. This can be undertaken through becoming a supervisor through practice education, supervision, mentoring, teaching, providing continuing professional development, and in research or practice publication. Placement educators and trainers regularly emphasise how their own practice grows through their working relationship with trainees and graduates early in practice. When a pioneering practitioner chooses to change path or leave an established role, it can be useful to reflectively consider succession planning in order to continue the principles and ideals of the work.

Conclusion

This chapter has explored the issues facing newly qualified graduates when approaching a career in music therapy, and also the variety of directions they can take. The following chapter presents some varied accounts of music therapists who have expanded their careers beyond music therapy practice, where contributors reflect on how music therapy thinking has inspired their development.

References

Aafjes-van Doorn, K. and Barber, J. P. (2023) Professional training and supervision after graduation: Is it worthwhile?, in Becoming Better Psychotherapists. [Online]. Washington: American Psychological Association. pp. 55–82.

Aasgaard, G. (2023) *Music Therapy Conversations*, BAMT Podcast No. 80. Available at: www.bamt.org/DB/podcasts-2/georgina-aasgaard (Accessed 9 January 2023).

Ahonen-Eerikainen, H. (2003) Using Group-Analytic Supervision Approach When Supervising Music Therapists. *Nordic journal of music therapy [Online]*, 12 (2), 173–182.

Ansdell, G. and Pavlicevic, M. (2008). Responding to the challenge: Between boundaries and borders: A response to Alison Barrington's article challenging the profession. *British Journal of Music Therapy*, 22 (2), 73–76. https://doi-org.ezproxy.uwe.ac.uk/10.1177/135945750802200205.

Austin, D. (2016) 'Vocal psychotherapy: Discovering yourself through the voice', Edwards, J (Ed) in *The Oxford Handbook of Music Therapy*. [Online]. Oxford Academic: Oxford University Press.

Barrington, A. (2008) Challenging the profession. *British Journal of Music Therapy*, 22 (2), 65–72.

Barrington, A. (2015) Perspectives on the development of the music therapy profession in the UK. *Approaches: Music Therapy & Special Music Education*, Special Issue, 7 (1) 118–122. Available at: https://approaches.gr/perspectives-on-the-development-of-the-music-therapy-profession-in-the-uk-alison-barrington/ (Accessed 6 January 2023).

Bonde (2011) Health musicing – Music therapy or music and health? A model, empirical examples and personal reflections. *Music and Arts in Action*, 3 (2), 120–140.

Bradt, J. (2018) Involving services users in music therapy evaluation, *Nordic Journal of Music Therapy*. 27 (1), 1–2.

Carr, C. E. et al. (2017) Understanding the present, re-visioning the future: An initial mapping of music therapists in the United Kingdom. *British Journal of Music Therapy* [Online], 31 (2), 68–85.

Cohen, N. S. (2017) *Advanced Methods of Music Therapy Practice: The Bonny Method of Guided Imagery and Music, Nordoff-Robbins Music Therapy, Analytical Music Therapy, and Vocal Psychotherapy.* London and Philadelphia: Jessica Kingsley Publications.

European Music Therapy Confederation (2023) *EMTS-Commission: Work in Progress: Developing Recommended Standards for Music Therapy Training in Europe.* Available at: https://emtc-eu.com/training/training-standards/ (Accessed 10 January 2024).

Frohne-Hagemann, I. (2017) Guided imagery and music (GIM): Reflections on supervision in training and therapy. *Approaches: Mousikotherapeia kai Eidikī Mousikī Paidagōgikī*, 9 (2), 252–266.

Gordon-Nesbitt, R. and Howarth, A. (2020) The arts and the social determinants of health: Findings from an inquiry conducted by the United Kingdom All-Party Parliamentary Group on Arts, health and wellbeing, *Arts & Health*, 12 (1), 1–22, DOI:10.1080/17533015.2019.1567563.

Health and Care Professions Council (2023). *Standards of Proficiency: Arts Therapists.* Available at: www.hcpc-uk.org/standards/standards-of-proficiency/arts-therapists/ (accessed 25 July 2024)

Health Education England (2021) *Art, Drama and Music Therapy Career Choice Factsheet.* Available at: Allied Health Professions (AHP) Careers Awareness Toolkit (Accessed 10 January 2024).

Jacobsen, S. L. et al. (2019) *A Comprehensive Guide to Music Therapy: Theory, Clinical Practice, Research and Training.* Second edition. London: Jessica Kingsley.

John, D. (2009) 'Getting better: Some thoughts on the growth of a therapist', in Odell-Miller and Richards, E. (Eds), *Supervision of Music Therapy: a Theoretical and Practical Handbook.* London: Routledge. pp. 83–89.

Kalsi, P. (2023) *Music Therapy Conversations,* BAMT Podcast No. 74. Available at: www.bamt.org/DB/podcasts-2/preet-kalsi (Accessed 11 January 2023).

Koch, S., and Fuchs, T.(2011) Embodied Arts Therapies, *The Arts in Psychotherapy*, 38 (4), 276–280, https://doi.org/10.1016/j.aip.2011.08.007.

Langenberg et al. (1996) *Qualitative Music Therapy Research Beginning Dialogues.* Gilsum: Barcelona Publishers.

Langford, A., Rizkallah, M and Maddocks, C. (2020) *British Association for Music Therapy Diversity Report.* Available at: www.bamt.org/resources/diversity-report. (Accessed 10 January 2024).

Leandertz, M., Danso, A. and Carlson, E. (2021) Adapting to change: How the COVID-19 pandemic has impacted the music therapy profession. *Journal of Music, Health and*

Wellbeing, Special Issue. Available at: /www.musichealthandwellbeing.co.uk/musickin gthroughcovid19. (Accessed 2 January 2024).

Li K., Weng L. and Wang X. (2021) The state of music therapy studies in the past 20 years: A bibliometric analysis. *Frontiers in Psychology*, 12, 697726–687726. Available at: DOI:10.3389/fpsyg.2021.697726. PMID: 34177744; PMCID: PMC8222602 (Accessed 8 January 2024).

Meadows, A. (2005) *Qualitative Inquiries in Music Therapy Research. Vol.2, 2005*. Gilsum: Barcelona Publishers.

Meadows, A., Shoemark, H. and Magee, W. (2023) Leadership and teamwork during the COVID-19 pandemic: Experiences of music therapy business leaders. *Journal of Music Therapy*. Available at: https://doi.org/10.1093/jmt/thad027. (Accessed 2 January 2024).

Moss, H. (2003) Service evaluation: Music therapy and medicine for the elderly. *British Journal of Music Therapy*, 17 (2), 76–89.

Moss, H. (2016) Arts and health: A new paradigm. *Voices; A World Forum for Music Therapy*, 16(3). Available at: https://voices.no/index.php/voices/article/view/2301/2056 (Accessed 10 January 2024).

NHS Digital (2021) Allied health professionals by selected equality and diversity metrics. https://digital.nhs.uk/supplementary-information/2021/ahps-by-protected-characterist ics-aug2021.

NHS England (2018) STOMP: Stopping the overmedication of people with a learning disability, autism or both, Guidance leaflet. Available at: NHS England » STOMP – Stopping the over medication of people with a learning disability, autism or both (Accessed 9 January 2024).

Nursing and Midwifery Council (2023) *Principles of Preceptorship*. Available at; www. nmc.org.uk/standards/guidance/preceptorship/ (Accessed 11 January 2024).

O'Grady, L. (2004) What Is the experience of a community musician who is also a music therapist? *Voices: a World Forum for Music Therapy* [Online], 4 (2). Available at: https:// doi.org/10.15845/voices.v4i2.181 (Accessed 9 January 2024).

Phillips, L. A., Logan, J. N. and Mather, D. B. (2021) COVID-19 and beyond: Telesupervision training within the supervision competency. *Training and Education in Professional Psychology*, 15 (4), 1–6. https://doi.org/10.1037/tep0000362.

Potvin, N. (2017) Review of 'An introduction to music therapy research', by Barbara L. Wheeler and Kathleen M. Murphy. *Nordic Journal of Music Therapy*, 26 (2), 200–201, DOI:10.1080/08098131.2016.1276952.

Procter, S. (2008) Premising the challenge. A response to Alison Barrington's article challenging the profession. *British Journal of Music Therapy*, 22 (2), 77–81.

Rickson, D. J. (2014) The relevance of disability perspectives in music therapy practice with children and young people who have intellectual disability. *Voices: a world forum for music therapy*, 14 (3). Available at; https://doi.org/10.15845/voices.v14i3.784 (Accessed 13th January 2024).

Robb, S. L. (2023) Opportunity and responsibility in music therapy research. *Journal of Music Therapy*, 60 (4), 378–391. Available at: https://doi-org.ezproxy.uwe.ac.uk/10.1093/ jmt/thad025. (Accessed 5 January 2024).

Roy, M. and Liersch, M. (2013) I am a better driver than you think: examining self-enhancement for driving ability. *Journal of Applied Social Psychology*, 43, 1648–1659. https://doi.org/10.1111/jasp.12117.

Stewart, D. (2000) The state of the UK music therapy profession – Personal qualities, working models, support networks and job satisfaction. *British Journal of Music Therapy*, 14 (1), 13–31.

Stige, B. (2002) *Culture-Centred Music Therapy*. Gilsum: Barcelona.
Tsiris, G., Spiro, N., Coggins, O. and Ania, Z. (2020) The impact areas questionnaire (IAQ): A music therapy service evaluation tool. *Voices: a World Forum for Music Therapy*, 20 (2), 1.
Warner, C. (2014) 'The evolution of group participation through sounds and musical play: Participatory action research', in De Backer, J. and Sutton, J. (Eds), *The Music of Music Therapy: Psychodynamic Music Therapy*. London: Jesssica Kingsley. pp. 162–171.
Wheeler, B. L. and Murphy, K. M. (Eds) (2016) *Music Therapy Research*. Third edition. New Braunfels: Barcelona Publishers.
Wood, S. (2016) *A Matrix for Community Music Therapy Practice*. First edition. Dallas, TX: Barcelona Publishers.

Chapter 9

The broader role of the music therapist

Tessa Watson and contributors

Careers within music therapy

In Chapters 2 and 8 of this volume we read of the development of music therapy and of pioneers within the profession. As this book draws to a close, we now consider broader contemporary careers within music therapy. In this chapter, we hear from music therapists who have used the springboard of music therapy work to take varied career paths, developing specialties in their specific areas of interest. Their career journeys are fascinating to read and are as diverse as the people behind them. Within these case studies we read of careers within management, consultation and commissioning, within specialist areas of clinical work, within research development, within the arts and health and of activism and advocacy.

Whilst the Psychological Professions Network includes music therapy within their career pathway (PPN 2023), the development of careers within the discipline of music therapy has not received much attention. Career development within the health and care professions is generally neglected across the board, with development work in the UK interrupted by Covid in 2020. In England and Scotland there are plans that aim to develop the health and care workforce and provide sustainable career pathways (NHS 2020, The Scottish Government 2018). Some fellow allied health professions consider career pathways, with Nashwan focusing specifically on nursing (Nashwan 2023). Other authors address the topic from the perspective of researcher-clinicians. In Australia, one researcher interviewee in a study by Brandenburg and Ward (2022: 8) stated that 'I can't see a pathway or structure unless you create that pathway...'. Music therapists are likely to feel similarly, wherever their country of work.

In 2016, Ledger wrote about developing new posts in music therapy, within their chapter drawing upon research and literature from change management. Within Ledger's chapter, skills of improvisation, flexibility and resilience were identified as assisting music therapists in developing new posts and breaking new ground (Ledger 2016). The case studies we read in this chapter reveal how their writers used these qualities to develop careers in their areas of interest and with their particular skills, taking new career pathways that enabled them to develop work that felt valuable, satisfying and necessary.

160 The broader role of the music therapist

We start with a case study from Stephen Sandford, who stresses the importance of listening, the value of mentors in his career journey and the importance of leadership within the careers of music therapists.

> **Box 1.1   Stephen Sandford**
>
> Every day is a music day for me, even if some days I don't appreciate it is. Sometimes I need to go searching for music, sometimes it's sounding me in the face. Other times, it's carried to me by colleagues or through *the tone* of the communities I serve. They all help me retune in to listening again.
>
> I'm a Music Therapist and Chief allied health professions (AHP) officer for one of the new Integrated Care Boards (ICB) in England. The role of an ICB is to join up health and care services, improve people's health and wellbeing, and make sure everyone has the same access to services and gets the same outcomes from treatment. There are around 6,000 AHPs in my ICB serving a population of around 1.8 million people.
>
> I got here by listening. Music therapists have such finely honed awareness of timbre, rhythm, intensity. We are trained to hear the harmony implicit in the melody of others around us as individuals and as groups. I've taken these listening skills into strategic service development. They are key parts of my leadership tool kit. I embraced them as my assets in working with and through others.
>
> It wasn't always like this. I have felt less than, incomplete, lacking and questioning of my potential, purpose and identity. But then I found my way to connect with some amazing leaders who were not music therapists. Their curiosity in *my sound*, and in my potential, fostered confidence, trust and a growing realisation of what I had to offer. I'll always be grateful to these amazing (often) women who supported my development. They challenged me to be authentic in my creative playfulness, to harness my listening sensitivity to others and to raise the voice of often vulnerable service users. I firmly believe it is our continuing will to listen that truly fosters our own leadership potential, not clinging to our cumulative years of experience.
>
> I'm glad I'm here. I'm constantly challenged and need to actively seek out ways to re-fresh, to stay connected and true to my values of care, respect and inclusion. I do this through seeking out playful listening with others.
>
> I encourage and challenge all music therapists to channel the essence of your listening skills – bring your disruptive creative turn-taking in response to your carefully honed listening. This is essential, much needed creative leadership.
>
> Key developmental aspects of my leadership journey so far...
>
> - A newly qualified peripatetic music therapist with a car boot full of instruments.

- An NHS music therapist with a wonderful team of listening music therapists.
- A range of leadership roles in vibrantly diverse busy multi-professional clinical teams, here my identity as a member of the LGBTQIA+ community was respected and celebrated.
- A strategic leadership role with many art, music, drama and dance movement therapists in an Outstanding rated NHS Trust.
- Expanding my view point in a lead role for Allied health professions in the same NHS Trust.
- A newly established lead AHP role in a new Integrated care board.

Helen Odell-Miller, a pioneer and innovator who has influenced music therapy not only in the UK, but worldwide, now shares thoughts about her career journey. Helen tracks her pathway from qualification to her work as director of CIMTR, noting some of the qualities and principles that have been important in her work.

Box 1.2 Helen Odell Miller OBE

Career journey

Since September 2023, I am Emeritus Professor and Founding Director of the Cambridge Institute for Music Therapy Research, (CIMTR) at Anglia Ruskin University (ARU). Qualifying in 1977, I was lucky enough to interview for, and be offered a new full-time post in the NHS, working with people with learning disabilities, who at that time were mainly living inside a hospital. Three years later I was inspired by colleagues there to move to work in the mental health field. Here I created a new post in the NHS at the nearby psychiatric hospital, where I worked with and learned from people of all ages with mental health issues, in the hospital and the community. I still hold an Honorary contract there, 43 years later, most recently undertaking research about music therapy for older people living with dementia in ward settings. As Head of Arts Therapies and day and therapy services for older people there, I learned that all approaches to music therapy are relevant; in-depth psychoanalytically informed work, open sessions involving the whole ward/community, and the use of music therapy group work as a tool for problem solving in management and business meetings.

Setting up the first official career structure for music therapists in the NHS, becoming Advisor to the Department of Health on Music Therapy, and later deciding to work with international colleagues, including undertaking my PhD at the international PhD programme at Aalborg University, Denmark, stretched me enormously and also opened up new possibilities. In 1994, I started a part time role at ARU, responding to that university's wish to set up a Music Therapy MA. We developed a course, linked closely to music therapy practice, and later we developed research and PhD opportunities.

I continued to work clinically as a music therapist throughout my career, maintaining a part time role in the NHS alongside my university role until 2006, when I applied for the post of Deputy Head of Music and Performing Arts at ARU. I always felt working as a therapist was crucial to training music therapists and I also always loved the clinical work. Some of my key decisions to apply for positions in leadership roles have been rooted in my belief that working from the inside is an effective way to bring about change and understanding about arts therapies.

Responding to the needs of organisations is crucial, and latterly we founded, in 2017, CIMTR, a large music therapy research institute where I was director for 6 years. ARU saw music therapy as a key research discipline, able to impact upon the lives of people in the community. Partnerships for research with health and social care settings was seen to benefit wider society.

Reflections on how being a music therapist has shaped my career

I believe that leadership is about human collaboration, and is embedded in everyone's role, whatever their tasks or responsibilities. If you do not lead your leaders, they will not be able to lead you, and vice versa. Leading multidisciplinary teams in the NHS helped me to recognise that barriers are often set between professions. I realised early on that any organisation is only as effective as the people within it.

Music involves nurturing relationships and 'attunement' – being attuned to the world and people around you. Whether it be in a music therapy, musical performance, or community music setting, music-making is not possible without collaboration, listening and following, turn-taking and adjusting pace, rhythm and melody, just like good leadership.

The third case study is from Fiona Ritchie, who began her career by developing a team of arts therapists in Birmingham, working with people with learning disabilities. Fiona Ritchie's writing in the *British Journal of Music Therapy* about her approach and experience of people who had been traumatised by institutionalisation was groundbreaking and inspiring reading for generations of music therapists, including the authors of this book. Fiona writes about her varied career pathway and the importance of advocacy and music therapy skills across all her work.

> **Box 1.3 Fiona Ritchie OBE; Director and Senior Intervenor**
>
> **Career journey**
>
> I am self-employed, working for not-for-profit organisations, Local Authorities, NHS services and NHS England. In my NHS England role as a Senior Intervenor I support multi-disciplinary teams in their work with people who are stuck in secure mental health services to move into less restrictive services or their own homes. I am also an associate for National Development Team for inclusion where I lead five programmes to develop small supports, my passion is around ensuring individuals have a voice and control and ambition in their life. I was delighted to be made chair of the British Institute of Learning Disabilities in 2020.
>
> I trained at Roehampton and after qualifying worked in a hospital in Birmingham with people with learning disabilities whose behaviour can challenge. I was the first music therapist appointed and I developed an arts therapy team, with music and drama therapists working in the hospital and the community.
>
> For several years, Roehampton music therapy students joined us for brief periods as part of the course, offering experience of the practical issues around delivery of therapy and of the hospital setting. I published articles about the work I did with individuals who were extremely traumatised and spoke at several international conferences. My career developed away from clinical work to effect change on a bigger scale because I felt I could influence people and staff lives for the better.
>
> I have always worked for people with learning disabilities and autistic people. After leaving music therapy I began managing an NHS day centre, and then moved to managing all community services in the Trust. When the Trust took a new direction which did not align with my principles I decided to leave.
>
> I went to the Strategic Health Authority and became their lead for learning disabilities focusing on public health screening, and concurrently studied for a Master's degree in public health. I then worked for the Health Care Commission (HCC) (now CQC) as the lead for learning disabilities. At this time, I was also privileged to be awarded an OBE for working with people with learning disabilities. With the change of the HCC to the CQC I felt my skill set was not what they were looking for, so I returned to an NHS Trust as Associate Director of Transformation, working to support change, streamline pathways and ensure better, timely care and support for individuals.

I then moved on to become Managing Director for Learning Disabilities and Mental Health in a large national charity. This was the most demanding job I have had, working to ensure service quality was good and that we were always person centred. Not easy when you have 4,000 staff and geography across England.

After eight years I felt I needed time to regroup, left and set up my own consultancy. I have always had a strong moral compass and I have made important career decisions based around this. Setting up on my own was a risk but I wanted to be able to control the work I did and to ensure everything I did made a difference to individuals.

Reflections on how being a music therapist has shaped my career

I always tell people that being a music therapist has shaped the way I work. It shapes the way I think about things, about depth and resilience, about always working with what people give you and getting underneath the superficial. I have and still use the observation skills that were honed during training in all aspects of my work. In my current job having been a clinician gives me expertise to constructively challenge senior clinicians in multidisciplinary meetings to ensure the individuals' voice is always heard and the least restrictive practices are used. It has helped me enormously to make connections with people, to be a good communicator, an active listener of people's needs and dreams to enable their care team to think differently and bigger. The training and supervision also gave me time to explore myself, to reflect and I still use this to this day.

I have been asked a lot of times if I would still undertake music therapy knowing what I know about my career. I always answer yes to this. It made me resilient to having to get my point across, to stick to my guns when I felt I was right and no one else was listening to the individuals, I loved seeing individuals take control through music and affect their emotional state, their resilience and determination to change. I see this now through the individual work I am doing as a Senior Intervenor by giving people a voice and by supporting the staff to think outside of the box individuals' lives are being transformed and they are starting to hold ambition for themselves. I do not believe I would have travelled the journey I did if I had not started as a music therapist.

Next, we read of Alexia Quinn's career as director of the Charity Music as Therapy International, which developed alongside her music therapy career. Alexia stresses how some of the skills she associates with music – listening, teamwork and resilience – helped her to develop her international charity.

Box 1.4 Alexia Quinn

As a teenager I was never without a Walkman in my pocket or a cassette playing in my room. Every moment of my adolescence has a soundtrack. And when I wasn't listening to music, I was making my own. An enthusiastic pianist and a reasonably proficient flautist, what brought me greatest musical fulfilment was playing with others or playing my favourite tracks to others; sharing music. But I also came to realise that I was one of life's accompanists, not soloists. As I began exploring a career in music therapy, I feared this might hold me back. Perhaps I wasn't a good enough musician to take centre stage. Was a lack of musical talent going to prevent me from studying music and then training as a therapist? Just as creativity in the visual arts shouldn't be reduced to whether or not you can draw an object or a person with realism. Over the course of my career, I've come to realise that musicianship is so much more than virtuosic performing. And that there are far-reaching skills developed through musical training – such as resilience, attention to detail and acute listening – that supplement expressive musical communication in music therapy practice.

My first steps into music therapy started young. Inspired by a conversation with Sybil Beresford-Peirse from Nordoff Robbins, I allowed my musical skills to develop naturally as I progressed through school and I focused on finding opportunities to explore every corner of the human condition. I read voraciously – personal accounts of living with disabilities and of working with people in vulnerable situations or facing challenges throughout the lifespan. I volunteered in places where I could meet people who might access music therapy. I worked with children and young people in wide ranging contexts. This included time spent overseas during my gap year and it was then, in Romania, where I found myself trying to make sense of an overwhelming experience. I paid attention to the rhythm, pitch and intensity with which people communicated to interpret what was going on around me when I couldn't understand the words being spoken. Perhaps a musical ear helped me in my attempts to learn the Romanian language as I sought closer involvement in the new world in which I was living. I watched everyone carefully, as they went about their daily lives that were so different to my own back in England. I noted people's different ways of doing things and tried to adapt to fit alongside them. I asked a lot of questions and I listened. I really listened. I learnt so much from my Romanian friends, colleagues and the children with whom I was working. And I learnt some uncomfortable truths about the international response to a country emerging from a complicated and devastating period in its history.

Ultimately this led me to found Music as Therapy International, a charity working worldwide to enable caregivers to draw on music therapy practice and incorporate music into their day to day activities with people living in vulnerable situations across the lifespan. Alongside this, I completed my music degree, my music therapy training and secured a clinical role within a paediatric NHS team. As I started honing my clinical skills I realised the relevance of these skills to international development: Meeting people in the moment and attuning as a way of understanding our starting point and building an authentic alliance, showing respect and unconditional positive regard, seeking to understand even when communication is complicated or behaviours are unexpected, careful observation, focusing on details and, above all else, acute listening and patience. Clinical supervision developed my understanding of preparation and the importance of clarity of thinking. I became increasingly adept at inviting engagement but remaining ready to be flexible in my response, guided by the individual I was with.

It transpires that these clinical skills are critical to building all sorts of effective partnerships. And it is genuine, thoughtful partnerships that underpin positive international development practice. So as my clinical skills strengthened through my music therapy work, I transferred them quickly into my work with the charity. Over the past thirty years I have learned that maybe I am not one of life's accompanists. A music therapist does not simply provide musical context for her client's experiences and self-expression. A music therapist also offers "intervention": Extending possibilities, encouraging our clients to take risks and try new things, to explore new competencies, and to build their confidence in doing so. I have come to realise that I am, perhaps, one of life's facilitators. It has been an unexpected discovery that my music therapy skills transfer so neatly into my ongoing work running a charity where, as a facilitator, I work with my team to support caregivers to embed music into their practice, in the UK or overseas.

The international theme is continued with the next case study from Risenga Makondo. Risenga has had a dual career as a performing musician and music therapist. He describes his journey to music therapy, and some of the notable aspects of his career, leading to his return to South Africa to direct his own arts centre.

Box 1.5 Risenga Makondo

My musical roots

From rural South Africa, Limpopo Province I am of mixed heritage. My father is Venda and my mother is Tsonga, also known colloquially as Shangaan. Music has always been central to rural life in South Africa. As for my early musical experiences as a young person, music provided a meeting point for the whole community inclusively. As a young person, whenever I heard the sound of music, I would follow it until I arrived. Wherever it was being performed whatever the style of music, I cannot recall ever being disappointed.

In the city of Johannesburg, Gauteng Province

At the age of fifteen, I left the countryside, my village and went off to look for work. I got a job working in a factory in Cleveland, the industrial area of Johannesburg. It was a rebellious act. Leaving my sleepy village meant that I did not have to join the army or police service and participate in the war with neighbouring Mozambique and Zimbabwe. So I bought my first brown suit and from that moment onwards — I felt I was a man, no longer a boy — little did I know that I was actually a child labourer. It was during this period in my young life that I came across people who were interested in what I loved so much: music, culture, traditions.

In and out of Soweto the Ghetto

The music of the village community that I experienced as a child became my guide. It nurtured me and redirected my path. I met people who were musicians, poets, visual artists, dancers, actors, who saw value in my musical background and I was invited to join their bands and theatre groups to perform. And I got paid too. I found myself exposed to other cultures and musical forms that I never knew existed within South Africa. In Soweto, I enrolled in a community arts centre named Funda Centre and it was here I started to speak English. Growing up during Apartheid meant that I had previously only had one kind of experience with white people, particularly in my home province, but my experience of performing introduced me to friendly white audiences. A few years later, I joined the Cape Town-based band Amampondo. We toured all five continents of the world. It was an exciting time and I realised how much I enjoyed performing and seeing the world.

But I yearned to be of service in the world. I especially wanted to be of service to those who were directly or indirectly excluded from society. My dream was to get an education and do something meaningful with it. And I certainly did!

My journey into music therapy

It took more years before I finally settled in Brighton and began my higher education studies. I completed an undergraduate degree in Visual and Performing Arts from the University of Brighton and then a postgraduate degree in Music Therapy from the University of Surrey Roehampton. My education as a music therapist opened my eyes to the multifaceted nature of the world. It gave me a greater understanding of humanity: as physical, psychological/mental, social, cultural and spiritual. The human diversities that co-exist within societies and cultures became increasingly visible for me. Music therapy also made me understand myself: I became more self-reflexive in seeing situations with a broader perspective. Rather than all the self-referential me-me-me stuff. I started to think more deeply about what I am doing. And why? Long before I became a music therapist, I would do things simply because I could. Developing an understanding of the therapeutic role of music also slowly began to shape my visual and performing arts work. I became effective in my work and receptive to new ideas.

My early career experiences as a qualified music therapist

I have worked as a self-employed music therapist with Sound Wave Southwest and Music Space in Bristol. I worked across many educational settings, hospices and family centres; it was a truly rewarding experience. It took me some time to realise that music therapy as a discipline began to enhance the quality of my music workshops and also my solo performances. I facilitated workshops and performed in festivals across Europe, Asia, Australia and Africa. I also started to nurture many young and seasoned artists, mentoring them to produce their own live shows. One of many examples is the band Sotho Sounds from Lesotho.

In 2012 I was offered a full-time job by Hertfordshire Music Service (HMS) to facilitate music classes and workshops that adopt a holistic approach. I worked in primary education for mainstream and special schools and I trained teachers to work with all young people in a more creative ways through music and visual performing arts. I formalised my approach and created Creative Music Nurture Groups (CMNGs) to meet the needs of those who could be easily forgotten. This approach was expanded across all primary schools in Hertfordshire, with the aim to expand nationally through a large-scale research project funded by Youth Music.

Limpopo Calling

I am now back in South Africa to establish Mashudu, translating as 'Blessings' in Tshivenda, an integral arts centre in Venda. The centre will eventually run flagship teacher training programmes, as well as a range of other classes, workshops and events centred on creative, spiritual and wellbeing practices in the local rural area. We have fertile land in the countryside and are now working on planning and saving the funds to complete the construction as it is a real feat!

Music therapy is a truly transformative career.

Our sixth case study is from Eleanor Tingle. Eleanor trained at Bristol and now works as Dean for Welfare at St Peter's College, University of Oxford. Eleanor unfolds her pathway and the centrality of her music therapy skills in being with others through all her work.

Box 1.6   Eleanor Tingle

Introduction

Music has always been the lens through which I experience the world. It is a constant which enables connection, gives solace, expresses joy and translates what cannot be spoken into something tangible. When I was a child I dreamt in music.

Exposition

Training as a music therapist enabled me to begin to understand music as a complex and powerful clinical tool. The most crucial lesson, and the most difficult, was to be fully present, to 'just be there' with each client. Through my training and early work, I embraced client-centred practice as the cornerstone of clinical thinking and I continue to explore what this means. As a peripatetic music therapist working in many different institutions, I learned to listen to the complex dynamics, harmonies and dissonances of each setting, and of the systems around myself and those referred for music therapy. I worked to understand their impact on each note played in the therapy room.

Development

A client-centred focus and a desire to understand more about music as a clinical tool, has led me forwards. The vision of an independent team of music therapists, able to provide a wraparound client-centred service outside the limits of the education authority setting in which I was first employed, led to the creation of what was to become the charity Music Therapy Works (MTW). Providing the best possible CPD and professional support for the growing team of music therapists at MTW was driven forward by looking at what would best enable us to support our clients. Developing ideas and learning about music as a clinical tool led me to undertake training in Guided Imagery and Music and in Neurologic Music Therapy; to research; and to develop an undergraduate music therapy module at Birmingham University (and so very nearly a music therapy training course!). At the centre of everything was being in the therapy room. Across more than 25 years, the MTW team thrived and together we explored different permutations of funding, clinical delivery, research, supporting each other and enhancing client-centred practice.

Recapitulation

The other part of the story is the support I received at an early age, almost always from musicians, and almost always from gay men. I was seen and encouraged in a way which enabled me to flourish, although acute early illness and childhood trauma remain strong influences. In my own therapy the realisation that I had worked to create a safe place in which traumatised and sometimes unwell young people might thrive through music was gently reflected back to me. The move to become Dean for Welfare at St Peter's College, Oxford, came about through an emerging realisation that whilst I could continue to work to transform and 're-orchestrate' MTW for many more years, it was in a strong position to move forwards with different leadership which might enable fresh thinking and greater diversity. I looked around for somewhere my skills at 'being with' and understanding systems might be used, chanced upon an advert for the Dean for Welfare role and applied. The role requires the use of all of the transferable skills I learned in music therapy training and pretty much every piece of clinical knowledge and understanding I have accumulated across the years. I miss using music directly in my meetings with students but it is still there, underpinning these interactions. I have gained a new community and work within the wider university arena too in considering new ways of providing support. In 2021 I was delighted to be made a Supernumerary Fellow of St Peter's.

Coda

Noting a professional journey in a few hundred words leaves out a great deal, in particular the interplay of the personal and professional, the times of doubt, anguish, illness and struggle. What has sustained me is the presence of music, a belief in its inviolability and in the transformative power of music therapy. I remain to my core a music therapist and continue to seek to serve the profession. In 2021 I applied to become Chair of the British Association for Music Therapy, a role I am currently privileged to hold.

Now to Northern Ireland, where Jenny Kirkwood unfolds her journey from clinician to leader within the Public Health Agency of Northern Ireland. She lists some of the qualities learnt as a trainee that have stood her in good stead in her leadership role.

Box 1.7   Jenny Kirkwood

From music therapy to AHP leadership: A journey of transferable skills

In my role as AHP Coordinator for Children and Young People's Emotional Health and Wellbeing at the Public Health Agency of Northern Ireland, I reflected on the skills that working in public health requires:

Critical thinking, analysing detail but also seeing a broader perspective.
Making connections and 'systems thinking'.
Collaborative work, fostering relationships with effective communication.
   Empathy and listening.
Adaptability and flexibility, encouraging different viewpoints.
A commitment to population health and supporting diverse communities.
Addressing challenges and finding resourceful solutions.
Creative thinking and openness to new ideas.

Don't these qualities align closely with those of a good music therapist? In my experience, the broader role of music therapists as Allied Health Professionals (AHP) is not always realised, but if you re-read that list for a music therapist, the breadth of our skillset and its transferability across health and social care roles is clear.

   I was introduced to music therapy by my school music teacher, who facilitated my work experience with a local therapist, Julie Sutton. From then, I knew that using my music studies in a healthcare profession was a perfect fit for me. After my music degree a year in Italy turned into more, and I was lucky to discover a UK music therapy course in Bologna allowing me to stay there to study. My entry into the profession was delayed by the arrival of my first son, but I began working for a Northern Ireland music therapy charity in 2007 and remained there for over 11 years working in various settings and clinical areas, and later in management roles.

   In 2018 a change in the organisation's management style and priorities ultimately led to my acceptance of voluntary redundancy. This was a very challenging time. I loved clinical work and had never expected to fully leave it, but limited opportunities for music therapists in Northern Ireland forced me to reconsider my next step.

At this time of reflection and reorientation, a temporary role at the Public Health Agency (PHA) provided a pivotal opportunity to experience working within the health service, and a transition from clinical practice to a broader AHP remit.

The AHP team at the PHA provides professional advice for commissioning and service development and supports public health by improving outcomes and reducing health inequalities. Since 2019, my work has taken me through diverse areas, including reviewing services for children with sensory impairments, pandemic contract tracing, evidence reviews to inform service improvement and policy, regional support for adults with swallowing difficulties, health literacy and my current role in children's emotional health and wellbeing. Navigating the insecurity of temporary roles and feeling unaccustomed to the statutory system has presented challenges. Yet having that different perspective becomes an advantage at other times. Throughout this work, those skills developed as a practicing music therapist have been called upon daily and have proven invaluable. It is clear that we AHPs have more that unites us than divides us, and I encourage music therapists considering paths outside of clinical practice to recognise the value they can contribute.

Conclusion

The inspiring case studies in this chapter illustrate how the experience of becoming a music therapist can enrich many other areas of work and development. These examples of creative, innovative careers may lead readers to consider more broadly their own careers within music therapy, and muse upon pathways that music therapists might choose to take. Future issues such as climate change and sustainable communities (United Nations, ND), a continually developing understanding of trauma and of the experiences of, for example, displaced people and new developments in technology may lead music therapists along new and innovative paths in their future careers.

References

Brandenburg, C., and E.C. Ward (2022) 'There hasn't been a career structure to step into: A qualitative study on perceptions of allied health clinician researcher careers', *Health Research Policy and Systems*, 20 (6), pp. 1–17. https://doi.org/10.1186/s12961-021-00801-2.

Ledger, A. (2016) 'Developing new posts in music therapy' in Edwards, J. (ed.) *Oxford Handbook of Music Therapy*. Oxford: Oxford University Press, pp. 875–893.

Nashwan A.J. (2023 May 10) 'The vital role of career pathways in nursing: A key to growth and retention', *Cureus*, 15 (5). Available at: https://www.ncbi.nlm.nih.gov/pmc/articles/PMC10254089/ (Accessed on 23 November 2023).

NHS (2020) *'We Are the NHS: People Plan 2020/2021 – Action for us all'*. Available at: https://www.england.nhs.uk/ournhspeople/ (Accessed on 23 November 2023).

Psychological Professions Network (2023) *Career Map for the Psychological Professions.* Available at: https://www.ppn.nhs.uk/resources/careers-map (Accessed on 23 November 2023).

The Scottish Government (2018) *Transforming Nursing, Midwifery and Health Professions' (NMaHP) Roles: Pushing the Boundaries to Meet Health and Social Care Needs in Scotland.* Scotland: The Scottish Government.

United Nations (No Date) *The 17 Goals.* Available at: https://sdgs.un.org/goals (Accessed on 23 November 2023).

Chapter 10

Coda

The future

Catherine Warner and Tessa Watson

And so the journey continues. Here we look back at some of the landmarks within the book, and walk through a possible future for music therapy.

Within **teaching and learning,** continued attention to diversity, anti-oppressive practice, promoting flexibility in practice, incorporating innovative new, ancient and indigenous ways of thinking about music and health and encouraging new music therapists to conceptualise, present and describe music therapy in a way that enables job creation and retention, all emerge as important themes.

Authentic learning and teaching co-production with people who access music therapy demands new institutional thinking, highly developed skills in reflexivity and teamwork, and imagination. This co-production should apply across training institutions employing service users, within placements where trainees co-create music therapy aims and work with clients, to engagement and consultation in the workforce and within professional associations. New frameworks for thinking about this might be needed within training programmes.

Within theoretical framing, there are several areas of research and knowledge that are likely to continue to develop. It will be important to continue to embed insights and research from **neuroscience** within music therapy training. Deeper understanding of how music affects the brain, how trauma is embodied and passed on generationally (epigenetics) and how early musical relationships begin, is developing apace (Sokira et al 2022). Most music therapy training courses now incorporate trauma informed approaches, exploring ways in which the rhythms and cycles of music can help us self-regulate and remain present in the moment.

The challenges and opportunities of **Artificial Intelligence** (AI) for teaching and learning will unfold in future years (Crompton and Burke 2023). From a trainee and practitioner perspective, AI is increasingly becoming part of digital music and the person in therapy and responsive therapist will find ways to make use of this (for example, in lyric generation). From a trainer's perspective, new assessments harnessing AI need to be explored creatively in order to assist trainee understanding of how to use AI in productive and ethical ways.

The lack of clinical tariffs and therefore the lack of payment for placement educators (supervisors) means that the **development of placements** in new areas, and where there is demand from training, continues to be challenging for trainers, despite the possibilities of role emerging placements. This is an area of development for the professional association and for those working in senior roles in placement settings.

New routes to training are needed: As more musicians choose music therapy as a career and life choice, more affordable, diverse and graduated career routes need to become available. It might be useful to pose the question of whether undergraduate routes, as in some European countries, can be considered, not at the entry point to the profession, but in terms of gaining better access to music therapy training. **Degree Apprenticeships** are starting, and will need resourcing and monitoring, ensuring that the curriculum delivers robust graduates who have the necessary knowledge, skills and self-care capacity to practice. Encouraging **career awareness of music therapy** amongst young people and raising the **importance of music education in schools is one task for future music therapists.** This will make differences to the diverse pipeline of younger people coming to train.

In practice, **entrepreneurship** is something to be celebrated, as can be seen by the inspiring career stories in Chapter 9. Identifying during training the importance of being agile and innovative, valuing our unique skills as music therapists and improvisers (in the broadest sense), and promoting narratives that align with identified needs and gaps in access to music therapy will be important skills for the future (Ledger 2016). Producing graduates who understand the key needs of the cultural and geographical area in which they work will also assist in meeting need in marginalised areas. Work with the **marginalised** and where there are **health inequalities,** including in health prevention and promotion will be an important strand of development for music therapy in the UK.

The profession needs to further identify and move into **geographic deserts.** There are efforts afoot to develop a training course in Northern Ireland, and with the newer courses in the North West and North East England, slowly recruitment and practice will flourish there. The music therapy community needs to support these areas of growth as much as they can.

Cultural humility and openness is essential for the future of music therapy across training and practice (Edwards 2022). It is hoped that the future of music therapy will see a development of willingness to learn from those in diverse and marginalised groups, including trainees and clients and to co-produce training and practice. With a strong focus on increasing accessibility to training, and therefore increasing diversity into the workforce in all settings, it is hoped that clients will see 'more people like me' in the therapy space.

More broadly, in terms of the interface with **arts and health** a collaborative and respectful future between these continuums of music, wellbeing and health is envisaged (Moss 2022). How will music therapists understand, articulate and develop how we can most effectively work with and alongside artists and community musicians?

Living and working in a more **sustainable** way is a challenge to all, but awareness of how music therapy can actively promote sustainability must be developed further. The United Nations Sustainable Goals include a focus upon poverty, zero hunger, good health and wellbeing, quality education, gender equality, sustainable practices, climate action, reduced inequalities and peace and justice (United Nations 2016). These are all goals that music therapy practice can be particularly well linked to if we are able to aim for equity in access to creativity.

The **development of the experienced workforce** through a prioritisation of CPD and through seeking CPD that is most relevant for practice and development will continue to be important. The related concepts of **lifelong learning** and **self-care** are emphasised in this book with many music therapists giving serious consideration to developing their practice through CPD. One such example for development is support to gain **supervision competence**. Currently, music therapy supervisors are not required to be trained as such, and the few good quality training opportunities available are costly.

New ways to **research and evaluate** music therapy will need development in the years that follow. It is hoped that there will be development of research relevant to health inequalities, the experiences of diverse music therapists and that which identifies new areas of practice. The need for the capacity to learn how to bid for funding and the confidence to undertake or promote service evaluation has been identified in this book. More broadly, **data about the NHS arts therapies workforce** is clearly inadequate, and is likely the case for music therapists across diverse practice settings, despite the efforts of the BAMT. Therefore, projects to map the profession as it develops are a priority, in order to make informed judgements about where to target resources.

Our book ends with the voices of two graduates and a placement educator, reflecting on their training and practice journeys:

> I think I went into the training thinking about how it might change my relationship with music and of course that I would train to be a Music Therapist but it was surprising to me how the process of that training had such a profound and positive effect across every element of my life. (Graduate)

> *My training journey in music therapy has been a tapestry of self-discovery, cultural awareness, and professional growth. Each element – from reflective practice to theoretical exploration – has contributed to a deeper understanding of myself, both as an individual and as a therapist, navigating the complex interplay of music, culture, and identity.* (Graduate)

> Will music therapy survive? Of course! Who's saying it won't? For millennia now, humans have used the arts to make sense of their world. Being the most nebulous art form, music will be the closest ally to our emotional selves and will always have a role in the psychological support of this species! (Placement educator)

References

Crompton, H. and Burke, D. (2023) 'Artificial intelligence in higher education: The state of the field' in *International Journal of Educational Technology in Higher Education*, 20 (22). https://doi.org/10.1186/s41239-023-00392-8.

Edwards, J. (2022) 'Cultural humility in music therapy practice' in *Trauma-Informed Music Therapy Theory and Practice*. London: Routledge, pp. 49–57.

Ledger, A. (2016) 'Developing new posts in music therapy' in Edwards, J. (Ed) *The Oxford Handbook of Music Therapy*. Oxford: Oxford University Press.

Moss, H. (2022) *Music and Creativity in Healthcare Settings: Does Music Matter?* London: Routledge.

Sokira, J., Allen, J. and Wagner, H. (2022) 'The resilience framework for trauma-informed music therapy' in Beer, L. and Birnbaum, J. (Eds) *Trauma-Informed Music Therapy Theory and Practice*. London: Routledge, pp. 30–39.

United Nations (2016) *The Seventeen Sustainable Goals*: Department of Economic and Social Affairs. Available at https://sdgs.un.org/goals: (accessed 8th January 2024).

Index

ability to reflect 102, 127
ableism 7, 111, 113, 127, 131
access meetings 86
accreditation 139
acoustic screen 125
adjusting 60, 134, 162
advocacy for profession 123, 151, 159, 163
affect attunement 55, 64
affect regulation 64
affordances 62
Ahonen, H. 83, 98, 129, 130, 136, 155
Aigen, K. 35, 40, 45–6, 62, 68, 74
Allied Health Professions 36, 106, 120, 146, 156, 159–61
Allied Health Professions Federation (AHPF) 139
All-Party Parliamentary group for Music Education 107
altruism 84
Alvin, J. 33, 55
Amampondo 167
analytic listening 63
Anglia Polytechnic University Cambridge *see* Anglia Ruskin University
Anglia Ruskin University 33, 42, 58, 80, 153, 161
anti-oppressive practice 143, 152, 174
anxiety 10, 23, 27, 57, 103, 108, 112, 115, 131
applicants 52–8, 99–109, 112, 117
appraisal 11, 82, 85, 87
apprenticeships 34, 40, 48, 95, 106, 148, 175
apprenticeships, placement experience 4, 74, 91
arts and health 15, 105, 140, 159, 175
arts therapies 1, 38, 40, 42, 50, 53, 75, 82–3, 97, 106, 110, 119, 127, 129, 140, 147, 149, 156, 161–2, 176

assessment of applicants, suitability for training 112
assessment: accessibility 113; alignment 16, 21, 27; artificial intelligence 174; essay 6, 28, 44, 70, 78, 83, evidence of learning 16, 82; formative 26, 58, 81, 86, 89; learning outcomes 26, 27, 115, 128; live classroom assessments 66, 68; peer feedback 26; performance 26, 125; placement 79, 82, 87, 89, 93, 114, 116; presentations 26, 125; reflective accounts 26; student experience 10, 19, 22, 25; summative 26, 58, 87; theory and practice: 5, 16, 26–7, 111, 112, 114, 174; viva examinations 26
assessor subjectivity 112
associate lecturers 150
Associated Board of the Royal Schools of Music 56
Association of Professional Music Therapists 33
authenticity 2, 37, 96, 103
autobiography 6, 58, 111
autoethnography 152

BAME communities 152
barriers: beat-making technology 72; between professions 162; to disabled access 113; financial 56, 105; to health and social care 44; to personal development 127; to placements 92, to training 7, 21, 56, 92, 105–11, 113, 147–8
Big Data analysis 152
Bion, W. 65
boundaries 18, 19, 24, 35, 42, 116, 128, 141, 144
Bristol University 33, 80, 168, 169

British Association of Music Therapy (BAMT): area groups 153; conferences 9, 40, 49–50, 136; CPD 97; curriculum guidelines 51; disabled student guidance 114, 120; diversity report 7–8, 12, 152; history 34, 170; international workers 151; lived experience groups 153; mentoring scheme 91, 146; podcasts 155–6; special interest groups 153; supervision register 154; training and education committee 146; workforce survey 141, 146
British Institute of Learning Disabilities 163
British Journal of Music Therapy 9, 33–5, 37, 38, 162
British Society for Music Therapy 33
broadening practice 153–5
Brown, S. 35, 47, 68, 82, 98
Bunt and Hoskyns 41, 52, 61, 101
Bunt, L. 11, 22, 30, 34–5, 41, 44, 52, 61, 70, 83, 101, 105, 118
burnout 132–4
bursaries 106
business model 11

Cambridge Institute of Music Therapy Research (CIMTR) 153, 161–2
Care Quality Commission 44
careers in music therapy 1, 139, 151, 159, 160, 173
carers 14, 40, 51, 71, 96, 104, 150
caseloads 80, 144
Casement, P. 130
cause for concern 115–16
Charitable Boards of Trustees 150
charities 8, 84, 99, 148, 150, 163–4, 166, 170–1
Clare Maddocks 146, 152, 156
client-led approach 20, 167, 169
climate emergency 8
clinical: notes 79; scenarios 66; seminars 82
co-creation 18, 30, 52, 53, 69
collaboration 11, 13, 33, 36–7, 42, 44, 47, 49–50, 98, 104, 145, 152–3, 162
colonialist perspective 9, 47, 110, 122
commissioning 41, 45, 141, 159, 172
commitment: to cultural thinking 73; financial 106; to musicianship 61 (see also musicianship); to music therapy profession 10; to personal development 96, 104

communication: around experiential groups 128; between placement, trainee and educator 28, 90, 93, 94, 116; between professions 44; of client 166; complex communication 45; diverse communication styles 109; for change 142; as a graduate skill 96; musical 53, 90, 165; song communication 67; within a team 143, 171
Communicative Musicality 64, 76
Community Music Therapy 49, 150, 158
community musicians 141, 150, 157, 162
compassion fatigue 132–4
complex of life skills 74
composition 55, 67–8, 76
constructive alignment 16
consultancy 155, 164
consumer culture 11, 12, 21, 150
containment 62, 65, 68, 128
continuing professional development 1, 97, 141, 145–6, 153, 155
Control of Noise at Work Legislation 125
co-production 37, 44–5, 100, 143, 150–1, 174
core curriculum 35, 72, 113
core principles in practice 133, 143, 170
Council for Professions Supplementary to Medicine (CPSM) 139
countertransference 11, 63, 68
Courses Liaison Committee 36
course websites 52, 106
Covid 19 pandemic 1, 8, 25–6, 43, 54, 83, 85, 90–1, 101, 105, 108, 114, 131, 141–2, 145–6, 152, 156–7, 172
creative therapies 47; see also arts therapies
creativity 3, 102, 135, 144, 165, 176–7
critical disability studies 7, 14, 49–50, 113, 121
critical thinking 9–10, 107, 113, 171
cross-modal matching 65–6
culture: client culture 73, 152; consumer culture 20; cultural adjustment 111, 167; cultural agendas 73; cultural awareness 41–2, 50, 71, 73, 95; cultural competence 73, 95; cultural diversity 168; cultural reflexivity 71, 73, 95, 111, 176; cultural humility 1, 33, 95; cultural relevance 69; cultural sensitivity 41, 61, 120; musical culture 41–2, 59, 76; of practice 91, 110, 119; safe spaces 14; song culture 69; trainee's own culture 109, 124, 143, 167; training culture 89

curriculum: apprenticeships 175; constructive alignment of 16; co-production 150; design of 8–9, 16, 150; diversity in 8, 15, 109–10; for educators 27; guidance 34, 36–7; HCPC guidance 34; hidden 22; history of music therapy 110; inclusive 115; National Curriculum for schools 107

Darnley-Smith, R. 34–6, 47, 49, 62, 75, 105, 120
Davies, A. 24, 127, 129
Davies, H. 7, 42, 115, 135
debriefing 81
defences: in experiential group 23; in music 63
development of new posts 159
difference: between courses 64–6; between trainees 42, 111; in groups 110, 111; making a difference to clients 164; as welcome 42
digital music 56, 72, 107, 174; *see also* beat-making technology
disability: disability studies 8–9, 41; learning disability 44; medical model; social model 66; student disability 94–6, 105, 111, 113, 127, lecturer disability 111
disabled trainees 113, 120, 121
discipline of music therapy 159
disclosure 11
diversity 3, 7–9, 25, 36, 38, 40–3, 60, 83, 93–6, 106, 109–15, 143, 147, 149, 153, 174–5
double loop learning 10
doubling 64
dynamic form 64

ear defenders 125
East London NHS Foundation Trust 150
efficacy in research 153
e-learning 1, 33, 43
electronic portfolios 82
embodiment 20, 43, 64, 129, 154, 156, 174
emotional labour 111, 144
emotional maturity 103–4
employment 20, 36, 86, 92, 96, 102, 141–2, 144–6, 150
empowerment: of client 143; of learner 18
energy: of client 65; of trainee 84, 125
engagement in arts-based practice 125
entrainment 66, 77
entrepreneurship 81, 175

equity and diversity 1, 7, 27, 41–2, 55, 56, 94, 110, 176
ethnography 152
ethnomusicology 110
European Consortium of Arts Therapies Trainers 38, 48, 140
European Music Therapy Confederation 38, 140, 156
experiences of trauma 126
experiential group 23–5, 126–8: confidentiality 128; encounter group 24; facilitator 24, 128; introduction to 124; power 128; themes 128
experiential learning 17, 20–2, 66–7, 124, anxiety 128; conflict 23
experts 74
external examiner 112

facilitation 16, 19, 68, 111, 128
family experience 105
feedback: accepting of 87; formal and informal 86–7; formative 58; summative 58
finance for student 100, 105–6, 121
financial barriers *see* barriers
first study instrument 56–7
fitness to practice 115, 125, 134
flexibility: qualities of music therapist 123, 140, 142, 159, 171, 174; in training journey 44, 114, 150
flexible working 105
flow 57, 61, 65, 70, 75–6, 85
freedom: of expression 24; in improvising 62; to learn 4, 14–15, 20, 31, 74; to practice therapy 140; with the voice 65
free improvisation *see* improvisation
freelance: consultancy 155; contract 144–5; educators 92; therapists 92, 146
funding 12, 15, 25, 39, 44, 141, 145, 152, 176
Futurelearn 55

gamelan 49, 72, 76
gaps in provision 149, 154, 175
GDPR (General Data Protection Regulation) 78, 154
Gelbert, P. 109, 120
gender and sexuality 7, 42, 110, 113, 120, 176
genre 60, 62, 72, 143
geographical aspects of provision 26, 148–9, 154, 175

GIM (Guided imagery in Music) 154, 156
Goldie Leigh Hospital 33
Goodman, K. 16, 17, 23, 27, 29, 37, 82
good practice: assessing and interviewing trainees 112; evaluating practice 146; on placement 28; in practice 36, 91; in supervision 144
grade 8 minimum 56
graphic score 68, 70, 75
grounding as musical technique 64
group experiential teaching 61, 127
group improvisation 54–5, 62, 66, 72, 102
Guildhall School of Music and Drama: introductory courses 55; PhD programme 153
guitar 72

Hadley, S. 8, 14, 71, 75, 110–11, 120, 137
Halford, E. 100, 120
Hardy, S. 113, 120
harmony 20, 65, 71, 101, 106, 160
Health and Care Professions Council (HCPC): Code of Conduct, Performance and Ethics 139; context for music therapy 9, 37, 41–5, 53, 65–7, 139–40, 151; curriculum 9; diversity 42; protection of public 116; registration 140; service evaluation 45, 151–2; Standards of Education and Training 14, 96, 139, 150; standards of proficiency 26, 37, 40; standards of proficiency, music 53, 65, 67; standards of proficiency, placements 82; standards of proficiency, self-care 108, 125, 127, 134; working with others and co-production 44, 96, 150
health and social care landscape 3, 45, 109, 162, 171
Health Education England 105, 120, 147, 156
health inequalities 149, 152, 172, 175–6
health musicking 14, 141, 156
Heaney, S. 136
hearing and hearing loss 125
higher education in UK 8, 9; consumerism 20, 117; current climate 34, 39; decolonisation 18; fitness to practice process 115; music 107; power 11, 12; satisfaction surveys 39, 116–17; research 153
Higher Education Institution (HEI): business model 11, 83, 117

high level of musicianship 53, 55
Hip-Hop see Rap and Hip-Hop
home country working 109, 151

identity: gender 42; musical 6, 57–61, 74; online 43; personal 20, 42; professional 6, 57; racial 42; self-care 6, 43
illusory superiority 153
impact of loud music 125
impact of past experiences 20, 24, 126
imposter syndrome 8, 143, 147
improvisation: clinical improvisation 53, 62, 28, 75; free 55, 63, 66; in communities 61, 67, 160; online improvising 25, 43, 54, 72, 91, 101; recording of 54; 58, 70, 82, 91, 102; response improvisation 54, 70, 82; structured improvisation 68, 83
improvisational potential 52–4, 64, 101–2
inclusion 7, 15, 51, 55, 92, 110, 131, 160, 163
independent learning 26
independent music practice 124, 125, 141
indigenous perspective 110, 121, 174
indirect exposure to trauma see secondary trauma
induction 80, 111
infection control 78
inner indexing 70
inner supervisor 83
innovation assessment 82; covid 19 pandemic 25, 54; curriculum 10, 27, 175; service delivery 144, 145, 172
insight 21, 30, 99, 105, 110, 123, 127, 129, 132, 174
institutional dynamics 3, 81, 144–5, 150
integrating: approaches 35, 40
interactive musicianship 35, 52, 54, 61
interdisciplinary learning and working see interprofessional learning and working
intergenerational trauma 110, 126
internal supervisor see Casement
international trainees 57, 109, 150
interpersonal contours of music 68
interprofessional learning and working 1, 3, 33, 43, 44
interruptions to training 130
intersectionality 11, 13, 42, 110, 121
interviewer subjectivity 112
interviewing skills 145
introductory courses 33, 55, 99
investment in training 4, 105
isolation 131, 146, 153–4

Index

job interview 87, 142
job satisfaction 34, 123, 132
Journal of British Music Therapy 33

key attributes of trainees 96, 100–5
keywords in research 153
Kirkwood, J. 45, 171
knowledge: of music therapy 104; knowledge loss 153
knowledge exchange 38
Kolb, D. A. 17, 21

language: body 54; cultural 111, 165; harmonic 72; no language 69; professional 42, 142–3; reflexive 150; music as universal 109
leadership 40, 44, 68–9, 102, 160, 162, 170–1
learning and teaching: co-creation 18, 53, 69; experiential learning (*see* experiential learning); helicopter technique 17; learning styles 5, 17; personal learning style 17; quiet learning 22; relational security 19; theories 3, 16–29
learning and teaching pedagogy: active learning 22; blended learning 26; context 1, 8; deep and surface learning 10, 16–17; flipped classroom 18; interprofessional 43; problem based learning 21–2; role play 21, 52, 61, 65–6, 85, 102; theories 10, 16–30; tutorial 18, 57, 134
learning differences, dyslexia, dyspraxia 5, 114, 130
learning journey 5, 96
learning needs 94, 114
learning to learn 3
leaving the profession or training 116, 131–2, 136
Lee, C. 68, 70, 72, 75–6, 83
LGBTQ+ 8, 111, 113, 161
Lifelong learning 3, 5, 10, 17, 18, 176
lifespan model 80
listening: in leadership 148; 160–6, 171; to music 53, 57, 63, 66–7, 69, 91, 124–5; as part of learning 17–18; in supervision 129; to trainees 5, 96
listening diary 124
lived experience 3, 15, 64, 66, 95, 105, 112–14, 135, 143, 150, 153
lockdown 25, 43, 54, 75, 83, 90, 105, 108, 131, 146

Lockett, B. 53–4, 61, 66–8, 70, 76
long-arm supervision *see* supervision
low morale 36, 144
lyrics 69, 76; *see also* Rap and Hip-Hop; song

major projects 57
Makondo, R. 166–7
management 11, 39, 135, 160, 161, 171
managing tax 145
manual handling 78, 94
matching as musical technique 64–6
medical professions 8, 113, 139
mental health: mental health nursing 148; music therapy work in 44, 46, 50, 110–11, 115, 120–2, 133, 136, 161, 163–4; of trainee 11, 39, 88, 94, 100, 108, 138
mental imagery 107, 121
mentorship 80, 91, 114, 145–7, 155, 160, 168
microanalysis 70, 77, 118
microprocesses 25, 66, 70
mistakes 84, 98
moderation in marking 112
monitoring: of learning 26, 81, 85; of programmes 12; of self 134
mother-infant observation 79
motivation 5, 21, 84, 147; to train 126–7
movement play 66
moving and handling musical equipment 125
multi-disciplinary team (MDT) 43, 50, 80, 92, 137, 143, 150, 161–4
music: analysis 29, 70–1 (*see also* microanalysis); autobiography 6, 58, 111; background 56, 58, 60, 167; case formulation 21, 154; childhood 54, 167; connection 59, 63; cultural accumulation 60, 73; evaluation 70; experience 6, 111, 167; flexibility in music 66, 73, 140, 159, 174; genres 62, 72, 143; identity 6, 58–61, 124, 128; personal practice 125; personality 63; play 63–5, 68, 70, 90, 158; qualities 43, 101; structure 55; traditions 95; in training 52–74; transference 63
Music as Therapy International 166
music-centred approach 46, 49, 62, 70
music education barriers 106; *see also* barriers
Musician's Union 107, 120–1, 125, 137

musicianship: expressive 165; high-level 53, 55
Music Therapy and Remedial Music 33
music therapy as a second career 148
music therapy assistants 98, 122, 142
Music Therapy: Intimate Notes 105, 121
music therapy musicianship 52, 54, 61, 68
music therapy training: co-production 37, 44, 147; discourse 7, 8, 20, 36, 37, 52, 110, 115, 150; in Europe 34, 37–8, 61, 63, 127, 140, 175; historical pathway in UK 1, 22, 29, 33–8
Myerscough, F. and Wong, D. 7, 14, 42, 49, 109, 111–12, 121

National Curriculum 107
National Development Team 163
negative capability 136
neuro-affirmative model 113
neurodiversity 13, 48, 110–11, 113–15, 120, 137
Neurologic Music Therapy (NMT) 66, 77, 154, 170
neurorehabilitation 66
neuroscience 64, 70, 122, 153, 174
newly qualified therapist (NQT) 146
NHS: careers 8, 36, 37, 161–6, 176; outcome measures 45; psychological professions network 139; student experience 149; workforce 148–9, 155, 159
Nordoff and Robbins 33, 35, 55, 61–2, 68, 100, 105, 143, 153, 165
Nordoff and Robbins PhD programme 153
Nordoff, P. 33, 48, 55, 61–2, 68, 76, 105, 121, 143, 153, 156, 165
Northern Ireland 171–2, 175
nursing preceptorships 147, 157

observational placements 79; *see also* placements
occupational therapy 36, 44, 80, 154
Odell-Miller, H. 34, 35, 45, 153, 161
Office for Students 39
off-site placement support 80, 149; *see also* placement
older adults 47, 153
Oldfield, A. 44, 58, 65, 72, 76
online placements *see* lockdown
online reflective practice groups 83, 98, 154
online security *see* GDPR

online work: artificial intelligence 44; learning 25–6, 43, music 54, 72, 97; pandemic 90–1, 108, 118; publications and resources 34, 42, 55, 104, 145; selection process 101; social media 8, 43, 149; supervision 83, 154; work with service users; 44, 92, 142
on-site placement support 3, 28, 78–80, 83, 115, 129
Open Access publishing 142
open groups 145
oppressive practice 42, 143, 152, 174
osteopaths 149
othering 110, 131
outcome measures 45

pair work 66
participatory action research 152, 158
Paul Nordoff 33, 56
Pavlicevic, M. 35, 37, 40, 64, 68, 76, 105, 121, 126, 140–1, 150, 155
pedagogy: 3, 7, 14, 50, 61, 121, 137
peer learning 59–61, 72
peer supervision 81, 83, 130
pentatonic 67
performance: academic 12–13; anxiety 57, 75; musical 22, 26, 62, 68, 117, 125, 162, 168; professional 139
personal identity 42, 147
personality of therapist 63, 127, 138, 144, 146
Personal Protective Equipment 90
personal qualities 50, 53, 138, 157
personal therapy: cost 25, 104, 127; group (*see* experiential group); purpose 24, 57, 104, 124, 126–7, 132; student experience 24, 88, 108, 128, 131, 132
personhood 58
phone working 91
physical: impact of music therapy work 88, 125–6, 133–4; responses 66, 72, 168; self-care 134; student experience 94–5, 101, 113
piano 125
Pickard, B. 7, 9, 14, 42, 49–50, 113, 121
pilot studies 13, 145–7
pioneers 35, 55, 159, 161
placement educators: assessing students 28; central role 1, 19, 27–9, 84–96, 174–5, communication 28, 90, 94, 115, 116; covid 19 pandemic 90; description of role 73, 85; expectations 87, 97,

150; experience 23, 84, 134; feeling observed 29; involvement in curriculum 9; learning opportunities 93, 95, 132; motivation 84, 142, 155; payment 149, 174; training 27, 86, 91; triangulation 28, 82, 90

placement observation 78–9, 85

placements: communication 28, 90, 94, 115, 116; fail 28, 94, 115, 116; portfolio and passport 78, 82; preparation 78–9; support 81

placement supervisor 81, 84, 115, 130; *see also* placement educator

play 64; *see also* musical play

plurality 40

postgraduate loan 56, 74, 105, 121

power 3, 7–12, 27, 37, 63, 82–3, 126, 128, 140, 170

practice mentor 80; *see also* placement educator

pre-composed music 62

preparation for training 99–100

presentations 26, 28, 34, 38, 40, 58, 83, 88, 131, 142

Priestley, M. 41, 43, 50, 63, 64, 68, 76

private organisations 147

privilege: concepts 7, 96; monetary privilege 8, 95–6; student experience 131; trainer 12, 132, 164, 170

professional conduct 139

professional structures 39, 142, 144–5, 147

professional suitability 115; *see also* fitness to practice

professional, statutory and regulatory body 9

prosthetics and orthotics 148

protected characteristics 114

protected job title 139

protection of public 140

psychoanalytic perspective 14, 35, 46, 71, 90, 136, 154, 161

psychodynamic perspective 12, 50, 59, 62–3, 68, 70, 72, 74, 158

Psychological Professions Network 159, 173

public organisations 147

Quality Assurance Agency 39

Queen Margaret University 33, 144

Quinn, A. 165

race 42, 95, 110–11

Rap and Hip Hop 72, 107, 122

readiness to train 100

reading music 106

reasonable adjustments 113

referral 80, 84–5

reflective practice: centrality of 123–4, 128; how to reflect 135–6; in staff team 29; in interprofessional learning and work 44; music 82, 124; personal development 126; play 64–5, 134; student experience 117–18, 176; supervision 29, 82, 90, 115–16, 129–30

reflective practice groups 82, 108, 115, 126, 129–30; *see also* clinical seminars and supervision

reflexive spaces 57

reflexivity 14, 73, 82, 110–11, 116, 174

regulation: art psychotherapy 36; dramatherapy 36; music therapy pathway 33, 36, 41; occupational therapy 36; paramedics 36; power (*see* Health and Care Professions Council)

relationship: between client and therapist 24, 35, 62–3, 68, 96, 113, 132, 136; between trainee and trainer 19, 155; with client's parents 80; in a group 24; to music 6, 59, 117, 124; power relationship 37, 63; with instrument 58; with other professions 141; with mentor 142; with supervisor 115, 155

research: alignment 8; equality 152; ethics of 152; European arts therapy standards 38, 140; into higher education 20; into therapy and music therapy training 52, 53, 81, 132, 159; literature 151; pathways of music therapy research 35, 161–2, 168, 170, 174, 176; relationship to curriculum 9; representation 152; research excellence framework 39; service evaluation and research 45, 153; service user involvement 152; student research whilst training 89, 119, 131, 151–2; within professional practice 44–5

Research Excellence Framework 39

research methodology 152

resilience: of client 164, 177; developing on training 86, 88–9, 132–3; experiential group facilitator 128; of experiential group leader 128; self-care as 133; skill for career 159, 164, 165; of trainee 86, 89, 132, 136, 159, 164

resistance: of client 81; in music 63; of professional change 37; of trainee and trainer 14, 30

response improvisation *see* improvisation
responsibility: of music therapist 113, 116; of placement educator 28; in research 157; of trainee 22, 28, 63, 87; of trainer 9, 11, 28
Richards, E. 108, 129
right to resit 116
risk assessment 125; physical impact of work 126; volume of music 125
Ritchie, F. 162–3
Robb, S. 152
Robbins, C. 33
Roehampton Institute of Higher Education 34; *see also* University of Roehampton
Rogers, C. 4, 20, 23
role-emerging placement 149; *see also* long-arm supervision
role play 21, 52, 54, 65–6, 85, 102
Royal Welsh College of Music and Drama 33
RSL 56, 76

safeguarding 19, 78, 81, 115
Sandford, S. 41, 160
SATTIE (The State of the Arts Therapies Training in Europe) project 140
Schesi 40
school businesses 142
scope of placements 78; *see also* placements
secondary trauma; 123, 132–3
secure base 117
self-care: activities 134–5; concept of 1, 5, 123, 132–6; learning in training 103, 111, 115, 124; in professional practice 43, 108, 141, 144; physical self-care 126; for sustainable future practice 175–6; for trainers 135; music as self-care 124–5; student experience of 44; wounded healer 126–7
self-employment 141, 145, 163, 168
self-reflection 3, 17, 83, 86, 123–4, 143
self-taught musicianship 107
senior jobs 142, 148, 163–72, 175
service evaluation 33, 44–5, 145–6, 151, 157–8, 176; *see also* research
service user 3, 6, 9–10, 20–1, 24, 35, 37, 40–1, 43, 45, 96, 111, 116, 123, 126, 135, 143, 145, 150–1, 160, 174
simulated clinical skills 25
Skilled Worker Visa 150
skill-sharing 145

Sobey, K. 35, 124
social enterprises 145
social model 7, 62–3, 66
social stories 96
social support 100
social welfare systems 151
song 6, 60, 62, 65–9, 73, 76, 91
songwriting 46, 53, 55, 62, 67, 69, 72, 75, 154
special experiences 70
speech and language therapists 36, 80, 154
spiritual beliefs and practices 126, 135, 143, 169
Standards of Proficiency *see* Health and Care Professions Council
stereotyping 111
Stern, D. 64–5, 76
stigma: of disability or mental health 110–11, 122; of therapy 104, 107, 143
STOMP (Stop OverMedicating Patients) 149, 157
storytelling 69
stress: during pandemic 43, 145; for educators 28, 117; for music therapists 126, 133–4, 137–8; for trainees 39, 103, 106, 108, 121
structural dynamics 142
student satisfaction surveys 116–17
succession planning 155
summative feedback *see* feedback
supervision: Balint group 129; challenges 115; clinical 79, 85, 91, 93, 144; concept of 28–9, 126, 128–9; developmental stages of 82; embodied experience 154; for experiential group facilitator 128; group 82–3; internal supervisor 130; long-arm 81, 93, 149; managerial *vs.* clinical 144; music 83, 130; observers, on placement 78, 80–2; online 154; parallel process, peer supervision 83, 130, 154; post training qualification 38, 176; in professional practice 144, 146, 154; sliding scale of costs 144; style 87, 90, 92; supervisor as assessor 81, 115; as support 88, 95, 132, 134; tensions 90; trainee reflection 118, 165–6; use of music (*see* reflective practice)
surface indexing 70
survey (BAMT) 141
suspension of musical wishes 73
sustainability 1, 10, 39, 123, 134, 146, 175
systemic thinking 90

Talwar, S. 110, 121
teaching assistants 148
Teaching Excellence Framework 11, 39
technology: music 67, 85, 107, 111; within music therapy 1; 25, 33, 172; within training 18, 41, 43 (*see also* E-learning)
Teesside University 34, 148
tenth world congress of music therapy, Oxford 37
theoretical stance 89–90, 142
therapeutic alliance 113
therapeutic presence 68, 81
time-limited working 97
Tingle, E. 169
tokenism 150
trainee: background 7, 53, 55–6, 58, 60, 72, 95, 106–8, 111, 124, 167; cultural wealth 42–3; enhancing workplace 88; expectations 5, 16, 17, 73, 80, 82, 87–9, 108, 116; disability 94–5, 105, 111, 113, 127; gender identity 42, 110–11, 113, 176; identity 5–6, 20, 42–3, 57–61, 74, 111–13, 127–8, 147, 160–1, 176; learning style 5, 17; motivation 5, 21, 126–7, 147; racial identity 42–3, 95, 111; relationship with music 6, 58–61, 124, 128; self care 44, 103, 111, 115, 124–7; sexuality 7, 42, 111, 113; vulnerability 59, 95, 103, 128, 135; workplace presentations 142
trainee health *see* self-care
trainee pregnancy 95, 131
trainers: approaches to selection 52–7, 60, 99–107, 111, 112; clinical practice 10; curriculum development 10, 41; modelling 18–19, 90; power 7–8, 11; pressure 39–40, 117, 135; privilege 12; styles of teaching, learning and assessment 17–29, 42–4, 58–74, 79–97, 115, 116, 126, 128–30; supporting students with disabilities 5, 111, 113; role 4–5
Training and Education Committee of BAMT 9, 36, 146, 149
training discourse 2, 7, 8, 15, 36–7, 41, 52, 110
training selection 53–8, 100, 102, 112
training values 143
trauma: in body 77, 174, 177; of childhood 170; of music college 117; of service user 111, 113, 162, 163, 170, 172; of trainee 19, 31, 57, 103, 110–11, 123, 126, 132–3, 137
treatment 36, 47, 49, 143, 160
Trevarthen, C. and Malloch, S. 64, 76

unconditional positive regard 94
undergraduate study 38, 147–9, 168, 170
undervaluing: music education 107; music therapy 142
University of Derby 34
University of Edinburgh 33
University of Limerick 34
University of Roehampton 33–4, 47, 55–6, 148
University of South Wales 34, 55–6, 143
University of the West of England 33, 56, 58, 80, 81
unsafe practices 144

videos of music therapy practice 79, 91, 104
virtual platforms 90
virtual practice 142
visa requirements 57
Vocal Psychotherapy 154–6
voice: of placement educator 84–5; singing 53; of trainee voice 83–4
volunteering 97, 99, 105
vulnerability *see* trainee vulnerability

Western Music 56, 60, 71
Wetherick, D. 8–10, 15, 35, 51–2, 54, 68, 77
widening participation 9, 34, 40
Wigram, T. 7, 34, 36–8, 52, 61, 64, 66, 67, 69, 72
world music 71
work-based learning *see* placements
work environment 114, 142
work experience 97, 99–100, 104–5, 143, 146, 171
working whilst training 106
working with difference *see* difference
work shadowing 148
workshops and workshopping 17, 20, 44, 61, 62, 69, 72, 93, 124, 168
work with colleagues 20, 44, 71, 92, 97, 123, 133, 160, 161, 165
wounded healer 126

Youtube material 142

For Product Safety Concerns and Information please contact our EU representative GPSR@taylorandfrancis.com
Taylor & Francis Verlag GmbH, Kaufingerstraße 24, 80331 München, Germany

www.ingramcontent.com/pod-product-compliance
Lightning Source LLC
Chambersburg PA
CBHW061714300426
44115CB00014B/2691